Payback

Payback

Why We Retaliate, Redirect Aggression, and Take Revenge

DAVID P. BARASH, Ph.D.
and
JUDITH EVE LIPTON, M.D.

OXFORD
UNIVERSITY PRESS

OXFORD
UNIVERSITY PRESS

Published in the United States of America by Oxford University Press, Inc.,
198 Madison Avenue, New York, NY, 10016
United States of America

Oxford University Press, Inc., publishes works that further Oxford University's
objective of excellence in research, scholarship, and education

Oxford is a registered trade mark of Oxford University Press
in the UK and in certain other countries

Library of Congress Cataloging-in-Publication Data
Barash, David P.
 Payback : why we retaliate, redirect aggression, and
take revenge / David P. Barash, Judith Eve Lipton.
    p. cm.
 Includes bibliographical references and index.
 ISBN 978-0-19-539514-3 (hardcover : alk. paper)
 1. Pain. 2. Revenge. 3. Aggressiveness. I. Lipton, Judith Eve. II. Title.
 BF515.B36 2011
 155.9'2—dc22   2010040162

978-0-19-539514-3
1 2 3 4 5 6 7 8 9

Typeset in Chaparral Pro
Printed on acid-free paper
Printed in the United States of America

To our children. We celebrate Eva, her husband, Jeremy, and their son, Isaac; Ilona and Yoav; and Nanelle and Lizzy. We also dedicate this to our friends and colleagues who have struggled with these issues along with us, and who are committed to personal as well as global healing. We thank our patients and students, who have taught us while allowing us the privilege of teaching them. Finally, we note those remarkable individuals who are living examples of peace and equanimity, whose very presence is like a glass of cold water on a hot day. Such people bring peace and in their gracefulness, they help others relax, and explore alternatives to retaliation, revenge and redirected aggression.

PREFACE: 1984 TO NOW

The winter of 1984 was a perfect storm in the Barash/Lipton household. George Orwell himself would have been impressed with the misery. Politically, two "Big Brothers"—Ronald Reagan and Leonid Brezhnev—were at each other's throats, flaunting enough nuclear weapons to poison life on earth if war broke out. Whether the end was to be by fire (global incineration) or by ice (nuclear winter), it looked like everything we knew and loved, including the entire process of biological evolution, was threatened by two competing empires with more interest in dominance than in preserving life on our shared planet. The authors, Barash and Lipton—the former an evolutionary biologist specializing in animal behavior, and the latter a biologically oriented psychiatrist—were totally immersed in the peace movement, trying to stop nuclear war. This meant that the house was littered with picture books about Hiroshima and posters saying things like "Life itself will end if there is a nuclear war." In addition to our own professional writings, we had already written a book called *Stop Nuclear War, a Handbook* (Grove Press, 1982), which included a detailed description of the medical effects of thermonuclear war, along with the history and politics of the Cold War. Another book—*The Cave Man and the Bomb: Human Nature, Evolution, and Nuclear War*—was underway, eventually published in 1985 by McGraw-Hill.

One of us, David, although a biologist by training and inclination, was a tenured professor of psychology at the University of Washington, in Seattle, and the other, Judith, was a highly respected physician. For all our professional success and recognition, however, our house had become a toxic environment, especially for our children by previous marriages. Trying our best to save the world, we absorbed a lot of pain in the process and were unintentionally passing some of it to our children. We recall with some shuddering pain a sardonic ditty by "Weird Al" Yankovic," whose song *Happy Birthday* coincided with our 13-year-old's birthday, helpfully advising that thanks to nuclear weapons, we would all be "crispy critters" after the next war. Our pain had become theirs; happy birthday indeed.

In addition to fighting to prevent World War III, we also fought about trivia: the correct tempo for *Für Elise,* whether to have white sugar in the house, whether to require the kids to clean their own rooms and do laundry. We fought about bedtimes, playtimes, and sports. We fought so much about food that Judy eventually resigned from cooking altogether. And we fought about our stepchildren.

Eva left first, in 1980, deciding to live with her biological mother. And on August 1, 1983, Jenny—age 13—died when her bicycle was hit by a pickup truck. Our stepfamily had been vaporized, as surely as if it had been hit by a bomb. We were left with "our own" child, Ilona, then age five, a quiet little girl who knew how to make herself invisible. Our relationship was strained, almost to breaking. It was unclear which of us was the worst offender when it came to making our home such a difficult place for children. Obviously, we were both responsible.

In January 1984, on a bleak and especially miserable day in the Pacific Northwest, in the cold, empty house where children used to play and now there was only one, Judith struggled with anger, fear, and depression. Then something changed, and very quickly. She happened to read an essay by the Buddhist monk Thich Nhat Hanh, which later became his wonderful book *Being Peace* (Parallax Press, 1987). In it, Hanh describes how suffering begets suffering, entreating his readers to look deeply into the origins of things, especially bad things. He explains that all actions are born from others—a non-theological perspective on *karma*—and how it is that many betrayals, assaults, critiques, and defections are brought about by previous experiences of loss and pain. In the end, Hanh enjoins us all to stop the cycle of suffering . . . simply by recognizing the problem and, despite recognizing that some degree of suffering is inevitable, making it our private mission to minimize the world's burden of pain. How to do this? By taking personal charge of our actions—specifically, deciding that "the pain stops here," and therefore no longer passing it along like a hot potato. It is asking a lot, but it also offers a lot.

Judith thinks that until that day she did not have a clear "moral compass," although she had always tried to be a reasonably good person. She was good or bad, depending on circumstances and emotions, fighting to prevent nuclear war (good) but also fighting with stepchildren (bad). Good and bad were automatic, not calculated. It was good to save a kitten and bad to run over a dog in the road. Good to give money to charities, bad to give money to panhandlers. Good to be a physician, bad to be sloppy about collecting payments. It was good to play the piano, bad to play *Für Elise* too fast. It was good to read fiction, bad to watch TV. And for David's family, who had run a small flower shop in the subway of New York City, it was good (albeit regrettable) to pay off the thugs for protection, good to sell old flowers in artful bouquets, bad to buy retail, and even worse to vote Republican.

Most people, we submit, have a similar inner algebraic system for calculating moral dilemmas, although the metric and substance of that system is not conscious. "Do unto others as you would have them do unto you" is an excellent and nearly universal rule, but in practice, terribly difficult. The Ten Commandments and Islamic Shar'ia law have algorithms for making moral decisions, but these, too, are not easily internalized and are often stretched. In this sense, we were not alone in our moral quandaries during that snowy winter of 1984. It was good to fight and work for peace, to study animals and evolution, and to minister to the psychiatric needs of suffering patients, but bad to deal incessantly with nuclear war, to the point that dinner table conversation with 10-year-olds was mostly about politics and the possible end of the world. Judith called her revelation of January 1984 the Principle of Minimizing Pain, and we offer it, unblushingly, as the 11th Commandment (see Chapter 8). It yields a clear—albeit difficult—ethical guideline, a way to calculate actions that includes recognition of feelings, both in oneself and others, but one that is not based on feelings or intuition alone. It is a slow process, because actions have consequences, and it is difficult to think through the ever-growing circles of cause and effect that any given action may provoke. Sometimes the effects are obvious. For example, after Jenny died, we took the books, posters, and movies about nuclear war out of the kitchen, dining room, and living rooms, confining them to the study where they did not poison the children with fear and foreboding. (We did not stop our anti-nuclear activism, however.)

It also became clear that it was better to accept a stepchild's foibles than try to make him or her into a different person. Better just to grieve our losses —rather than sling blame back and forth. We were far better as a team than as competitors or opponents. Better to offer and receive love, within a family, than to rail against imperfections. If the children wanted to live on pizza or macaroni and cheese instead of specialty vegetarian dishes, what did it matter? No one was going to die of malnutrition, but clearly we were suffering over trying too hard to eat just the "right" things.

David was smitten, as well, with the concept of "pain-passing," not only for its interpersonal insights, but because it helped make sense of some of the most troublesome things that people (and animals) do, while uniting facts and theories from physiology and evolution to the behavior of nations, connecting ethology, history, anthropology, philosophy, and psychology. Even literature, law, and theology. As we now hope to show, it is a paradigm that offers not only a powerful dose of practical day-to-day wisdom, but also a means of tying together an impressive array of seemingly disparate findings—loose ends no longer, they emerge as parts of a coherent whole.

In Judith's work as a physician, it became clear that in order for the Principle of Minimizing Pain to work, it had to include provisions for reconciliation and forgiveness, which, in turn, morphed into another algorithm, a Forgiveness

Protocol that became a handout and methodology in her psychiatric practice (see Chapter 7). In order to minimize pain and not pass it to others, a complicated social dance must occur, in which grievances are noted, errors are acknowledged, and the perpetrator of pain asks the recipient for forgiveness, or at least non-retaliation. Many religions and ethical systems have procedures for doing just this, for healing wounds and reconciling differences without rage and violence, yet the process is not easy, nor is it translated into principles that can easily be taught to others. We attempt to fill this gap, ending the present book with a methodology for minimizing suffering and achieving peace and reconciliation.

This book began in a snowstorm in the state of Washington, and ends in the sunshine of Costa Rica. After more than 26 years, we feel that we can address some of the causes of violence, and offer some solutions for achieving nonviolent conflict resolutions. We have been thinking about this book for decades, and we are grateful to Lori Handelman at Oxford University Press for seeing merit in this project, and especially to Abby Gross and Joanna Ng, who helped to bring these thoughts to you, the reader. We are also delighted to thank the following students at the University of Washington who assisted in evaluating ideas and catching errors: Christine Bender, Chaz Casassa, Nicole Clopper, Karin Frank, Andrew Geels, Emily Leickly, Brian Stamer, Jennifer Trnka, and Nicole Vongpanya. Of all the books we have written, this one is closest to our hearts, and we hope that it will become close to yours as well.

—David P. Barash and Judith Eve Lipton
Playa Grande, Costa Rica, 2010

CONTENTS

8. Conclusion: The Principle of Minimizing Pain (an 11th Commandment)

Payback

1

Passing the Pain Along

Pain is not popular. No one likes it . . . except for a few weirdos such as sadists (who enjoy the pain of others) and masochists (who relish their own). In fact, when we initially proposed calling this book "Passing the Pain Along," our wise editor at Oxford University Press urged us to find a different title, since "not very many people are going to be attracted to a book about pain." We have followed her sage advice but have kept our original formulation for this chapter because, even though pain is, well, a pain, it is also universal, important, and what this book is about.

But what is pain?

Pain is a living thing's response to a particular current of energy, a neurological signal within an individual that reverberates throughout its being, whether that being is a simple creature or a complex mammal, including *Homo sapiens*. Pain is an inner SOS, a distress signal, something that is not only highly subjective but that—initially, at least—is profoundly inward-focused, involving only the affected individual and his or her welfare. But often enough, it moves from the individual outward in circles and spirals that involve friends, enemies, relatives, strangers, and sometimes expands to affect entire communities and even nations. Time does not heal all wounds. Rather, the wounded often act in ways that magnify further wounds, for the injured self and others.

That is the basic point of this book. Pain, according to the International Association for the Study of Pain, is "an unpleasant sensory and emotional experience associated with actual or potential tissue damage."[1] "Suffering," by contrast, although sometimes used as a synonym for "pain," should be seen as deeper, more general, and perhaps more conceptual, something that can be evoked by diverse experiences—including thought alone—and not merely by the activation of certain sensory neurons. For our purposes, however, "pain" will mostly suffice, flying as it does from being to being, human to human, human to animal, animal to animal, and animal to human, resulting in a constant network of reverberations that most individuals do not perceive, because its presence in their lives is incessant, a kind of ongoing background noise. Pain is in fact ancient and omnipresent, with much of human history concerned with efforts to minimize it, or alternatively, to extol or exaggerate it, and on occasion to transcend it.

Rarely recognized, however, is this troubling fact: After experiencing pain, there is a powerful tendency for a victim to respond by passing it along to someone else. In short: payback.

If you were to interview a hypothetical intelligent fish and ask for a description of her world, the chances are she would not volunteer that "It's very wet down here." Similarly, as we will see, pain-passing, in one form or another, is so prevalent that nearly everyone takes it for granted. Payback is the ocean in which we swim. In the pages to come, we will explore that ocean, sound its depths, and map its contours, providing what the French would call a *tour d'horizon*.

In the end, we will provide an overview of how different religions and philosophies have attempted to stop this terrible cycle, adding a recipe or two of our own. We fully expect that this will not be the final word on the subject but rather an introduction, and that nearly everyone will have something to add, resulting in a vital conversation about how to mitigate suffering in this sad and beautiful world. Some suffering, to be sure, is inevitable. But much of it is preventable, and it is toward this end that we write.

* * *

What are the Three Rs? Not the usual reading, writing, and 'rithmatic, but rather the pathways of social relationships that deal with the infectious transmission of pain: Retaliation, Revenge and Redirected Aggression.

When one being hurts another, several things may happen. Sometimes, the pain is immediately reflected back onto the perpetrator: This is retaliation. It is prompt and straightforward. It doesn't require a sophisticated nervous system, or indeed, any brains at all: Touch a jellyfish and you will be stung. Try to destroy a hornet's nest and you will be mobbed by furious insects. Tom attacks Dick, and Dick hits back. Often the reaction is quick, proportionate, and unconscious. One kick in the pants leads to another kick in the pants.

Then there is revenge. Once again, Tom attacks Dick, which leads to Dick's hitting Tom, but not right away. And not with equal and balanced intensity. When revenge is afoot, its more like Tom hits Dick . . . time passes . . . then Dick clobbers Tom. The response is delayed—often for a long while and with much prior contemplation (Sicilians say that "revenge is a dish best served cold"). And typically, revenge is disproportionate: An eye for a tooth, or a life for an eye. So far, so bad.

The strangest form of payback, the oddest of the "Rs," and hence, the one that most occupies this book, is redirected aggression: Tom goes after Dick, who responds by going after *Harry*, who had nothing to do with the initial problem at all! This seems illogical, yet it happens all the time. Strictly speaking, it isn't so much payback as "pay-forward," or—more precisely—"pay sideways," since Harry did not "deserve" his treatment. Sometimes, when Harry isn't available, Dick may pound his fist on a table, slam the door, or kick the dog. Or he may develop high blood pressure or road rage, or beat his wife or child. Maybe he will even commit murder or suicide.

Redirected aggression—the targeting of an innocent bystander in response to one's own pain and injury—seems not only absurd but also morally bankrupt and downright dangerous. Although explicitly condoned by very few societies (perhaps by none), it is so widespread as to be essentially universal, and also, not coincidentally, often overlooked.* If Tom hurts Dick, the popular expectation is that Dick will either retaliate against Tom, choose to practice nonviolence, or exact revenge, not that he will take it out on Harry. The fascinating reality, however, is that he often does; the pattern of *A hurts B, who then hurts C or D* is remarkably common, and it cries out to be identified, understood, and ultimately overcome.

Although huge cultural differences exist within and between different societies, "retaliation, revenge, and redirecting aggression" reflect a broad trend of diminishing social legitimacy. Retaliation—direct and immediate payback—is widely perceived as acceptable or even necessary, so that "self defense" is not typically viewed as a crime. In fact, many consider it laudable, and the failure to defend oneself deplorable, although many cultures urge restraint or at least strict proportionality ("an eye for an eye, a tooth for a tooth"). Revenge is more complex, sometimes even socially mandated, although a minority of cultural traditions urge victims to forego this kind of payback and to forgive and forget.

There do not appear to be any human groups, however, that go out of their way to recommend redirected aggression, although at the same time, there are no laws or precepts that explicitly prohibit it, probably because the phenomenon itself is not widely acknowledged outside the narrow confines of ethology, the science of animal behavior. People know redirected aggression when they see it, whether manifested as road rage, sadism towards animals, or violence against vulnerable people. Once we recognize that someone is simply having a bad day, many of us avoid that person, instinctively knowing that he or she is liable to "take it out" on someone else. The point cries out to be made: Pain and violence are frequently and compellingly intertwined, across cultures, time, geography, and even species.

Pain and suffering are inevitable for everyone. The Buddha proclaimed it the first of the Four Noble Truths. Every organism faces aging and death, and human beings experience suffering due to competition, disappointment, neglect, abandonment, illness, and injury. Scientists distinguish different varieties of pain, from the simplest "noxious stimuli" experienced even by unicellular organisms, to the most complex, perhaps "existential angst" for those more philosophically inclined. Pain and hurting in human beings can be physical, like a stubbed toe,

* Remember that talking fish!

or it can manifest as emotional suffering such as a "broken heart" after a love affair has gone awry. The basic idea of this book is that these two kinds of "hurting" are intimately related, so that when people are hurting—in pain themselves—they are especially likely to respond by hurting others. Often these new victims are innocent bystanders who had nothing to do with the initial provocation, but who are then recruited into the ranks of eventual victimizers.

Pain, in short, is infectious; it is passed along like a demonic bucket brigade, which, instead of putting out a fire, burns its victims, who respond by causing yet more pain, which leads to yet more victims. Thus the sad pattern continues. In the pages to come, we will take a close look at this process, one that warrants all the attention that concerned people can muster. We will also look at ways to stop passing the pain along.

* * *

"Attend the tale of Sweeney Todd. He served a dark and an angry god. . . ." Thus begins Stephen Sondheim's ghastly masterpiece, *Sweeney Todd: The Demon Barber of Fleet Street*. Who is this dark and angry god? How—and why—did Mr. Todd serve him? (And what does a Sondheim musical have to do with self-aware fish and the tragic transmittal of misery?) *Sweeney Todd* is the tale of one Benjamin Barker from Dickensian London whose lovely wife, Lucy, unfortunately caught the eye of the lecherous and villainous Judge Turpin. Turpin has Barker arrested on false charges and transported to hard labor in Australia so that he can take advantage of Lucy and adopt Barker's infant daughter, Johanna. After fifteen years, Barker escapes and returns to London, bereft of his wife, his daughter, and his place in society. To create a reason for living, he reinvents himself as "Sweeney Todd," superficially an enterprising middle-class barber but actually a focused embodiment of hatred and loss. Not surprisingly, Sweeney Todd vows revenge on Turpin, but just as Act I is concluding and the judge is about to get his just reward, courtesy of a straight razor expertly wielded by barber Todd, he escapes and Sweeney is cheated of his vengeance.

But not altogether. Mr. Todd proceeds to "take it out" on the citizens of London, slitting the throats of his clients and then serving them up as meat pies, owing to a clever business plan devised with his new lady-friend, Mrs. Lovett. Who, or what, is Sweeney's angry god? To begin with, it is revenge. But more than that. Only one of his victims turns out to be the evil judge—the source of our "hero's" pain—and this comeuppance only arises toward the end of the show. Prior to its *dénouement*, Sweeney kills left and right, fully aware that his various "customers" have never harmed him, his wife, or his daughter.

Why did Sweeney Todd do what he did? It wasn't simple revenge; that, after all, was reserved for the dastardly judge. Rather, a more interesting, more complicated, and more irrational motivation is afoot, one that sits at the root of revenge and of much additional nastiness. Sweeney's tale is an iconic case of "passing the pain along," or redirected aggression. If revenge or retaliation are possible in such cases, so much the better. But when they are out of reach, redirected aggression will have to do! Judge Turpin injured Benjamin Barker/ Sweeney Todd, who, unable to injure Judge Turpin in return, redirected his anger onto his innocent tonsorial clients. Why? At first glance, it seems utterly senseless, even comically absurd to "take it out" on someone who had no responsibility for the initial transgression. Turpin hurt Todd, who became not only a serial killer, but one who tricked the surviving innocent citizens of London into cannibalism.

We never discover, incidentally, why Judge Turpin is such a creep, but it seems more like plain old male dominance and sexual voraciousness rather than either "retaliation, revenge, or redirected aggression." Turpin is the embodiment of turpitude, steeped in power, lust, and greed. In real life, a Turpin character could have had a bad childhood, but he could also be a garden-variety sociopath, which seems to have a genetic basis. In real life, too, some people commit evil and violent acts without having first been injured themselves. The main events in *Sweeney Todd*, however—the title character's magnificent, horrifying, occasionally hilarious and bloodthirsty murderousness—comes from the title character's redirected aggression.

But of course, *Sweeney Todd* is fiction. What about real life?

* * *

Attend the tale of Geronimo, who became one of the most renowned and feared Native American war chiefs. Here is how he got started.

One day in 1858, a squadron of Mexican cavalrymen ambushed a group of Apaches in peacetime, while the men were away. The following year, a large force of Apaches, looking for revenge, caught up with a detachment of Mexican soldiers—who may or may not have been those who committed the massacre— and a young man named Geronimo was given command. Why him? Because his mother, wife, and three young children were amongst those slaughtered the previous year. Here are Geronimo's own words:

> I was no chief and never had been, but because I had been more deeply wronged than others, this honor was conferred upon me. . . . In all the battle I thought of my murdered mother, wife, and babies—of my father's grave and my vow of vengeance. . . . Still covered with the blood of my enemies, still holding my conquering weapon, still hot with the joy of battle, victory, and vengeance, I was surrounded by the Apache braves and made war chief of all the Apaches. Then I gave orders for scalping the slain. I could not call back my loved ones. I could not bring back the dead Apaches, but I could rejoice in this revenge.[2]

The entire Mexican force, two companies of infantry and two of cavalry, was wiped out. Apache losses were also high, but for Geronimo and his fellows, as for millions of others before and after, it seems to have been worth it.

But Geronimo's actions took place 150 years ago. What about more recent times? Does redirected aggression operate today?

"This week two Hamas gunmen raided a Jewish settlement in the Gaza Strip and killed two Israelis," wrote *New York Times* columnist Anthony Lewis on October 6, 2001. "In response, Israeli tanks shelled a town, killing six Palestinians—who may have had nothing to do with the raid—and bulldozers destroyed Palestinian farmland. The result: more funerals, more deprivation, more rage." There is nothing terribly unusual about this exchange. That is the point.

"Two Hamas gunmen," "two Israelis," "six Palestinians," all real people, but without names and stories. For a more personalized case, like Geronimo's, consider the tale of Hanadi Jaradat, a 27-year-old lawyer who, on Saturday morning, October 4, 2003, waved goodbye to her parents in the town of Jenin, on the West Bank.[3] Six hours later, she had removed her traditional Palestinian clothing and put on jeans, replaced her headscarf with a ponytail, strapped an explosive belt around her waist, and proceeded to blow herself up in the city of Haifa, killing nineteen Israelis in the process: fourteen Jews, three of whom were children, and five Arab Christians. Two days later, a *New York Times* reporter asked the young woman's mother if she had any message for the Haifa victims and their families. "Tell them," she said, "they should think about why our daughter did this." It is something we should all think about.

Four months before this particular suicide bombing, in one of its harshest crackdowns since the *intifada* began, the Israeli Defense Forces had forced their way into Hanadi Jaradat's city of Jenin, whose 30,000 people, not far from Lebanon and Syria, seethed with anti-Israeli hostility. Tanks, infantry, and bull-dozers had killed dozens of Palestinians and left an entire neighborhood in rubble; the simmering came to a boil.

It turns out that Hanadi Jaradat—young, intelligent, full of promise—had been not only devoutly religious, awakening before five every morning to pray and read the Koran, but also enraged by the death of her brother, Fadi, age 23, and her cousin, Saleh, 31, both killed in the earlier Israeli military crackdown. "She was full of pain about that," lamented Mrs. Jaradat. "Some nights, she woke screaming, saying she had nightmares about Fadi." A new radicalism crept into her remarks about Israelis after her brother died. Mrs. Jaradat went on to note that, "I don't want to talk about my feelings, my pain, my suffering. But I can tell you that our people believe that what Hanadi has done is justified. Imagine yourself watching the Israelis kill your son, your nephew, destroying your house—they are pushing our people into a corner, they are provoking actions like these by our people."

Nor are Palestinians alone in being thus provoked. We can only imagine, for example, the rage, pain, and suffering experienced by Hanadi Jaradat's victims and *their* families.

Also worth noting: two days later, the Israeli Defense Forces responded by bombing a site in Syria that had once been a terrorist training camp. Incidentally, the camp had long been abandoned, and Ms. Jaradat had never been there.

There seems to be no end to this kind of thing. On January 22, 2009, an article appeared in the *New York Times* that dealt not only with the fraught question of whether international law had been violated in the brief 2009 "Gaza War," but also with something equally if not more troubling: the impact that violent, pain-inducing events have on their victims—not just the immediate damage inflicted, but also their subsequent inclinations. The *Times* reported on the anguish of Sabah Abu Halima, a Gazan woman whose husband and four children were killed in a fire that, according to Palestinian officials, was started by Israeli use of banned white phosphorus munitions. The article concluded with the following account, as chilling as it was tragic: "She wept with fury, saying that as farmers she and her family had good relations with Israelis, selling them produce in past years. But now, she said, she wants to see Israel's leaders—she named the foreign minister and president—'burn like my children burned. They should feel the pain we felt.'"

Admittedly, Hanadi Jaradat was merely one person. As were Sabah Abu Halima and Geronimo. Is there any evidence that redirected aggression operates among groups?

* * *

Turn, now, to Bosnia. Here is journalist Lawrence Weschler recounting an experience he had in the Bosnian town of Banja Luka, which used to consist of a majority of Muslims, nearly all of whom had just previously been murdered or driven out ("cleansed") by their Serb neighbors:

> As I was standing alongside the rubble-strewn parking lot on the site of what had until recently been one of the most splendid ancient mosques west of Istanbul, I asked a passing Serb student by what justification this and all the town's other mosques had been leveled. "Because of what the Ustasha did to us during the Second World War—they leveled our Orthodox churches," he replied without the slightest hesitation. Only the Ustasha were Croats. I somehow felt transported into a Three Stooges movie: Moe wallops Larry, who then feels entirely justified in turning around and smashing Curly.[4]

In short, Serbs had long been nursing a grudge against Croats; in response, they attacked Bosnian Muslims! This would be slapstick, if it were not tragedy.

Nor are Americans immune. This little ditty, to the tune of the children's song, *If you're happy and you know it, clap your hands,* made the rounds on the Internet during the run-up to the invasion of Iraq in 2003. It appeared in various versions, making authorial attribution impossible; yet its basic message is easily attributed to redirected aggression.

> If you cannot find Osama, bomb Iraq.
> If the market's hurt your Momma, bomb Iraq.
> If the terrorists are Saudi, and they've repossessed your Audi,
> And you're feeling kind of rowdy, bomb Iraq.
>
> If your corporate fraud is growin', bomb Iraq.
> If your ties to it are showin', bomb Iraq.
> If your politics are sleazy, and hiding that ain't easy,
> And your manhood's getting queasy, bomb Iraq.
>
> If we have no allies with us, bomb Iraq.
> If we think someone has dissed us, bomb Iraq.
> So to hell with the inspections,
> Let's look tough for the elections,
> Close your mind and take directions, bomb Iraq.
>
> Fall in line and follow orders, bomb Iraq.
> For our might it knows no borders, bomb Iraq.
> Disagree? We'll call it treason,
> Let's make war not love this season,
> Even if we have no reason, bomb Iraq.

There are actually many possible reasons why the Bush Administration chose to bomb Iraq and then either "liberate" or "invade" it (depending on one's perspective). What is clear, however, is that Saddam Hussein was not responsible for the terrorist attacks of September 11, 2001, but that in the minds of most Americans, the agony of that attack demanded that something be done—something violent—and that someone be held accountable and made to suffer, preferably someone already known to be nasty, and who could readily be defeated.

Here is Thomas Friedman writing in *The New York Times,* in June of 2003: "The 'real reason' for this war, which was never stated, was that after September 11 America needed to stick it to someone in the Arab-Muslim world. . . . Smashing Saudi Arabia or Syria would have been fine. But we attacked Saddam for one simple reason: because we could, and because he deserved it, and because he was right in the heart of that world." According to former chief U.N. weapons inspector Hans Blix, in his book, *Disarming Iraq,* "It is clear that the U.S. determination to take on Iraq was not triggered by anything Iraq did, but by the wounds inflicted by Al-Qaeda." Sweeney Todd would have understood.

U.S. counter-terrorism expert Richard Clarke noted that, "Having been attacked by Al Qaeda, for us to go bombing Iraq in response was like our invading Mexico after the Japanese attacked us at Pearl Harbor."[5] Richard Clarke, again: "Secretary Rumsfeld complained that there were no decent targets for bombing in Afghanistan and that we should consider bombing Iraq. At first I thought Rumsfeld was joking. But he was serious. . . ." The Three Stooges redux, and once again without the humor.

And yet, aside from its obtuse venality and blinkered ideological rigidity, it seems clear that in one respect at least, George W. Bush and his Administration were not stooges at all, but quite brilliant. They read the need of most Americans at the time: to hit someone, hard, so as to redirect their suffering and anger. The evidence is overwhelming that for the Bush Administration's "neocons," the September 11 attacks were not the reason for the Iraq War; rather, it was a convenient excuse for doing something upon which they had already decided.[6] Their accomplishment—if such is the correct word—was identifying the post-9/11 mood of the American people, and manipulating this mood, brilliantly, toward war. Yet, despite the terrible illogic of Geronimo, the Bosnian Serbs, the Israeli-Palestinian conflict, and the Iraq War, there is nothing unusual about such happenings. *That's the point.*

If this tendency is as deep-seated as we believe, then the urge to respond to pain by inflicting yet more pain on others should show up even in the daily lives of normal people who are removed from the terrible exigencies of war. It does.

* * *

On September 29, 2004, Channel 8's "Eyewitness News," in Las Vegas, Nevada, reported:

> A valley woman has two broken arms and possibly a broken neck from a road rage accident. A silver Pontiac forced the driver of a white Pathfinder off the road at Eastern and Warm Springs. The SUV slammed into a palm tree. . . . A man in the Pontiac told police he and a friend were speeding because *they were angry that another driver had cut them off*. Eighteen-year-old Joseph Archuleta drove off but later called police. He's charged with felony hit and run.

If Mr. Archuleta is unusual, it is not because he felt as he did, since psychologists have found that redirected aggression is especially likely among motorists,[7] but that his behavior was so flagrant. Road rage, however, is not the only quotidian manifestation of redirected aggression. From the child taunted by her playmates, to the office worker who feels stifled or insulted in his daily routine, to the political activist frustrated by the failure of other people to understand what she sees so clearly, people take out their pain and anger on others: sometimes inanimate things, sometimes animals, sometimes other people. They may slam a door, kick the dog, or, in more extreme cases, abuse a spouse or a child. Think of how many abused children grow up to be abusive parents, thereby maintaining those well-known yet poorly understood "cycles of domestic violence."

To understand how (and why) people pass their pain along is to gain startling insight into seemingly disconnected events. For example, current psychological theory holds that families often establish a "designated transgressor" who is blamed for any existing dysfunction. This leads us to a more general phenomenon that is as powerful and troublesome as it is ubiquitous.

The ancient Israelites used to hold a ceremony in which the high priest would lay both his hands over the head of a live goat and "confess over him all the iniquities of the people of Israel, and all their transgressions and all their sins; and he shall put them upon the head of a goat, and send him away into the wilderness . . . the goat shall bear all their iniquities upon him to a solitary land" (Leviticus 16:20–23). Sometimes, after the sins of the community were symbolically placed upon the goat, the animal was ritually slaughtered instead. Either way, the people were purified and the term *scapegoat* was later introduced into the Western vocabulary.

Goats are not slaughtered these days, but in advance of Yom Kippur, the Day of Atonement, Orthodox Jews perform a ritual known as *Kaparot*, whereby a chicken is swung over one's head, by which it is believed that one's sins during the past year are transferred to the chicken. The poor vertiginous and suddenly sin-filled fowl is then slaughtered and the meat given to charity.

Scapegoating is probably the most clear-cut historical example of passing the pain along and doing so in a socially accepted manner. In some cases, such as the Old Testament ceremony or modern-day *Kaparot*, the symbolism is acknowledged and up-front. In others, it is kept in the background, although it generally remains no less real. Jews, who may have invented scapegoating as a formal ritual, have, ironically, been victimized by it for thousands of years, from medieval times through the Inquisition, to Russian *pogroms*, to the Nazi holocaust: "I know we are the Chosen People," laments Tevye in *Fiddler on the Roof*. "But next time, couldn't you please choose someone *else*?"

Of course, Jews have not been alone as the chosen scapegoats. In the United States, African-Americans have been the foremost recipients of this dubious honor. In a now-classic study, bearing the excessively modest title "Minor Studies of Aggression,"[8] psychologists Carl Hovland and Robert Sears found that they could predict the number of southern lynchings taking place during any given year between 1882 and 1930, by knowing the price of cotton during that year. When cotton prices went down, the frequency of lynchings went up. Not that white southern racists literally blamed African-Americans every time cotton prices declined on the northern mercantile exchanges; rather, a bad economy (low prices for cotton) led to an outpouring of anger, resentment, and frustration, which was then turned against a conspicuous and powerless minority. The economic and social pain of poor whites was passed on to blacks, without any conscious awareness of the scapegoating involved. Although recent scholarship has cast some doubt on the clarity of the Hovland/Sears interpretation,[9] their research remains an iconic reminder of how scapegoating can link seemingly disconnected events.

In some ways, it is a matter of simple common sense, something that W. H. Auden saw clearly when he declared:

> What all schoolchildren learn:
> Those to whom evil is done, do evil in return. [10]

As we shall see, not all people respond to evil by "doing" it, but many do; pain-passing qualifies as what anthropologists call a "cross-cultural universal," found among the aboriginal people of Australia and indigenous inhabitants of the Amazon; among Wall Street financiers no less than inner-city gangs. You can find its imprint from neo–Stone Age tribal conflicts, through medieval pageantry, to modern warfare. As we shall see, it has left its mark in the genocidal wars of the twentieth century, as well as those that threaten to overwhelm the twenty-first, just as it underlies many of the most prominent, enduring themes of literature, history, psychology, and religion. It haunts our criminal courts, our streets, our battlefields, our homes, and our hearts. It lurks behind some of the nastiest and seemingly inexplicable things that otherwise decent people do, from road rage to yelling at a crying baby. It exists across boundaries of every kind—culture, time, geography, and even species.

Thus, there is growing evidence that the human penchant for passing along one's pain is not merely a human trait, nor is it limited to humanity's unspoken cultural traditions. Rather, as we shall see, it is something that we share with many other living things, firmly lodged in biology no less than in history and in unspoken cultural tradition.

* * *

Previous attempts to analyze aggression and violence have looked only at the first stage of the Tom-injures-Dick-who-injures-Harry sequence; that is, they asked what happened to "Tom." "Dick," by contrast, is our primary subject of inquiry. We will look at the victim's behavior *after* he has been victimized. Bear in mind that everyone is Dick, at least on occasion; no one avoids being the recipient of pain. The initiator in our example may in fact be Tom, literally a person seeking to better his situation at Dick's expense, or responding to his own pain initiated by someone else. Or "Tom" may stand for bad luck or the vicissitudes of life itself, such as cancer, a drought or flood, losing your job, being subjected to a neighbor's persistently barking dog, rejection by the college of your choice, and so forth. Bad things happen.

An important question then arises: What happens to those to whom it happens? Let's agree with Auden that in many cases those to whom evil is done are liable to do evil in return. That is the subject of this book. But we are not unaware that there are many other potential responses to evil, including depression, post-traumatic stress disorders, anxiety reactions, and a whole devilish load of psychiatric disturbances. Of course, not all people with depression have previously been victimized, nor do all victims develop aggression directed toward themselves or others. But there may nonetheless be substance to the old psychoanalytic notion that depression, at least on occasion, is anger turned inwards, becoming self-destructive and even suicidal instead of being redirected outwards.

The psychiatric community characterizes some individuals as "resilient."[11] Consider, for example, a middle-aged woman who came to Dr. Judith Lipton's office years ago, requesting an antidepressant. Her husband had divorced her for a younger woman, her daughter had breast cancer, her house was in foreclosure, her business was failing, and she had severe, crippling arthritis. Aided by 25 mg of Zoloft, within two weeks this woman was feeling strong and well again. She came back six weeks later, announcing that she was coping well and had stopped taking the Zoloft. What should we make of this? Was she lying, perhaps because she had terrible side effects and did not want to take the medicine any more? Or was she so resilient that a humble dose of a simple serotonin-booster helped her surmount her difficulties? How could she have lost or be losing everything in her life, and yet still feel "pretty good"?

We are not attempting to prove that all evil is a reaction to pain, nor that aggression is the inevitable outcome of loss and suffering. In fact, we are especially interested in cases where people suffer gently and with grace, harming nobody and hating no one. We are, moreover, inspired by them.

This brings up an important point: the flaccid notion of biological determinism. Ever since Darwin's Very Big Idea, especially when combined with advances in genetics, people have used biology and the science of natural selection to justify behavior, as in "my genes made me do it." At the same time, and at the other extreme, some have righteously declaimed that biology literally has nothing to do with behavior, and that either people are the beneficiaries of unlimited free will or that parents, the environment, or some other social circumstances induce every human action. To follow the logic of this book, not to mention that which connects behavior, biology, and environment, such dichotomous thinking must be discarded. There is a logic and predictability to violence and aggression, just as there are basic patterns for knitting socks. But each person comes into his environment with a unique set of genes, yielding a mass of imponderables that make each life one of a kind. From the same sock pattern, you can knit wool socks, silk socks, matching ones, big or small, and each individual with her own ball of yarn and needles will knit something unique. People are not machines, and genes are not computers. To explain what happens when bad things happen, one must look at the big basic patterns while also acknowledging those small, individual variations—including, but not limited to, free will. For now, however, as a first approximation to understanding how pain-passing works in people, we are especially interested in the big stuff, which means that we can learn a lot from fish and other animals, because it turns out that the evolutionary logic to aggression and its variants is both deep and wide.

* * *

Redirected aggression is not limited to human beings. Consider this account:

> [W]hen the going gets tough, the first thought is to find someone else to pay for it. A guy loses a fight and spins around and chases someone younger who, cheesed off, lunges at a female who swats an adolescent who knocks an infant over. All in about fifteen seconds. . . . [A]n incredible percentage of aggression consists of someone in a bad mood taking it out on an innocent bystander. . . . [T]his time, L trounced . . . N [who] sprinted off, badly in need of someone weaker to take his defeat out on. He lunged at the screaming J, chased some kid, and then smacked B as she leapt to get out of the way.

This comes from Robert Sapolsky's book *A Primate's Memoir*, and it describes a common event among East African baboons. Sapolsky's narrative highlights a revealing aspect of redirected aggression: it happens among animals no less than human beings. This, in turn, strongly suggests that nature—and not just nurture—is involved.

It is not even necessary for the creatures to be primates, or, for that matter, mammals. Ethologists have known for some time that when animals are inhibited from attacking whoever has actually victimized them, aggressiveness will instead be redirected toward someone else. Interestingly, even "primitive" animals frequently indulge in redirected aggression in the early stages of courtship and mating. In his book *On Aggression*, Nobel Prize–winning ethologist Konrad Lorenz described the following courtship interaction among a species of freshwater cichlid fish:

> At first nervously submissive, the female gradually loses her fear of the male, and with it every inhibition against showing aggressive behavior, so that one day her initial shyness is gone and she stands, fearless and truculent, in the middle of the territory of her mate, her fins outspread in an attitude of self-display, and wearing a dress which, in some species, is scarcely distinguishable from that of the male. As may be expected,

the male gets furious, for the stimulus situation presented by the female lacks nothing of the key stimuli which, from experimental stimulus analysis, we know to be strongly fight-releasing. So he also assumes an attitude of broadside display, discharges some tail beats, then rushes at his mate, and for fractions of a second it looks as if he will ram her, and then ... the male does not waste time replying to the threatening of the female; he is far too excited for that, he actually launches a furious attack which, however, *is not directed at his mate but, passing her by narrowly, finds its goal in another member of his species.* Under natural conditions this is regularly the territorial neighbor.[12]

Lorenz further recounts that when he kept a male and female together in an aquarium tank, without any other fish, domestic violence often developed. Things typically calmed down, however, (at least between the mated pair) when other suitable targets were included within the aquarium. The best arrangement, Lorenz found, was to have an elongated tank, with several male-female duos, each separated from neighboring pairs by glass partitions. The researcher could tell whenever these partitions were getting overgrown with algae because as the glass became increasingly opaque and the inhabitants found themselves unable to discharge their aggression upon their neighbors, squabbles would break out *within* each domestic unit.

But what about the underlying basis for passing the pain along? The fact that it is not limited to *Homo sapiens* makes us ask whether there is something deeply rooted in nature—and not just human nature—that makes sense of all this.

* * *

It turns out that there is.

Place a rat in a cage with an electrified floor and subject it to mild but repeated shocks. When necropsied, the victim will be found to have oversized adrenal glands as well as frequent stomach ulcers, both indicating serious stress. Also likely: Hypertension as well as reduced testosterone levels.

Now, repeat the experiment but with a wooden stick in the cage alongside the rat. When shocked, the rat chews on the stick, and as a result, it can endure its experience much longer without burnout. Moreover, at autopsy, its adrenal glands are smaller, and stomach ulcers fewer.[13] The rat buffered itself against its stressful situation by chewing on the stick, an act that evidently "feels good"— and *is* good—for the rat, even though it does nothing to get him out of his predicament.

Now, the kicker: Put two rats in the electrified cage. Shock them both. They snarl and fight. Do it again, and keep doing it: They keep fighting. At autopsy their adrenal glands are normal, and, moreover, even though they have experienced numerous shocks, they have no ulcers. It thus appears that when animals respond to stress and pain by redirecting their aggression outside themselves, whether biting a stick or another individual, they are essentially self-medicating, protecting *themselves* from stress.[14] (Robert Sapolsky asks us to think of the guy of whom it is said, "He doesn't *get* ulcers, he *causes* them.") By passing their pain along, such individuals minister to their own needs. It may not be ethically "good," but it is definitely "natural."

Behavioral endocrinologists have discovered similar patterns in many different species. Animals—and by all accounts, people, too—who lose a social confrontation experience what is called "subordination stress." Their blood pressure and adrenal hormones go up, while neurotransmitters that influence the sense of well-being go down. But if these same animals have the opportunity to "take it out" on another individual, their stress hormones and neurotransmitters return to normal levels. In short, living things can reduce their own pain-induced distress by passing that pain to another. Think, once again, of the pattern: "A hurts B, B hurts C." By displacing his aggression, B down-regulates his stress and upgrades his neurotransmitters by dumping his pain on someone else, who is then inclined to offload his or her burden, giving rise to "C hurts D," and so on. Alternatively, as in the case of Sweeney Todd, pain-wracked "B" may well proceed to wreak havoc, in turn, on "C," "D," "E," etc., since Mr. Todd's victims were unable to redirect their own aggression once they were dead.

For now, let's grant that there is a biochemical, hardwired basis for redirected aggression (and perhaps for retaliation and revenge as well), manifesting itself in human beings as well as in many other animals. But why is it there? It seems strange that living things would partake of such a strange and counterintuitive system, involving mechanisms that cause harm to themselves unless they cause harm, in turn, to someone else. Nor is it a satisfying explanation simply to point to eventual stress-reduction as a presumed payoff, because that begs the question of why subordination stress exists in the first place, not to mention the question of why stress should be diminished by evoking stress in someone else.

* * *

Our next step, accordingly, is to search for the "adaptive significance" of this near-universal tendency to pass along one's pain and to engage in redirected aggression in particular. If our premise is correct, and pain-passing—whether immediate (retaliation), delayed (revenge), or redirected—is responsible for much of the world's violence, human as well as animal, then it should be possible to glimpse its basis in evolution.

In short, we will go beyond questions of immediate causation to explore the deeper biological underpinnings of such behavior: Why have living things evolved with stress mechanisms that work this way? What, as biologists are inclined to ask, is the adaptive significance, the ultimate reproductive value, of relieving one's own stress by increasing another's? Our answer, which we will develop in detail in the next chapter, is that individuals who responded to painful situations by striking out at someone else have probably been more successful than those who sat back and "took it," because by signaling their continued vigor and stubborn selfhood (by demonstrating that even after being victimized, they can still dish it out), such individuals were less likely to be victimized in the future. Better, in short, to be a predator than prey, pain-causer rather than pain-wracked. The particular connection to redirected aggression would be that in a social species, the cost of being victimized almost certainly involves more than a short-term injury or loss of something (food, mate, nest-site) to the aggressor; rather it includes a loss of reputation—that is, being seen as exploitable.

In most social species, individuals are exquisitely aware of "who–whom?" a version of Lenin's famous rhetorical question, and with similar implied politics: Who is oppressing whom? Who is doing what to whom? It's bad enough to suffer someone's aggression, worse yet if in the process one is marked as vulnerable to further exploitation. In a rigidly hierarchical species, such as baboons (and human beings?), victims may well be unable to retaliate or avenge themselves against a higher-ranking perpetrator—after all, that is part of what it means to be a rigidly hierarchical species. Natural selection would therefore reward victims who conspicuously "take it out" on someone else, thereby announcing that "I may be down, but I'm not out," or "Don't get any ideas: I'm not a patsy." Thus, those who redirect their aggression aren't just a problem; they're also a solution.

Anthropologist Napoleon Chagnon reports that among the Yanomamo people of the Brazilian and Venezuelan rainforests, individuals with a reputation of being "fierce" were relatively immune to attack; they also accumulated more wives and, thus, more children. Moreover, tribes with a reputation for ferocious retribution were less likely to be raided in the first place, whereas those known to be vulnerable were more liable to be preyed upon by their neighbors.[15]

If Tom kicks Dick, who *doesn't* kick Harry, then Dick may be kicked in turn *by* Harry, as well as by others in the social group. Back to our lead-off example of Sweeney Todd: Had Sweeney not responded after being victimized, he might well have been further abused by others. In fact, early in Sondheim's dark musical, the barber is identified as an escaped convict by a previous colleague, who attempts to blackmail him, only to end up as Todd's first victim. Animals, people, even nations are painfully aware of the downside of being considered a doormat.

To recapitulate: Physiologically, as we have seen, it feels good to pass one's pain onto another, because it diminishes the accumulated stress. Evolutionarily, it is adaptive, almost certainly because it makes further victimization less likely. And historically, as well as in the modern world, it is all too common. Is there further evidence of a pervasive role for redirected aggression and its nefarious allies?

* * *

Think about "justice." There are, of course, victimless crimes, but the offenses that generate the most attention and outrage are those that result in someone being injured, if not physically, then financially and emotionally (and, as just suggested, socially). When these victims then demand justice, could they be insisting—although not in so many words—that their pain be offloaded onto someone else? Ideally, justice demands that punishment be meted out to the guilty. That is a large part of why we have courts of law: to assign guilt and determine punishment. But isn't it possible that what really matters is that once the wheels of pain have begun to spin, someone—anyone—must suffer in turn, must be made to "pay"?

We offer, therefore, this suggestion: that justice itself derives at least in part from the primitive yearning to exact retribution, for victims to pass *their* pain along. "What can be more soothing, at once to a man's Pride and to his Conscience," asked Edgar Allen Poe, "than the conviction that, in taking vengeance on his enemies for injustice done him, he has simply to do them justice in return?"[16] Moreover, the urge among victims to discharge their aggression is so strong that society steps in to make sure that this powerful impulse is given an outlet, while also being handled decorously. For all its biological propriety, revenge, after all, has a bad reputation, whereas "justice" is a different matter!

The boundaries between justice, redirected aggression, and revenge become uncomfortably blurred when outraged victims and their families demand a murderer's execution, typically insisting that only with the perpetrator's death will the surviving victims be able to achieve, as it is revealingly called, "closure." The road to justice runs through the territory of pain, in its diverse manifestations, and the differences between "just" punishment and revenge or redirected—even misdirected—aggression may be largely a matter of semantics. All of them are likely to "feel good" to the offended party, because they all operate at the same primitive level, that of passing the pain along.

Both justice and redirected aggression reestablish the social status as well as the internal physiological balance of the offended party, diminishing the initial victim's stress by subordinating someone else. This may help explain why so many crime victims respond to exculpatory evidence with outrage rather than gratitude that an innocent accused person has been spared. It also illuminates why forgiveness is also so difficult, despite the ardent recommendations of the world's greatest ethical and religious leaders. "To err is human," quipped S. J. Perelman, "to forgive, supine." To the extent that Mr. Perelman was correct, it is because to be victimized is to suffer doubly: not only the actual injury but also an accompanying risk of social subordination. "Getting even," therefore, is a goal whose meaning is literal no less than figurative, involving a more genuine leveling than most people realize, since it includes regaining lost social status along with a reconstituted internal hormone balance. There is more to "an eye for an eye" than meets the eye.

* * *

Let us also consider the intriguing possibility that modern science owes its existence, ironically, to scapegoating . . . or rather, to the people and societies who were able to *overcome* the urge to scapegoat and to redirect their anger and pain. Consider, for example, Oedipus, king of Thebes. In the famous myth, the people of Thebes are suffering from a terrible plague, which leads to the automatic conclusion that their pain must be due to someone's misbehavior. Sure enough, it is revealed that Oedipus had unwittingly killed his father and married his mother, whereupon the pain of Thebes is ultimately lifted once Oedipus heaps a hefty dose of pain upon himself.

The pattern, in a nutshell: When bad things happen to good or otherwise innocent people, the sufferers have long tended to cast blame on others, whose transgressions not only explain the ill-fortune, but whose subsequent pain and punishment lifts a burden on the initial sufferers. Whereas the Theban "plague" is the stuff of legend, along with Oedipus himself, the bubonic plague is unquestioned history, and was especially devastating in Europe during the Middle Ages. European Jews dreaded its arrival, less for the epidemic itself than for the epidemic of anti-Semitic violence it inevitably unleashed. Here is testimony by one Guillaume de Machaut, a French writer of the mid-fourteenth century, whose *Judgment of the King of Navarre* includes the following:

> Then came those false, treacherous and contemptible swine: the shameful Jews, who were wicked and disloyal, who hated the good and loved that which was evil, who gave so much gold and silver and promises to Christians, and who then poisoned several rivers and fountains that had been clear and pure, so that many lost their lives; for those who used them died suddenly. Ten times one hundred thousand undoubtedly died from it, in the countryside and in cities. Finally, then, this mortal disaster was noticed. He who sits high and sees far, who governs and provides for everything, did not want this treachery to remain hidden; he revealed it and made it so widely known that they [the perpetrators] lost their lives and possessions. Thus, every Jew was destroyed, some hanged, others burned; some were drowned, others beheaded with ax or sword.[17]

According to Guillaume (whose judgment must be considered at least somewhat suspect) one million people died from the plague, whereupon it was assumed that such devastation must have been caused by someone: the Jews. This assumption, in turn, gave license to terrible additional slaughter as those who survived the epidemic redirected their pain, anger, and aggression—satisfyingly, we must assume—upon their own chosen victims. And although the exact numbers are not known, historians are in no doubt that a terrifyingly high percentage of the European population died in medieval plagues, which in turn unleashed an orgy of killing against Jews, who were lethally scapegoated.

Of course, we know today that bubonic plague is caused by pathogens, not the "evil eye." The point is that in order for science as we now understand it to have developed, it may have been necessary for people to stop looking for the causes of disasters, and thus, of their pain, in social transgressors and instead, to begin responding to difficult circumstances by looking to natural phenomena for the causes of natural events. When plagues arrived or drought threatened, it may have satisfied a primitive need to blame other people, and to vent one's pain upon them, but genuine science requires looking instead for genuine causes, out there in the world. In short—as first suggested, in somewhat different form, by philosopher and historian René Girard—we didn't so much stop burning witches because we had science, but rather, we developed science because we stopped burning witches!

This is not to claim that all science owes its origin to restraint upon aggression, any more than all aggression derives from unrestrained pain-passing. We do suggest, however, that the Three Rs offer a novel trio of lenses through which to scrutinize human behavior. This leads to the following question: If pain-passing is so deeply rooted in the human psyche, where else might its imprint be found? If it—or rather, getting over it—helped power the advent of science (and thus, insight into that which is real), what about works of the imagination, those stories we tell ourselves, and that constitute "fiction"?

* * *

Fiction is supposed to be made-up, accounts of events that did not really happen, and yet, paradoxically, one of the most serious criticisms to be leveled against any work of fiction is that it isn't believable. The characters in question must behave with fidelity to our often-unspoken presumptions about what "human nature" really is.[18] Not surprisingly, literature, theater, poetry, and movies are awash with the Three Rs.

Pain-passing—often via redirected aggression—is a widespread theme in fiction no less than in life. It pervades Western literature, from *The Iliad*, through Shakespeare's tragedies, to the most current blockbuster flicks. It is noteworthy that even in works of the imagination—where, one might think, anything goes—only rarely are bad guys presented as doing evil for evil's sake: the mustache-twirling villain who gleefully ties the heroine to the railroad tracks because he is simply cruel, for no particular reason. Almost inevitably, for an evil character to be believable, he or she must be shown to have suffered some injury. Then it all makes sense. ("Those to whom evil is done. . . .")

Later, we will examine some of the archfiends of the human imagination, including Shakespeare's Iago and Richard III, and Nathaniel Hawthorne's Roger

Chillingworth (of *The Scarlet Letter*), looking for evidence that these malefactors were responding to their own burden of pain. Captain Ahab's inhumanly obsessive pursuit of the White Whale was rendered believable, which is to say, more in tune with what the reading audience knows to be human nature, by the "fact" that Moby Dick had bitten off his leg. *Moby Dick* may or may not be the great American novel, but there is no question that it is a great story of pain-powered revenge.

As for redirected aggression, consider James Joyce's story "Counterparts," appearing in his collection, *Dubliners*. It is the poignant tale of Farrington, a lowly clerk in a large firm, who had a bad day. Harassed by his overbearing boss, Farrington was in danger of losing his job. "He longed to execrate aloud," we are told, "to bring his fist down on something violently." But he couldn't. He had to "take it." So Farrington bore his pain and humiliation in silence until his painful workday was over at last. Then, seeking to "let off steam" in typical Joycean fashion, he went drinking with his buddies, only to spend most of the money he had obtained from pawning his precious watch. While at a pub, he even lost two arm-wrestling matches to someone much younger (Mr. Farrington, we learn, is a large man, much esteemed for his strength).

As a result, it was a sullen Farrington who headed home that evening, full of smoldering anger and vengefulness:

> He felt humiliated and discontented; he did not even feel drunk; and he had only twopence in his pocket. He cursed everything. He had done for himself in the office, pawned his watch, spent all his money; and he had not even got drunk. He had lost his reputation as a strong man, having been defeated twice by a mere boy. His heart swelled with fury and . . . his fury nearly choked him.

Farrington's young son came running down the stairs to meet him, small and vulnerable, pitifully eager to do his father's bidding, altogether innocent of his misfortunes, and unaware of the older man's pent-up rage:

> "What's for my dinner?"
>
> "I'm going . . . to cook it, pa," said the little boy.
>
> The man jumped up furiously and pointed to the fire.
>
> "On that fire? You let the fire out! By God, I'll teach you to do that again!"
>
> He took a step to the door and seized the walking-stick which was standing behind it.
>
> "I'll teach you to let the fire out!" he said, rolling up his sleeve in order to give his arm free play.

The little boy cried "O, pa!" and ran whimpering round the table, but the man followed him and caught him by the coat. The little boy looked about him wildly but, seeing no way of escape, fell upon his knees.

"Now, you'll let the fire out the next time!" said the man, striking at him vigorously with the stick. "Take that, you little whelp!"

The boy uttered a squeal of pain as the stick cut his thigh. He clasped his hands together in the air and his voice shook with fright.

"O, pa!" he cried, "Don't beat me, pa! And I'll . . . I'll say a *Hail Mary* for you. . . . I'll say a *Hail Mary* for you, pa, if you don't beat me. . . . I'll say a *Hail Mary*. . . ."

Mr. Farrington is not a very likeable character. In some ways, he isn't really a character at all but rather a conduit for anger and pain. We have all known Farringtons, and to some extent, most of us have probably been Farringtons as well. Furthermore, one need not be a specialist in developmental psychology or psychopathology to predict what sort of father, and victimizer in his own right, Farrington's young son is likely to become when he gets his chance.

* * *

Physiology, zoology, evolutionary logic, social and cultural traditions, history and literature—all are consistent with Auden's maxim: Those to whom evil has been done, do evil in return. We know that it happens, and at last, we have a pretty good idea why. Just as the first step in overcoming any challenge—from alcoholism to global warming—is to identify the problem, we would like to think that merely by alerting people to the ubiquity of the Three Rs, we will have performed a service, practical no less than intellectual. While revenge and retaliation are commonplace concepts, redirected aggression has been a more specialized notion, and we want to make it part of the common parlance as well. Moreover, redirected aggression—like violence generally—is not inevitable; there *are* ways out. Most of the world's great religions and ethical systems have struggled to teach people how to swim, not drown, in that ocean of pain-passing.

Take the many formulations of the Golden Rule, which are remarkably consistent across greatly different cultures, and that notably do *not* say, "do to others whatever has been done to you." There is a large and thoughtful body of jurisprudence and moral guidelines—often religion-based—that address matters of self-defense, retaliation, revenge, and justice; in short, how to respond to pain, and by implication, how *not* to. Even without explicitly identifying the Three Rs as the central problem that they are, enormous energy has already been expended and some wisdom accumulated, exploring not only how aggression is typically misplaced or displaced, but also how it should be placed, which is to say, the same way that porcupines are reputed to make love: *very carefully*.

So take heart! Solutions exist, based on a truth that is no less deep or widely shared than the tendency to respond to pain with the Three Rs of payback: that human beings, perhaps uniquely among animals, are capable of rising above some of their innermost promptings. We can cultivate resilience along with its sweet cousin, emotional stability, by eschewing violence and its counterparts, without sacrificing self-esteem and social status. Just as physical pain can be managed medically, so, too, can the various human responses to pain and suffering be managed—mindfully, carefully, and humanely.

References

1. J. J. Bonica (1979). The Need of a Taxonomy. *Pain* 6(3): 247–252.
2. Geronimo and S. M. Barrett (1996 [1906]). *Geronimo: His Own Story: The Autobiography of a Great Patriot Warrior*. New York: Plume.
3. John F. Burns (2003). The Mideast Turmoil: The Attacker; Bomber Left Her Family With a Smile and a Lie. *The New York Times*, A13, October 5.
4. Lawrence Weschler (1997). Mayhem and Monotheism. *The New Yorker*, Nov. 24, pp. 131–133.
5. James Bamford (2004). *A Pretext for War: 9/11, Iraq, and the Abuse of America's Intelligence Agencies*. New York: Doubleday.
6. Richard Clarke. 2004. *Against All Enemies: Inside America's War on Terror*. The Free Press: NY; Jim Mann. 2004. *Rise Of The Vulcans: The History of Bush's War Cabinet*. Viking: NY.
7. Rebecca Lawton and A. Nutter (2002). A Comparison of Reported Levels and Expression of Anger in Everyday and Driving Situations. *British Journal of Psychology* 93:407–423.
8. Carl Hovland and R. R. Sears (1940). Minor Studies of Aggression. VI. Correlation of Lynchings with Economic Indices. *Journal of Psychology* 9:301–10.
9. John Shelton Reed, Gail E. Doss, and Jeanne S. Hurlbert (2007). Too Good to Be False: An Essay in the Folklore of Social Science. *Sociological Inquiry* 57:1–11.
10. "September 1, 1939," copyright 1940 & renewed 1968 by W. H. Auden, from *Collected Poems of W. H. Auden* by W. H. Auden. Used by permission of Random House, Inc.
11. G. Vaillant (1993). *The Wisdom of the Ego: Sources of Resilience in Adult Life*. Cambridge, Mass.: Harvard University Press.
12. Konrad Z. Lorenz (1966). *On Aggression*. New York: Harcourt, Brace & World.
13. Jay Weiss (1972). Psychological Factors in Stress and Disease. *Scientific American* 226: 104–109.
14. S. Levine, C. Coe, and S. Wiener (1989). The Psychoneuroendocrinology of Stress: A Psychobiological Perspective. In *Psychoendocrinology* (S. Levine and R. Bursh, eds.). New York: Academic Press.
15. N. Chagnon (1988). Life Histories, Blood Revenge, and Warfare in a Tribal Population. *Science* 239: 985–992.
16. Edgar Allan Poe (1849). Marginalia, *Southern Literary Messenger*, 1461. Reprinted in *Poe: Essays and Reviews* (G. Thompson, ed.). New York: Library of America, 1984.
17. We thank Rene Girard (*The Scapegoat* [Baltimore: The Johns Hopkins University Press, 1986]) for pointing out the work of Guillaume de Machaut: *Guillame de Machaut, Oeuvres, Société des anciens textes français*, vol. 1. (Paris: Ernest Hoeppfner, 1908).
18. David P. Barash and Nanelle R. Barash (2005). *Madame Bovary's Ovaries: A Darwinian Look at Literature*. New York: Delacorte.

2

Biology

Animals and Molecules

Carefully rappelling down to a golden eagle's nest in Montana, the biologist was intent on putting leg bands on the recently hatched chicks so their fate could be monitored. As he descended the cliff, getting ever closer to the nest, the enraged eagle mother also flew closer and closer, screaming ever more loudly. Finally—beak snapping and claws extended—she dived at her tormentor, who was more than ten times her weight. At the last instant, the physical mismatch was too much, and the great bird swerved aside and, still screaming, flapped madly after a small gaggle of canyon wrens, which had been innocently fluttering nearby.

In fact, the eagle did not merely chase those little wrens away, she pursued them for nearly a quarter of a mile; unsuccessfully. At some level the eagle must have "known" she wouldn't catch them. Wrens are much too fast, too small, and too agile to be prey for such a large predator. The eagle was not chasing them in hope of a meal but "because" she couldn't chase her real target, the biologist.

At the time, more than 40 years ago, the biologist in question (David Barash) simply wanted to know more about eagles. He climbed into the eagle nest to learn how eagles live, to understand them and their ecosystem, and only secondarily—if at all—to inquire about what eagle biology says about evolution or behavior in general, including, perhaps, that of human beings. In the past, students of natural history studied living things to categorize them, and to describe and analyze their behavior, anatomy, physiology, embryology, ecology, and so forth. Darwin spent eight years studying barnacles, simply to understand barnacles, just as his consequential work on finches on the Galapagos Islands was undertaken because of his fascination with these animals.

Fascination with animals for their own sake thus has a place of honor in the annals of biology, although sometimes it is criticized as mere "stamp-collecting." Stamps, however, can be beautiful, fascinating, and instructive; animals, even more so. Moreover, it sometimes happens that an "album" of natural history facts, accumulated in the pursuit of what philosopher of science Thomas Kuhn called "normal science," can morph into something that is not just aesthetically pleasing but conceptually exciting: a new paradigm.[1] This certainly happened with Darwin. We are under no illusions that anything remotely comparable will occur with respect to the Three Rs, but we are nonetheless eager to share, in this chapter, an array of natural history examples, which, taken together, constitute a picture of how redirected aggression in particular manifests itself in the animal world.

Among the early twentieth-century attempts to make sense of animal behavior, one of the most prominent was that of "ethology," an approach that emphasized the study of instinctive behavior and was in many ways a healthy antidote to the focus on strictly learned behavior that dominated "comparative psychology." The earliest studies of retaliation and redirected aggression were conducted by "classical" ethologists, students of animal behavior like Konrad Lorenz and Niko Tinbergen, who watched animals and conducted experiments prior to the grand synthesis of animal behavior, population genetics, and ecology that came to be known as *sociobiology* roughly in the 1970s. The first generation of ethologists observed behavior, described it in impressive—sometimes obsessive—detail, and came up with a number of ideas and phrases to describe what was happening and why. But they lacked the tools and concepts to develop a "gene's eye" view of causality, and so there is a discrepancy between their older accounts and today's models.

Virtually anyone familiar with animals has observed the Three Rs* at work, without necessarily labeling them as such. But if these phenomena are as deep-rooted as we claim, proximally generated by underlying physiological mechanisms and ultimately buttressed by natural selection, they should also be widely distributed and not limited to *Homo sapiens* or just a few anecdotal animal examples. Hence, it should be worthwhile to look at the living world more generally. Merely listing examples, of course, can be suggestive, rather like case histories in psychoanalysis. But as psychoanalytic "research" has sadly demonstrated, anecdotes prove nothing, although the results can be entertaining in their own right, yielding good stories, sometimes with an astoundingly large scope.

The standards of proof in biology and in science generally continue to evolve, so that nowadays case histories simply do not make the grade as proof. In this chapter, nonetheless, we shall offer many examples of redirected aggression in animals and then offer some ways to understand these stories, first as a matter of physiology, and then at the deeper causative level of evolution.

Biologists use the term *proximal causation* to mean the immediately preceding events—chemical, physiological, anatomical, and experiential—that make

---

* More likely, two of the Rs—retaliation and redirected aggression—since, as we will see, revenge appears to be found only in human beings and chimpanzees. We would not be altogether surprised, however, if it were eventually discovered in other species as well; look for revenge in the smarter species: primates, dolphins, perhaps dogs, cats, and so forth, but not in worms or amoebae.

something happen. "Testosterone is a chemical that causes physical and bio-chemical changes in individuals that result, among other things, in male-pattern structures and behaviors." "*Clostridium perfringens* is a bacterium that causes food poisoning and gas gangrene." The two preceding sentences are examples of proximal causation. We know what makes something happen, and can prove it with a variety of experiments. When most biologists or physicians seek to answer questions of causation, such as what causes acne or heart attacks, they think in proximate terms. The answers have to do with hormones, chemicals, germs, genes, and environmental factors. These are all "How" questions.

By contrast, "ultimate causation" has come to mean answers to questions that begin with "Why?" The more technical questions of this sort begin with, "What is the adaptive significance of . . . ." A sociobiologist or evolutionary biolo-gist would ask, "What is the adaptive significance of acne?" or "of heart attacks?" (and, given our current ignorance in these cases, would probably be hard pressed to come up with a good answer!).

Retaliation and redirected aggression have been studied both at the proximal level and the ultimate level, in different animal species. In our earlier example of the irritated golden eagle and the anxious, dangling biologist, the biologist was not studying redirected aggression. If he had been, and if his focus were on prox-imate causation, he might have attempted to implant electrodes in the eagle's brain to see what regions were activated when she chased those innocent little canyon wrens. Or he might have taken blood samples before and after the event, looking for changes in hormone levels. Had he been concerned with ultimate causation, on the other hand, he would have sought to learn what effect, if any, chasing wrens has on the eventual success of those chicks our hapless biologist was seeking to monitor.

In this chapter, we will cite a large number of animal examples to show that redirected aggression is commonplace, with both proximal physiological causes and ultimate adaptive value.[†] However, don't expect proof. The science simply isn't there yet. Our hope is that some of our readers will take up the challenge, and refine these examples with both kinds of evidence.

* * *

Like people, animals typically do not go out of their way to cause mayhem. At the same time, like people, animals are liable to retaliate if attacked. Presumably this helps prevent further victimization and may also reduce the probability of being attacked in the first place. The first of the Three Rs, retaliation, is therefore not especially surprising or interesting.

[†] Also, because it is great fun to peek inside the world of other living things; all the more so, perhaps, when accompanied by a *frisson* of recognition.

On the other hand, and at the other extreme, revenge is very rare among animals, and is close to being a human specialty (more on this later). In between lies redirected aggression. As the Cole Porter song goes—albeit referring to sex, not redirected aggression—"Birds do it, bees do it, even monkeys in the trees do it." We're not so sure about the bees (although we wouldn't be altogether surprised), but it is abundantly clear that many animals engage in redirected aggression. As we'll see, this includes species as diverse as birds and horses, not to mention monkeys, whether in the trees or on the ground. It also includes fish—in fact, every major group of vertebrates. The fact that redirected aggression is widespread in the natural world certainly doesn't legitimate its occurrence among human beings. But it adds credibility to the claim that redirected aggression is "natural," and thus, explicable in terms of certain general principles that apply to the living world more broadly.

When it comes to the Three Rs, we are not alone.

Back at the ranch, a dominant mare, impatient because dinner is a half-hour late, kicks a young gelding when he gets too close, and the gelding in turn chases the pony away from the salt block. On the African savannah, a young adult vervet monkey who has just been threatened by a dominant adult proceeds to chase a bewildered adolescent bystander. Once alerted to it, you can observe redirected aggression all around you. Researchers have seen the phenomenon, too. When rainbow trout, for example, are kept with others of their species, they are somewhat aggressive, but not especially so. But when exposed to other trout that are larger and more aggressive than themselves, on the other side of a Plexiglas partition, they respond with a 77% increase in their tendency to attack any colleagues that are smaller than they are—which they had previously ignored.[2] The social life of rainbow trout is in fact quite simple, although evidently more complex than many would think.

The African cichlid fish, *Astatotilapia burtoni*, by contrast, partakes of a complex and sophisticated dominance hierarchy, one that has only recently been unraveled. In this species, a small proportion—generally fewer than 20%—of the males are socially dominant, and also readily identified because they are large and brightly colored, either yellow or blue, with a dramatic black stripe through their eyes, plus a conspicuous red patch on their bodies. These big, brightly colored fish are also reproductively active, for which purpose they aggressively defend territories against other large, dominant males. Most males of this species, the remaining 80% or so, are small, drab-colored, and socially subordinate; they typically school with the females, and indeed, until recently, they were thought to *be* females. Being territorial or non-territorial, however, is not a permanent condition among these animals. Unlike rainbow trout, male African cichlids can switch between the two roles in a matter of days.

The social system of *A. burtoni*, with their two kinds of males, is regulated by male–male aggression. These interactions be can either direct: A threatens or attacks B, who retaliates in kind—or redirected: A attacks B, after which B thrashes C. Since males are readily identifiable as either territorial or non-territorial, the question arises: Is there a difference in how the two kinds of males respond to conflicts? To find the answer, researchers showed both territorial and non-territorial males the same film clip of a large, dominant male displaying aggressively. (Admittedly, this is less realistic than using a genuine animal, but the filmed fish does exactly the same thing each time the film is played.) The results were unequivocal: Territorial males were substantially more likely to directly threaten the video display, whereas non-territorial males shown the same image were more likely to engage in redirected aggression toward other non-territorial tank mates.[3]

Despite the different social systems of rainbow trout and African cichlid fish, two common features can be identified for both species. First, redirected aggression is readily evoked in each case. And second, individuals pass aggression down the dominance hierarchy, with those who experience aggression responding to their victimization by attacking others who are subordinate to themselves. A dominant fish, when threatened, fights back, while a subordinate threatens someone else. If, for whatever reason (such as a Plexiglas partition), a dominant individual is not able to respond to the outside threat, then he is especially likely to redirect his response toward whoever is available, notably a subordinate.

This is a widespread pattern, one that can readily be evoked even in artificial circumstances. Train a pigeon, for example, to receive food in response to pecking a key. Then, if the food is no longer forthcoming, the pigeon will attack another, innocent bird, housed in the same box.[4]

Breeding behavior often sets the stage, which is not surprising, given that reproductive competition is typically a major source of aggression. Among mice, females are not ordinarily subjected to much aggression by males. But exceptions occur—at least under laboratory conditions—when a resident male is presented with a male intruder, especially if the two opponents are kept apart but the resident is left with his mate nearby; under such circumstances, the agitated male frequently attacks his own female.[5] When paired with females that have been hyped up on extra estrogen, male rhesus monkeys show increased sexual interest and decreased aggression toward them; once more, no surprise here. Interestingly, however, they also show an *increase* in the amount of redirected aggression displayed toward everyone else.[6]

Many animals—and perhaps most mammals—employ some kind of harem mating system, in which one male gathers together a number of females. In such cases, the harem-keepers are especially likely to be aggressive toward other males, as is the case, for example, among African impalas. Of these graceful antelopes, a single dominant adult male works hard to maintain a harem of females, among which a handful of subordinate, immature males will also be tolerated, largely because these juveniles don't constitute a serious threat to the harem-keeper. But other male adults are another story. During the breeding season, full-grown bachelor impala bulls regularly approach the dominant male and "his" females, thus threatening his suzerainty (and, more to the point, his evolutionary success), whereupon a fight may well ensue among the would-be harem-masters. If the conflict is resolved quickly, especially if the challenging male runs away before an actual fight ensues, the dominant male is liable to attack the juvenile males within his group . . . the ones he had previously ignored.[7] It is as though, having become competitively aroused, the dominant male has accumulated so much "aggressive energy" that he cannot simply turn it off once the situation is suddenly resolved; the built-up agitation—whatever that is— seems to spill over to other, innocent individuals (more on this particular proximate explanation later).

Depending on the species, competition over food can also be sufficient to set off a cascade of redirected aggression. As one field researcher noted, among spotted hyenas, "A chases B, B chases C, C chases D, and D chases vultures."[8] When it comes to nonhuman primates, however, although food and sex contests sometimes evoke redirected aggression, almost anything will suffice. During the first minute after they have been attacked by another individual—regardless of the reason—Japanese macaque monkeys are considerably more likely to attack other members of the group, compared with matched controls who have not been similarly victimized. It is, as statisticians like to say, a very "robust effect."[9] In another species, rhesus macaques, within the first minute of having been attacked, victims are ten times more likely to harass a bystander who, nearly always, is lower-ranking than themselves.[10]

People tend to find what they are looking for. Although this is less the case in science than in other areas of human endeavor, there is nonetheless a tendency for researchers to report results when they confirm expectation or if they are novel and therefore especially exciting. Only rarely does the world learn of research that is basically disconfirming. And so, we feel obliged to mention the following technical article, inspired by the observation that Australian magpies are often seen to attack members of other species. Its title: "Can redirected aggression explain interspecific attacks by Australian magpies on other birds?"[11] And its conclusion: "No, it can't."

So let's be clear. Redirected aggression is definitely *not* responsible for all of the fighting, biting, and chasing that goes on in the world of animals, any more than among people. It is surprisingly difficult to ascertain exactly how much violence is due to redirected aggression, but we suspect that it is far more than generally acknowledged.

In many cases, of course, the phenomenon is obvious, although the interpretation is not. Thus, it isn't uncommon for dogs who have been chasing another animal on the opposite side of a fence to suddenly turn and fight vigorously— although nearly always without injury—among themselves. Similarly, two angry dogs separated by a fence and thus prevented from attacking each other will often turn and attack another animal, typically one who is socially subordinate and (equally important) accessible.

People who deal professionally with domestic animals have long been familiar with the problem of redirected aggression, since human beings are often the innocent bystander-victims. An article in *Newsday* recounted how Pepper, a boxer dog described as "friendly . . . [with] no signs of aggression," attacked two young girls. It seems that a few days before the seemingly unprovoked attack, Pepper's family had adopted a new dog—which may well have induced Pepper to attack the weakest members of its "pack."[12]

Redirected aggression also takes place among species not normally considered to be especially hierarchical, such as domestic cats.[†] And in fact, among the various behavior problems commonly encountered when it comes to *Felis domesticus*, redirected aggression ranks particularly high. In an article titled "How to Keep Your Cat from Going Crazy," the reader is introduced to Lucy and her five-year-old cat Ramises. Ramises had suddenly and viciously attacked Lucy, who had owned Ramises since he was a kitten, and who reported that the cat had never acted this way before. After a complete blood analysis to rule out any pathology, the author, a clinical assistant professor at the Tufts University School of Veterinary Medicine, concluded that Ramises was suffering from the all-too-common feline problem of redirected aggression. It turns out that Ramises had recently witnessed an especially vigorous fight between two other cats, after which he turned on his owner, who was simply in the wrong place at the wrong time.[13]

This, in turn, highlights the most common circumstance in which animal redirected aggression becomes salient for human beings: when people become the victims. The University of Pennsylvania maintains a highly regarded animal behavior clinic that deals specifically with "problem animals," aggressive dogs and cats in particular. It appears that cats are especially prone to such (mis) behavior. For example, out of 27 cases of cats attacking humans, 14 were clearly diagnosed as due to arousal, and "the most common arousing stimulus was the presence of another cat. Other arousing stimuli included high-pitched noises, visitors in the house, a dog, an unusual odor, and being outdoors unexpectedly." As the veterinarians who analyzed these cases point out, "Sudden, apparently unprovoked attacks are particularly frightening, and owners may suffer severe bite and claw wounds."

[†] It is worth pointing out, however, that cats are not really as solitary as commonly believed. Most are certainly capable of living comparatively isolated lives in which they interact, one-on-one, with a human owner or family. But their repertoire makes it clear that they are also capable of complex social interactions.

However, in many of these cases, the attacks are not as unprovoked as many indignant cat owners might think. It turns out that redirected aggression is by far the most common identifiable cause of such cat-human attacks. In a typical example, the owner was bitten when attempting to break up a fight between two animals, or after disturbing a cat that had been threatening or merely observing another cat, even when one animal was outside and the other inside, watching through a window. Interestingly, owners often reported that their cats remained aroused and aggressive—exhibiting "hissing, growling, loud yowling, dilated pupils, and piloerection when approached"—for up to several hours after the initial provocation.[14] Cats who witness an aggressive incident, even through a window, may in a sense experience the aggression vicariously, perhaps via so-called "mirror neurons." In any event, domestic cats in particular are liable to persist in redirecting their aggression against the same person, even with no obvious provocation from the bewildered human.[15]

* * *

At first glance, it might seem peculiar that redirected aggression sometimes takes place interspecifically; that is, individuals not only pass their pain along to someone else (A hurts B, B hurts C), but even, on occasion, to someone else (individual C) from an entirely different species. But given that a subordinate hyena will chase a vulture, or a helpless, frustrated person might kick a cat, perhaps it isn't really all that odd that an agitated cat should occasionally bite a human.

Victims may attack whatever they can get hold of, even if their victims occasionally are not even animals at all. According to one researcher's report, a young female rhesus monkey once found herself surrounded by a number of higher-ranking individuals, including genetic relatives of the social superior who had just pushed her around. Kept from redirecting, she "proceeded to energetically and noisily pursue several lizards and a rat before peering intently into and repeatedly threatening a small bush (completely devoid of vertebrates)."[16]

When a highly "riled up" animal attacks another animal, or a person (or a lizard, rat, or even a small bush), it is tempting to conclude that at some level, the attacking individual is simply "letting off steam." And this interpretation may well be correct, as far as it goes (although as we will see, it almost certainly does not go far enough). Ethologists in the tradition of Konrad Lorenz and Niko Tinbergen paid special attention to the fixed behavior patterns that constitute much of an animal's repertoire. In the course of cataloging and interpreting such actions, these pioneering animal behaviorists developed a conceptual model that posited a buildup of behavioral motivation—something called "action-specific energy"—that was eventually released when an animal encountered an appropriate stimulus.

This so-called hydraulic model quickly lost favor among most biologists, largely because it could not specify exactly what was building up, not to mention how "it" was released, and why such release caused a reduction in such "pressure." The concept of action-specific energy was simply too reminiscent of those old, discredited and untestable non-explanations such as "phlogiston," "caloric" or "interstellar ether," whose proponents seemed to believe that to name something is to make it go away. We might call this belief the "Rumpelstiltskin effect," after the fairytale whose title character magically disappears as soon as he is named; the real world of scientific explanation operates somewhat differently, although the temptation persists to substitute nomenclature for comprehension.

On the other hand, the classical ethological approach works surprisingly well—almost distressingly so—when it comes to "explaining" redirected aggression as well as displacement activities, which are similar. The two phenomena have so much in common that the words are often interchanged, so that what we here term "redirected aggression" is frequently (but in our view, incorrectly) called "displaced aggression."

Displacement activities are seemingly irrelevant behaviors that occur when an animal is in a situation of internal conflict, such as during a dispute between two territory owners taking place on the margins of their adjoining properties. Under such conditions, each participant is motivated to run away, but also, simultaneously, to stay and fight. It cannot do both, but is highly agitated and energized to do *something*. If the animal in question is an avocet,[§] for example, that "something" is likely to be really incongruous, notably tucking its head into its wing feathers, in a posture otherwise seen only when the bird is asleep. According to the early ethologists' model, such peculiar actions occur because the animal is highly aroused—its action-specific energy at a high level—but it is inhibited from discharging that underlying energy in any appropriate way. So, the energy is *displaced* into another behavioral channel. Recall the harem-keeping impala who, all revved up but with no one to attack after an intruding male is driven away too quickly, "takes it out" against resident juveniles he normally ignores.

There is in fact some evidence that animals actually do accumulate a need to perform certain actions, as though some sort of undefined energy has built up and demands release. Some time ago, for example, a beautiful ocelot, one of the stars of the feline house at the Woodland Park Zoo in Seattle, had begun looking distinctly less beautiful. This heretofore gorgeous cat was losing substantial patches of his fur, leaving the bare skin discolored and raw. The zoo staff treated this worrisome dermatological disorder with a variety of antibiotics (suspecting a skin infection), and when this didn't work, with vitamin supplements. Finally, the head veterinarian suspected that the problem was behavioral rather than

---

[§] Lovely, stilt-legged shorebirds with distinctive up-turned bills; hence, their Latin genus name *Recurvirostra*

nutritional. He contacted David Barash, who noticed that the animal was actively conniving in his disorder. The ocelot's fur was not falling out, he was *pulling* it out. His diet had been impressively complex and complete, including a well-balanced mixture of beef heart and chicken carcasses. But something was nonetheless missing. Ocelots in nature primarily eat birds; however, the chickens supplied to this well-cared-for zoo inhabitant lacked feathers (they had been donated—as an ocelot-supporting community service—by a local supermarket). Under natural conditions, ocelots pluck their avian prey before consuming them, so the next step was to suggest that the increasingly-naked ocelot be given whole chickens, feathers and all.

Immediately, he started plucking his food . . . and stopped plucking himself.

Observations of this sort had led ethologists such as Konrad Lorenz and Niko Tinbergen to hypothesize their "hydraulic model" of motivation. Conceptually, if not physiologically, it might be only a small step from displacement activities (the strange case of the self-plucking ocelot) to redirected aggression. In the latter case, after losing an aggressive confrontation, or even, as with the house-cat watching through a window while two other cats fight, an individual is aroused but unable to discharge its accumulated emotional energy by fighting back (or, in the case of the observer cat, joining in the fray), it does something unsuitable and seemingly even silly. Instead of tucking its head into its shoulder, like an aroused but inhibited avocet, it may attack an innocent bystander.

Let us grant that the ethologists' hydraulic model lacks any genuine explanatory power. It nonetheless remains appealing, not least because most people find it subjectively satisfying; when asked to "explain" such actions as displacement activities or redirected aggression, people are intuitively inclined to reach for a similar interpretation. When we get angry or otherwise upset, it can often feel good to "get the anger out," by going for a run, pounding a table, yelling at the top of one's lungs, or, for some people, taking "it" out on someone else.

One of the foundational descriptions of redirected aggression occurs in a research article published in 1953, titled "Some Comments on Conflict and Thwarting in Animals."[17] It described some seemingly incongruous behavior on the part of black-headed gulls during the mating season, making full use of the ethologists' assumptions about drives and energy:

> During pair-formation among black-headed gulls, a male adopts a territory, where females visit him from time to time. The male is quite placid when alone on his territory; spending much of his time sleeping or preening in a relaxed fashion. When a female arrives, however, his demeanor changes abruptly. Her arrival stimulates the attack, escape, and sex drives of the male. These drives are, of course, incompatible. The activated attack drive is manifested, not only by actual attacks on the female, but also by the variety of threat postures the male shows

her. In addition, the male often rushes to vent his attack drive on other animals: other black-headed gulls, shelducks, lapwings, oystercatchers, and even human observers. It is obvious for several reasons that these sudden attacks are not provoked by any behavior of the attacked animals. First of all, many of the attacked birds are not showing any of the behavior normally liable to provoke attack. In the second place, although the male is certainly aggressive (he screams attack or threat calls) when he rushes away from the female, he may then have to fly a considerable distance and quite obviously have to search around for a scapegoat.

The authors went on to suggest that "this type of behavior would seem to deserve a name, and we suggest that it should be called a 'redirection activity.'"

The neighbor-attacking behavior of a male black-headed gull is somewhat different from more traditional cases of redirected aggression, since the male gull is not responding to his own victimization (neither by the female nor by anything else), but rather, at least in the interpretation of traditional ethologists, to an excess of conflicting motivations, which result in his acting out his suppressed aggression toward innocent bystanders. The underlying similarity of the behaviors, however, seems obvious. Maybe there is even similarity in the physiological mechanisms that underlie these acts, although modern biologists are unlikely to join the classical ethologists in hypothesizing some sort of "spark-over" or "overflow," despite such strange, suggestive cases as that of the aroused impala or the plucked ocelot.

Many examples of similar behavior have been described, involving several species of birds, such as herring gulls,[18] Ross's gulls,[19] and prairie falcons.[20] Coincidentally, the prairie falcon case describes situations that are very similar to that of the female golden eagle with which we opened this chapter:

> When these falcons are disturbed at the nest, by a human intruder, they usually begin to swoop at the intruder. Most of these swooping attacks, however, are not quite completed. Within a few feet of the intruder, the falcons will suddenly swerve to one side or another. . . . Under these circumstances, Prairie Falcons will attack other birds, such as Barn Owls or Ravens that happen to be passing by.[21]

And of course, such behavior is not found only among birds. Many zoo visitors report being occasionally threatened by some of the animals they watch, especially certain monkeys and apes. Unsophisticated animal-watchers are liable to see this behavior as comical, which often leads them to threaten back, hoping to evoke yet more reactions. When sophisticated zoo-goers see animals behaving in this way—threatening human visitors on the other side of their glass walls or fenced enclosures—they are likely to interpret such events as cases in which the animals have been inappropriately harassed, which, sadly, is often the case. It takes greater insight yet, however, to consider that sometimes the behavior involves redirected aggression and, paradoxically, may actually help keep the peace among the animals in question, just as the redirected aggression shown by male black-headed gulls appears to facilitate—somehow—benevolent courtship between male and female.

Consider, for example, the not-very-peaceful life of captive chimpanzees. Among the animals maintained at the Yerkes Regional Primate Research Center in Atlanta, Georgia, fighting among adult chimps generates an average of 3.55 wounds per individual per year. At another facility, the University of Texas M. D. Anderson Cancer Center Science Park, the average is 4.5. These wounding rates are 2.5 times and 3.0 times higher than those experienced by chimps housed at another research site, the Chimpanzee and Human Communication Institute (CHCI) at Central Washington University in Ellensburg, Washington. Although every animal facility is different—in physical layout as well as the specific individuals composing each social group—Roger and Deborah Fouts of the CHCI believe that the substantial difference in wounding rates is due to a substantial difference in the animals' social environment, notably the way human caretakers are instructed to behave.[22]

Thus, the Foutses insist that all human personnel at the CHCI adopt submissive chimpanzee postures when dealing with the animals, as a result of which CHCI caregivers are the "lowest-ranking" individuals in the chimp social hierarchy. The humans therefore provide a safe outlet immediately following chimp–chimp conflicts: When trouble erupts among these animals, the loser threatens a human instead of another chimpanzee. Nearly two-thirds of post-conflict aggression at the CHCI is redirected at a human being, and only one-third to another chimp. By contrast, at typical biomedical facilities (Yerkes, University of Texas) where human beings do not present themselves as targets for redirected aggression, the numbers are reversed, and then some: 22% of post-conflict aggression generates threats that are redirected toward people, and 78% toward other chimpanzees. And many of these latter threats result in actual injury.[23]

This is not to argue that people should get in the habit of harassing animals, whether captive or not, thereby providing an outlet for their (i.e., the animals') aggressive "energy." Nor do we support the deservedly defunct hydraulic model of behavior motivation, which assumes that a buildup of energy demands eventual release, producing a situation that is regularly resolved by "venting" the accumulated energy upon a third individual, or even an object. Nonetheless, there is simply no doubt that under conditions of conflict, and especially just after losing a confrontation with another individual—animals, and, we strongly suspect, people—frequently need to "let off steam."

But why?

* * *

First, a quick digression (not a redirection). Ultimate or "Why" questions are generally answered by evolutionary biologists with answers that relate to genetic success. Insofar as genes influence behavior, those genes must have increased the reproductive success of the individual who carries them[¶]; otherwise, they would have been selected against. In four billion years of evolutionary time, genes that made more copies of themselves prospered compared to those that made fewer. It is true that within the DNA of mammals lie genes that came from long ago, like genes that came from retroviruses, whose exact function now is not clear. They may have become freeloaders, genes that don't do anything useful right now, or they may have hitchhiked from previous infections. But overall, if there is genetic underpinning for a given behavior, it is a good bet that the behavior in question contributed to the reproductive success of its possessor.

When speaking of reproductive success, biologists often employ the word *fitness*, which may have little or nothing to do with *physical fitness* as used in ordinary language. If there are genes for aggression, be it directed or redirected, it is almost certainly because those genes helped project more of themselves into future bodies. Thus, when evolutionary biologists ask "Why do living things engage in redirected aggression?" they really mean "Insofar as redirected aggression may have a genetic basis, how does it increase the fitness of those animals that do it?" In short, why has it evolved? Or, what is its adaptive significance?

The short answer is that no one knows. Regardless of whether it is a matter of letting off "energy," "steam," or some sort of proximal, neurophysiological equivalent, one of the more intriguing questions about redirected aggression concerns its underlying evolutionary rationale. There are downsides to "releasing the anger" and "taking it out"—whatever *it* may be—on someone else. After all, a bystander receiving the brunt of someone else's pain may well fight back. And even if the redirector does not get him or herself into yet more trouble, it takes time and energy to redirect one's aggression in the first place. Why bother? If you think that "venting energy" provides an explanation, then you must ask why the biology of so many species has favored the accumulation of such "energy" in the first place, given that less-energetic individuals would seem to be better off. After that harem-keeping impala easily chased away his competitor, why didn't he just kick back, relax and congratulate himself, instead of spending time and energy kicking at those juveniles?

Scientists studying animal behavior have long devoted particular attention to animal aggression, and for good reasons: not only are there potential lessons here for a crucial human problem, but also the behaviors in question tend to be

---

[¶] More precisely, they must have increased the representation in succeeding generations of identical copies of those genes themselves. In the most obvious cases, this is achieved by increasing the number of offspring, but it also occurs via other relatives, with the importance of each relative devalued in proportion as he or she is more distantly related—and thus, less likely to carry the gene(s) in question.

dramatic and eye-catching. More recently, however, researchers have begun looking into *post*-conflict behavior, with particular attention to animal reconciliation.[24] After a fight, or even a nonviolent dispute, individuals of many species do things that calm down the participants and help rebuild social networks that may have become dangerously frayed. Not all animals are inclined to reconcile; some respond to conflict by distancing themselves, or simply remain grumpy, frustrated, and irritated with each other. An even smaller proportion partakes of what has been called "consolation," whereby third parties intervene to calm a distressed victim. For example, a dominant chimpanzee will sometimes literally extend a hand to an animal who has recently been threatened or attacked, thereby, it appears, helping the loser feel better.

It takes professional courage for modern scientists to investigate such actions, especially reconciliation and consolation, since the research itself comes perilously close to the third rail of animal behavior research: imputing human motivations to animals. (Touch it, and you might not get electrocuted, but you are less likely to get tenure.) As it turns out, however, "natural conflict resolution" is real, and has been described in objective, quantifiable terms. It is a genuine biological phenomenon. Moreover, a likely biological payoff for such post-conflict activities can be hypothesized and investigated: the supposition that individuals who reconcile—as well as those who facilitate the reconciliation of others—will experience a reproductive, evolutionary advantage as a result. This, in turn, can generate adaptive pressures for being a peacemaker and for accepting and facilitating the peacemaking efforts of others.

In fact, the pendulum appears to have swung beyond biologists' earlier fascination with aggression to a current focus on benevolence, the result being a flurry of articles with titles such as "Post-Conflict Behavior of Wild Chimpanzees (*Pan troglodytes schweinwurthii*) in the Budongo Forest, Uganda," "How to Repair Relationships—Reconciliation in Wild Chimpanzees," "Reconciliation and Variation in Post-Conflict Stress in Japanese Macaques (*Macaca fuscata fuscata*)," and so forth. Interestingly, nearly all research studies on this topic involve nonhuman primates, perhaps because post-conflict reconciliation is more frequent in our closer animal cousins, or because its manifestation among primates is more identifiable by human researchers; or maybe simply because its occurrence in creatures that are evolutionarily close to *Homo sapiens* is seen as especially noteworthy.

In any event, we cannot help noting that hidden in the back, almost as an afterthought among those studies documenting what happens in the immediate aftermath of animal conflicts has been . . . redirected aggression. It may seem churlish to point this out, but the reality is that reconciliation is not the only post-conflict outcome; often, a loser proceeds to attack an innocent bystander. In fact, much of what has recently been learned about redirected aggression—especially among monkeys and apes—has come about as an accidental side-effect of research focused on its conceptual opposite: reconciliation. The result has been revived awareness of a behavior that had been nearly ignored since the early ethologists identified and then "explained" it, more than half a century ago.

Along with this awareness have come new explanatory efforts. Many researchers now include redirected aggression as part of a species' repertoire of ways to resolve conflict.[25] This may be stretching things, since redirected aggression necessarily involves *extending* conflict to yet another individual, one who had not previously been involved. On the other hand, redirection could actually help resolve an ongoing conflict if it is a diversionary ploy that distracts the current opponent and encourages him to join in attacking a third party. There is evidence, in fact, that this occurs among chimpanzees: After a fight, both winners and losers increase their rates of attacking bystanders.[26] A chimpanzee on the losing end of a fight could also proceed to attack another chimp in the hope of diverting his opponent's attention toward a new target. In such cases, it isn't so much that a loser redirects his own aggression as that he seeks to redirect the other chimp's aggression, and to channel it so that the two former opponents join in attacking someone else.[27] This, it appears, is reconciliation via redirection.

When it comes to consolation behavior—doing things to bring about reconciliation between two individuals in conflict—it is also possible that a bystander could do so as a way of avoiding redirected aggression toward herself,[28] in which case redirected aggression itself could be selected for as a way to motivate others to be consoling.

This is not the usual course of events, however. Indeed, consolation is quite rare, whereas redirection is common. Most often, something more devious, even downright Machiavellian is going on. In a twist that Mario Puzo's godfather would recognize (and doubtless approve), victims of one-on-one conflicts frequently proceed to attack their victimizer's *relatives*. If redirection as a diversionary ploy seems too devious to be undertaken by animals, it pales by contrast with the kin-directed retribution that has repeatedly been documented for vervet monkeys[29] as well as several different kinds of macaques.[30] "Kin-directed redirected aggression" is not only a mouthful, but a reality in which a monkey, having been attacked by another member of the social group, responds by attacking the attacker's niece, nephew, son, or daughter. "Attack me again," the initial victim is essentially saying, "and your kid gets it."

One of the most important insights into the evolutionary biology of animal social behavior has been the recognition of so-called kin selection, whereby individuals are moved to behave benevolently toward each other as a function of their genetic relatedness. While "fitness" means the reproductive success of an individual, "inclusive fitness" means the reproductive success of that individual plus his or her relatives, valued as a function of the probability that they hold genes in common as result of their shared ancestry. Closer relatives are more benevolent, or altruistic; more distant ones, less so. In the process, individuals are behaving in a way that enhances the fitness of their genes, which are likely to be benefited in proportion as the recipient is closely related to the one doing the behaving.

This, in turn, opens the door to manipulating the altruistic"—in this case, protective—inclinations of individuals and their genes, as follows: "Better stop attacking me, or think twice before attacking me again, because I could always take it out on your relatives—which is to say, on copies of your own genes, residing in these individuals." This does not necessarily imply that a redirecting vervet monkey, for example, recognizes different levels of genetic connection; rather, it would be sufficient if a victim—individual B—simply recognizes that his victimizer, A, is often closely associated with individual C, so A's victim could respond to an insult or attack from A by taking it out on C.

If so, then genes within A that induced that individual to refrain from subsequent nastiness would leave more descendants than would genes that allowed its body to continue its aggressive course, come what may. And by the same token, genes within B that sent out a godfather-like message would also prosper.

The arch-diplomat Metternich once famously observed that "diplomacy is the art of avoiding the appearance of victory." Why? It can be disadvantageous to press home a competitive success if, as a result, you so humiliate your opponent, or drive him into a corner, that he becomes dangerous and threatening to the victor. Otto von Bismarck, nineteenth-century chancellor of Prussia, architect of German unification, and hardly a pacifist, understood this principle. During the Austro-Prussian War, in 1866, the Austrians were badly defeated at the Battle of Koniggratz, far more soundly than anyone had expected. At this point, political pressure quickly developed within Prussia for a wider victory over Austria, including the dismemberment of the Austrian empire itself. But Bismarck insisted on limiting Prussian demands to the provinces of Schleswig and Holstein, thereby preventing a wider war with France and possibly Russia and Britain.[††]

There is little doubt that for anyone (people or animals) involved in a serious conflict, victory is nearly always the goal. But it can be gained at too high a cost; specifically, it may be important to avoid defeating your opponent so thoroughly that he feels constrained to take it out on others, or make new alliances, perhaps to your eventual disadvantage. The threat "I know where your children go to

---

[*] One could as well describe such tendencies as "selfish," since what appears altruistic when performed by individuals can be selfish—when directed toward gene-sharing relatives—at the DNA level.

[††] It is tempting to identify a parallel with George H. W. Bush's restraint, after kicking the Iraqi Army out of Kuwait in 1991, in not proceeding to Bagdad and overthrowing Saddam Hussein.

school" is thoroughly despicable, but it can also be chillingly effective, even among animals.

It is worth repeating that such threats—and the tendency to respond adaptively to them—would not require any cerebral calculations on the part of either victim or victimizer. Natural selection would simply ensure that individuals who behaved as though they knew the genetic math would leave more descendants.

For a loser in a serious fight amongst, say, Japanese macaques, to attack the winner's close relatives can nonetheless be a risky tactic, since a winner's relatives are likely to be dominant themselves. Moreover, it is always possible that to attack someone's kin is to raise the ante, a seemingly ill-advised strategy for an already defeated individual. When it happens, moreover, kin-directed redirected aggression seems closer to revenge than to the more familiar, reflexive phenomenon of plain old-fashioned retaliation, or what we hope is now becoming another readily identified event: redirected aggression. This may be due to the necessary imposition of a time lag, since locating and then attacking a victimizer's kin typically takes longer then simply lashing out at whoever happens to be nearby.

It would not always be strictly necessary, however, for would-be kin-oriented redirectors to know precisely who is related to whom in order to get back at relatives of whoever recently victimized them. A general tendency to strike out at anyone nearby would probably target relatives disproportionately, if only because kin tend to associate. In any event, low-ranking individuals often flee the scene of a violent conflict: not only because, as the African saying goes, "when elephants fight, the grass gets trampled," but also because a losing elephant may actually go out of his way to stomp on the nearest patch of grass.

* * *

Once upon a time, there was a patter-song called "Talking Union" that was popular among lefties. Part of it went: "You may be down and out, but you're not beaten. Pass out a leaflet and call a meetin'." The social benefit of redirected aggression may well be the first part of the song, a signal that "I may have lost a conflict but I'm not beaten," as well as elements of the second. While critters don't pass out leaflets, they can certainly recruit kin and cooperative "friends" to create coalitions, packs, herds, and cliques. There is a benefit to sending the message "Maybe I've just lost a conflict, but don't get the wrong idea. I'm not a pushover. And moreover, since you are my relatives and friends, we need to stick together to keep our status and resources."

To understand this argument, it helps to be familiar with the "loser effect." It is the flip side of the "winner effect," something familiar to managers of prizefighters or anyone concerned with developing and maintaining human self-esteem and success. In short, winning promotes winning, partly because of the internal physiological changes that result, partly because of the psychological importance of a positive self-image, and partly because others, knowing that someone has been successful, are likely to treat him or her with deference and the expectation of further success—all of which contribute to a self-fulfilling prophecy.[31] Ditto, inverted, for the "loser effect." Losers at time t are liable to lose again at $t + 1$. This is true for animals no less than for people.[32]

The "I'm not a pushover" hypothesis suggests that redirected aggression is one way that a loser attempts to minimize his or her losses, essentially by tacking a bit of "winner effect" onto the newly absorbed "loser effect." A growing body of evidence supports this interpretation, notably the finding that, for a number of species, from rodents to primates, losers who fail to redirect immediately after their loss are more likely to suffer further losses. Strictly speaking, such findings, even as they accumulate, do not *prove* anything. As followers of Karl Popper readily acknowledge, scientific research rarely if ever generates absolute proof; what distinguishes science from idle speculation is that it offers the prospect of *disproving* a hypothesis, thereby helping its practitioners get just a bit closer to what they unblushingly call "the truth." In the case of animal observations, the "I'm not a pushover" hypothesis has consistently been confirmed—or at least, not disconfirmed. But it will take many more studies on many species in many different situations to justify a high level of confidence that it is correct.[‡‡]

For now, it is the best explanation we have. Moreover, it leads to some interesting predictions, which could in turn lead to greater refinement of the concept, and thus, to yet more testing. The "I'm not a pushover" hypothesis suggests, for example, that species susceptible to "piling on" or social bullying should be especially prone to redirected aggression. More generally, social species (such as human beings) should be more inclined to engage in redirected aggression than are species that are more solitary, such as woodchucks or gibbons. This is because being a pushover is less problematic for solitary creatures, among whom social reputation is less relevant; in addition, compared to a social species, loners are by definition less likely to be watched by other conspecifics, making it less consequential how they respond to being victimized, or indeed, whether they respond at all. On the other hand, solitary species have less opportunity to engage in redirected aggression, if only because there are likely to be fewer bystanders—innocent or not—in the vicinity. So whereas we would predict less redirected aggression in solitary than social species, even if our prediction holds up, this could be for reasons other than the validity of the "I'm not a pushover" hypothesis.

---

‡‡ "Failure to disconfirm" sounds like thin gruel, particularly for those seeking nothing less than robust certainty, and yet—especially if it occurs repeatedly—such "failures" lead to a kind of success: heightened confidence that the hypothesis in question is valid.

Another prediction: Assuming that the species in question is intelligent enough to modify its behavior as a result of recent experience—that is, to learn—we might predict that "successful" redirected aggression, by reducing the likelihood of subsequent revictimization, should result in a higher probability of subsequent redirected aggression by the affected individuals, if they were ever victimized again.

* * *

Among macaque monkeys, where the phenomenon has been most intensely studied, individuals who lose a contest, after which they neither reconcile with their more successful opponent nor redirect aggression toward a third party, are liable to receive significantly higher rates of threats and attacks within the next few minutes—not just from the original attacker but also from previously uninvolved bystanders.[33] A similar pattern has been documented among gorillas[34] and baboons,[35] all of which is consistent with this interpretation: Those who don't send out the "Talking Union" message, who are down and out but who *don't* indicate, by attacking someone else, that they aren't beaten, are more likely in fact to get beaten again.[§§]

This presumes that bystanders are aware of what is going on, even when they seem to be uninvolved. And usually they are: Disinterested is not the same as uninterested. Baboons are so alert to Lenin's query, "who, whom?"—and also so accustomed to redirected aggression on the part of a defeated individual— that researchers Dorothy Cheney and Robert Seyfarth of the University of Pennsylvania were able to use this awareness-plus-expectation to examine the higher mental powers of these animals. Specifically, following disputes between two adult female baboons, Cheney and Seyfarth played a tape of a dominant female, the one who had been victorious in the dispute, giving a scream, of the sort normally vocalized when such an individual is herself attacked by another baboon who is even higher ranking. The effect was to generate a great deal of attention from subordinate females, who already knew and anticipated that when an otherwise dominant animal is herself bested by someone higher up on the social scale, she is likely to take it out on those below her.[36] Particularly in a highly social species, there are no pure bystanders.

Accordingly, "eavesdropping" is not uniquely human; it is a hallmark of animal societies as well.[37] And not surprisingly, individuals are especially poised to pick up information about each other's relative fighting abilities, as well as about who

---

[§§] Unlike immature and subordinate male gorillas, which typically redirect aggression and do so with great frequency, adult female gorillas do not. This appears to be because among gorillas, adult females generally retaliate directly and immediately against aggressors (except when it comes to beating up the dominant, silverback male; no one does that).

is up and who is down on the social ladder.[38] This is shown by the fact that, immediately after a confrontation, others treat the participants differently, depending on whether they won or lost. Some examples include Siamese fighting fish,[39] green swordtail fish[40] domestic chickens,[41] and great tits (relatives of the North American chickadees).[42] A similar phenomenon might help explain why human beings, too, are so preoccupied with inter-individual conflicts, even if they do not have a direct relationship with any of the participants, including why audience interest is so great when it comes to boxing or wrestling matches, as well as competitive events of all sorts, extending even to televised "reality shows."

As part of the evolutionary history of any social species, there has probably been particular pressure upon bystanders no less than on participants to obtain prompt, real-time information, since, unless it is reinforced, the "loser effect" is typically short-lived, making it important for third parties to act quickly if they wish to take advantage of any changing circumstance. This, in turn, would make it especially important for the loser to assert himself promptly to keep things from spiraling out of control. Consistent with this, most observed cases of redirected aggression, at least among animals, occur within a few minutes of the precipitating conflict. In two different monkey species, long-tailed and rhesus macaques—the average lag between a conflict and subsequent redirected aggression was 12 and 28 seconds, respectively.[43]

Biologists are increasingly aware of the power of social circumstances when it comes to driving evolutionary change; non-scientists, we suspect, not so much. Thus, when thinking about natural selection, it is tempting to focus on dramatic physical changes in a species' environment, of the sort that occurs over geological time: droughts, floods, snowstorms, ice ages, or even the movement of whole continents. Although these things are often important, and sometimes overwhelmingly so, the same applies to a species' social environment, typically with a much shorter time scale. For most species, an individual's likely reproductive success is crucially influenced by subtle aspects of his or her social situation, which includes but is not limited to the ability to make friends, recruit allies, maintain his or her status in the dominance hierarchy, obtain a suitable mate, etc., and all in real time, which, in the case of social interactions, may involve minutes, even seconds.

The "Red Queen hypothesis" is named for an event in Lewis Carroll's *Through the Looking Glass* in which the Red Queen insists to Alice that because the world is moving so quickly, it is necessary to run in order to merely stay where you are. To actually *get* anywhere, announces the Queen, you have to go twice as fast! Social circumstances, too, are always changing, sometimes to one's benefit, sometimes to one's detriment. Redirected aggression, as biologists see it, is a way of keeping up, making sure that even an apparent loser does not lose too much.

It is not clear exactly what influences the time-course of any particular event of conflict followed by possible redirected aggression, although the simple proximity of appropriate third-party targets is doubtless a factor. If redirected aggression were merely a means of discharging accumulated energy, it would not matter who is watching or lurking nearby, but it does: immediate, real-time "audience effects" have been well documented, especially for nonhuman primates.[44] Even among creatures as diverse as Siamese fighting fish[45] and songbirds,[46] individuals perceived to have lost a contest are liable, shortly there-after, to lose their mates.

There is simply no doubt that among most species, most of the time, audiences are closely attuned to what goes on between protagonists. When the observers are not "running with the Red Queen," they are carefully watching to see who else is doing so, and who is gaining and who is falling behind.

Further evidence for the "I'm no pushover" explanation for redirected aggression comes from the fact that attention goes both ways: Protagonists are typically influenced by whether or not they have an audience, or think they do. Everyone knows the difference between being simply humiliated, and being *publicly* humiliated. Social psychologists have found, moreover, that if someone knows that his social diminishment has been witnessed, he will be especially determined to get back at the provokers, or, failing that, at someone else.[47] This effect seems especially pronounced among men as compared to women[¶¶]. For example, when two men are having a public dispute, the presence of a third-party observer literally doubles the probability that a verbal argument will escalate into a physical fight.[48]

Further evidence for the importance of an audience comes from the fact that redirected attacks tend to be especially noisy as well as conspicuously eye-catching, at least among animals. This could be because the redirector is especially aroused, but also, perhaps, because it is in the redirector's interest to make sure that his actions are duly noted (the two explanations are not mutually exclusive). There is no intuitively obvious reason why enhanced arousal should produce enhanced noise; could it not as readily cause greater attentiveness and thus an unusual degree of quiet? On the other hand, if the underlying purpose of redirected aggression is to send a message, especially one of continued vigor, then it makes sense to be noisy and conspicuous. (If, as we suspect, redirected aggression among human beings tends to be on the quieter end, this may be because people, unlike animals, have to contend with a widespread moral sense that redirected aggression, despite its biological appropriateness, is ethically unjustifiable. This will be further explored in chapters 6 and 7.)

¶¶ Which is precisely what is predicted for a biologically harem-forming species such as *Homo sapiens*, in which social and thus reputational success correlates with additional mating opportunities.

The prospect that redirected aggression is in large part a social signal offers novel insight into what is otherwise something of a mystery: Why should defeated individuals go out of their way to threaten or attack someone else, given that doing so is both energetically expensive and potentially downright dangerous, especially for someone who has recently been bested by someone else and is likely to be fatigued and not at the top of his or her game? The answer may be, paradoxically, that it is precisely *because* such behavior is demanding, risky, and potentially costly that it occurs.

Thus, it is easy for someone—animal or human—to make optimistic or even grandiose statements about his capabilities. Talk is cheap. And insofar as individuals may be selected to exaggerate their quality, their prospective audience would be selected to ignore or see through the deception. As evolutionary theorists have recently come to appreciate, this in turn sets the stage for "honest signaling," in which communication about one's personal qualities is believable in proportion as it involves the use of unfakeable signals.[49] After all, anyone can claim anything. The key is to do so in a manner that commands credibility. Shakespeare's King Lear, for example, rails against his terrible daughters as follows:

> I will have such revenges on you both,
> That all the world shall—I will do such things—
> What they are, yet I know not: but they shall be
> The terrors of the earth! (From Shakespeare's King Lear, Act 2, scene iv)

This outburst is especially poignant because, at this point, Lear is altogether helpless, a pitiful old man reduced to blustering verbal threats with nothing to back them up. By the same token, it might be possible for a defeated animal to utter the equivalent of an empty, Lear-like statement of personal power . . . but no one would believe it. Our point is that redirected aggression is not a vain boast or an empty threat; it makes demands on the perpetrator no less than on the bystander-victim, which in turn makes it all the more suitable as a "down but not out" signal. Precisely because it is costly and potentially risky, it is not easily faked.

Finally, insofar as redirected aggression is ultimately driven by the payoff of sending a message that says "I may be down but I'm not out," there is no reason for this information to be transmitted only to bystanders. The current adversary might also be relevant, perhaps especially so. And in fact, it is common to see redirectors glancing back at their previous opponent/victimizer immediately before attacking a bystander or even while doing so.[50] There may therefore be a "reconciliatory component" in such cases—if not an effort to become friends with one's oppressor, then perhaps to induce him or her to have greater respect for the defeated individual. "OK, you beat me, but look at what I can still do!"

There is, in fact, an intriguing connection between post-conflict reconciliation and redirection, at least among long-tailed macaques, which, so far as we can determine, is the only species in which this relationship has been explored. Among these monkeys, the initial aggressor is much more likely to reconcile with his victim if that victim redirected its aggression shortly after being attacked; that is, if the victim proceeded to victimize someone else.[51] A reasonable interpretation is that the aggressor judges that his victim is worth reconciling with if he has the spunk to redirect. If so, then the very prospect that his attacker would react this way could motivate the victim to redirect after being attacked. Interestingly, in instances in which reconciliation occurs shortly after the initial attack, the victim—now reconciled with his attacker, and presumably also enjoying a reestablished position within the social group—is much less likely to redirect aggression onto anyone else.

* * *

We have briefly discussed redirected aggression among animals in particular, pointing toward the most likely underlying reason for its existence: what evolutionary biologists call "ultimate" or "distal" causation. As for its immediate occurrence—its "proximate" causation—we briefly considered and largely rejected early efforts on the part of ethologists, not because they are necessarily wrong, but because such "hydraulic" notions as "energy overflow," the "discharge of accumulated frustration," or "sparking-over of built-up motivation" are more like metaphors or verbal models than scientific explanations.

This is not to say, however, that the proximate cause of redirected aggression is a complete mystery. To the contrary, a coherent understanding is finally coming into view, one that makes intellectual and biological sense, promising a satisfying picture of what happens inside the central nervous system of animals, and, probably, at least to some extent, people, too.

The key proximate consideration, we believe, is stress. Everyone has a subjective understanding of stress and what it entails: agitation, discomfort, fatigue and—if prolonged—illness. Increasingly, there is also objective knowledge of the concomitants of stress at the physiological level. Much of the mammalian stress response is mediated by hormones produced by the adrenal glands, which are located just above the kidneys. Each adrenal gland is divided into two parts, an outer layer that secretes hormones derived from cholesterol, such as cortisol, aldosterone, and DHEA; and an inner layer that secrets catecholamines such as adrenalin (also called epinephrine) and nor-adrenalin (also called norepinepherine). The inner hormones mediate blood pressure, heart rate, and the "fight or flight" response in general. The outer hormones mediate glucose and salt metabolism, and various aspects of healing, such as inflammation.

The entire adrenal gland is intimately connected to the brain, including the pituitary gland, which regulates many different hormones, as well as other parts of the brain that deal with immediate vital functions such as breathing, memory, and learning. Prolonged stress can result in hypertension, lowered sex hormone levels, reduced immune responses, and autoimmune reactions due to inflammatory proteins known as cytokines. In the short term, the body's biomedical response to stress is adaptive; continued too long, however, it can be devastating. The pituitary adrenal-axis works quite well if there is an acute stress, because the inner and outer layers promote emergency responses that may be life-saving, such as extreme energy to run from a predator, or enhanced strength to stand and fight. However, prolonged stress such as domestic conflicts or workplace subordination can result in long-term secretions of these chemicals, which in turn have negative consequences.

Crucial to understanding the likely connection between stress and redirected aggression is to recognize that stress is not only caused by time pressure, heavy demands at work, free-floating anxiety about the future, the pressure of never-ending "to do" lists, or emotional and physical pain. For many living things, stress has a huge social component. Some of the most impressive research in this area has come from the laboratory of the husband-and-wife team of Robert J. and D. Caroline Blanchard, at the University of Hawaii. The Blanchards and colleagues have carefully documented something that has come to be called *subordination stress*, which is exactly what it sounds like; namely, the stress associated with being socially subordinate.[52]

Much of this research involves placing various combinations of rats in a "visible burrow system" (VBS), a laboratory habitat intended to mimic natural conditions. The Blanchards' VBS consists of underground tunnels and chambers that resemble burrows dug by the animals in nature, but illuminated under infrared light so researchers can see what is going on. So far as the animals are concerned, however, all is dark (like tunnels and burrows are supposed to be). The laboratory "surface" is kept on a 12-hour day/light cycle. In different studies, different combinations of adult rats have been introduced into this system, usually two females and three, four, or five males. Although food and water are always available, the males in particular generate their own social stress, with one individual typically emerging as dominant within each social group, while the remaining subordinate males find themselves unable to gain access to females and—perhaps worse, from their perspective—bossed around by the higher-ranking dominant male.

Most interesting for our purposes, levels of corticosterone—a steroid produced by the rats' adrenal glands and indicative of stress—tend to be sharply higher in subordinates. There are also distinct anatomical changes such as adrenal and spleen enlargement, reduction in thymus and testes, plus a number of other detailed biochemical changes, revealed in a dazzling series of research papers published by the Blanchards and their collaborators over the past decade and a half.[53] For readers eager for the precise biochemical details, here are just a few of those recently discovered effects on the brains of subordinate animals: increased tyrosine hydroxylase and galanin mRNA in the locus ceruleus, decreased glucocorticoid and mineralocorticoid mRNA in the CA1 region of the hypothalamus, an increase in 5-HT2 receptor binding in the cerebral cortex, as well as diminished arginine vasopressin mRNA expression in the bed nucleus of the stria terminalis and medial amygdala.

These details are all notable, but don't miss the greater conceptual forest for the precise biomolecular trees: Thanks to such work, we now know conclusively that as a result of subordination stress alone, there is a physiological cascade that results in corticosterone going up, sex hormones going down, and the stressed subordinate being definitely worse off.[54]

Stress has long been considered important, especially since the now-classic work of Hans Selye, begun in the 1930s. Interestingly, the role of stress was first recognized by the biomedical community at about the same time that ethologists were just developing their hydraulic model of animal motivation, later applied to redirected aggression. But no one connected the dots. These days it is increasingly clear that not all stressors are created equal and that subordination stress, in particular, is typically more severe than some of the previous laboratory models of stress, such as those involving learned helplessness or chronic mild physical duress. It is associated with increased frequency of atherosclerosis, insulin-resistant diabetes, reproductive failure, immune suppression, and so forth.[55]

Thus far, and regrettably, the Blanchards have not studied redirected aggression among their subordinated rats. If they did so, however, one can predict that they would find diminished stress profiles among the subordinates who responded to their subordination by redirecting their experience; in effect, by passing along their pain and in the process subordinating others. For this area of research, we turn to work by Stanford University primatologist, neuroendocrinologist and stress maven, Robert Sapolsky.

It turns out that among free-living olive baboons, certain subordinate males are most likely to initiate fights, and, should they lose, to redirect their aggression onto others . . . who are more subordinate yet, and who are further subordinated by the experience. These initiators (who, not coincidentally, appear to be en route to becoming dominant), are also likely to have lower cortisol and higher testosterone levels than do subordinates who "take it" rather than "dishing it out." In short, some baboons avoid subordination stress by passing that stress along.[56] Stress mitigation of this sort is not simply due to being involved in a fight, but rather is specifically associated with *initiating* a fight with another individual shortly after having lost one.

Nor is this pattern found only among subordinates. Picture a competitive contest between two individuals. As things proceed and the outcome becomes increasingly evident, winner and loser develop increasingly divergent neuroendocrine profiles: among the victors, levels of the neurotransmitter serotonin goes up, and testosterone also goes up, while peripheral concentrations of glucocorticoids decline to their previous, baseline levels[***]. Serotonin is a prominent brain chemical that mediates a sense of contentment, completion, and fulfillment in human beings. This is why selective serotonin reuptake inhibitors (SSRIs) such as Prozac, Paxil, and Zoloft, which increase serotonin availability, help alleviate severe depression. Murderers and suicide victims have low levels of serotonin metabolites, which further contributes to the conclusion that it does not feel good to be deficient in serotonin. Indeed, one can conceive of depression as a chronic state of feeling like a loser and having the brain chemicals to match.

A common research paradigm is to pair animals in a variety of laboratory circumstances, creating round-robin or tournament competitions, while monitoring the various brain chemicals of the participants. When this is done, losers consistently not only undergo greater initial increases in adrenally mediated stress hormones, but they also remain stuck with elevated levels for a much longer time.[57] These differences persist as long as the protagonists are kept together.[58]

Among the rewards of social success, the increase in serotonin levels and reduction in glucocorticoid levels presumably feels good to the victor, just as reduced serotonin and testosterone levels plus increased catecholamines and cortisol certainly feel bad to the loser. Interestingly, when subordinates are removed shortly after having been defeated, the now-lonely winners show less glucocorticoid down-regulation; in other words, deprived of their victims, they are less likely or less able to experience the "high" that otherwise comes from winning. This is true even for lizards and fish.[59]

The connection between neurochemistry and aggression is complex, however, and resists simple one-to-one conclusions. For example, when young golden hamsters are exposed daily to aggressive adults and then tested for their own aggressive inclinations, it turns out that these subjugated individuals are more likely to engage in redirected aggression—attacking others that are younger and weaker than themselves—but *less* likely to attack animals of their own age and size. Moreover, they experience a 50% decrease in brain levels of the hormone vasopressin—which facilitates aggression—along with a 20% increase in the density of serotonin-sensitive fibers (serotonin typically inhibits offensive aggression in this species).[60] This small example is just one case study highlighting that biology can be complex, often defying simple explanations.

[***] In primates, the most important glucocorticoids are cortisol and hydrocortisone; among many rodent species, the key chemical is corticosterone. In all cases, these are closely related steroid hormones secreted by the adrenal glands. The "catecholamine hormones" epinephrine and norepinephrine have effects that are similar to those of the glucocorticoids, but their actions are quicker, taking place in seconds rather than minutes.

Here is more complexity: In studies of free-living baboons, conducted with his student Justina Ray, Sapolsky found that, just as not all stress is created equal, not all individuals are equally stress-sensitive. Although some dominant baboons have cortisol concentrations indistinguishable from those of subordinates, others are literally in a class by themselves, depending on their personal behavioral styles. In particular, dominant males have reduced biochemical indices of stress if they are especially adroit at distinguishing between potentially threatening rivals and those who are just hanging around; if they are more likely to initiate fights that they end up winning; and if, after losing a fight, they are especially likely to redirect their aggression onto an innocent bystander.[61] Once again, the biochemical take-home message is if you are stressed, pass it along, "take it out" on someone else. By passing along their pain, victims modulate their own internal plight, at the same time generating trouble for the next one down the line.[62]

In any event, for the stressed individual who has just been bested in a fight or even a less-intense conflict, redirection leads to a kind of resolution; namely, resolving the internal physiological imbalance that the experience has generated. As we have already noted, redirected aggression must therefore be seen as not only a problem (and a very serious one), but also a solution, and one that appears to act on two different levels simultaneously: the proximate or physiological as well as the ultimate or evolutionary.

But why not just say that redirected aggression takes place simply for its proximate, physiological benefits; namely, because it feels good to reduce one's arousal and down-regulate the level of stress hormones? This would take a rather narrow view of causation, like saying that people eat food purely for its physiological and metabolic benefits: because they are hungry and, in such a state, consuming food feels good. A more complete biological answer must respond to the question, "*why* does it feel good?" In this case, the answer is easy: Under such conditions, it is adaptive to eat (prolonged starvation not being conducive to eventual reproductive success), so natural selection has outfitted animals with a physiological and behavioral reward system that induces them to consume appropriate quantities of food, and to feel good in the process.

We submit that by the same token, a fish, bird, mouse, or macaque who responds to losing a conflict by attacking someone else would also say that doing so "feels good." Similarly, the early ethologists who argued that redirected aggression was a way of discharging "surplus excitation" might also deserve another hearing, bearing in mind that "motivational pressure" generated by blocked behavioral outlets may simply be another way of describing the fact that selection has favored individuals who, upon experiencing situations of conflict and especially subordination, respond by doing something about it. Something that requires energy and that sends a message, despite its immediate cost. If so, it would have felt good to our ancestors whenever they responded to situations of personal pain and degradation by inflicting similar pain and degradation on those around them, just as it feels good to eat when hungry, or to sleep when tired.

Not that it always works. These days, we can fool ourselves by eating foods that "feel good," such as chocolates, or fats, but that actually do us harm. But most people nonetheless find them attractive, probably because in our evolutionary past, there was an advantage associated with eating sweets and fats, and our deeper selves have not caught up with the fact that times have changed and that advantage has been eliminated. Thus, our primate ancestors almost certainly profited from sugary food, since they ate large amounts of fruit, and fruit is ripest (and accordingly, most nutritious) when it is rich in sugar. Similarly, fats are high in caloric value, and rare in wild game; eating fat must have been a special treat for our Pleistocene predecessors. These days, however, we can fool our taste buds by creating sweet foods of all sorts that are virtually devoid of nutritional value, as well as devouring fatty meats—larded with cholesterol acquired in a commercial feed lot—which, like excessive pain-passing, are truly bad for us.

The point is that certain actions, such as passing along pain, may continue to taste "sweet" to us today, even though such apparent "sweetness" can be a poor criterion for judging its real desirability. "If it feels good, do it," we have been told, and indeed, in our distant evolutionary past, this may have been good advice. But in the twenty-first century, some things may feel good but actually be bad for us as well as for everyone else, as outmoded as valuing our foods in proportion to their sugar or fat content. Passing the pain may well be worse than passing the butter or the candy; a biologically persistent but currently misguided attempt to improve the situation of injured and diminished people by injuring and diminishing those around us.

Just as natural selection has orchestrated digestive physiology and neurochemistry to reward food-restricted individuals who "do the right thing" (not ethically right, mind you, but fitness-enhancing), the likelihood is that evolution has orchestrated aggressive physiology to encourage losers to pass along their pain, to demonstrate to bystanders and opponents alike that although they may be down, they had better not be counted out. In the past, such payback was probably biologically and socially adaptive. But not now.

References

1. Thomas S. Kuhn. (1962). *The Structure of Scientific Revolutions*. Chicago: University of Chicago Press.
2. Øyvind Øverli, Wayne J. Korzan, Earl T. Larson, Svante Winberg, Olivier Lepage, Tom G. Pottinger, Kenneth J. Renner, and Cliff H. Summersa. (2004). Behavioral and neuroendocrine correlates of displaced aggression in trout. *Hormones and Behavior* 45: 324–329.

3. T. S. Clement, V. Parikh, M. Schrumpf, and R. D. Fernald. (2005) Behavioral coping strategies in a cichlid fish: The role of social status and acute stress response in direct and displaced aggression. *Hormones and Behavior* 47: 336–342.

4. N. H. Azrin, R. P. Hutchinson, and D. F. Hake. (1966). Extinction-induced aggression. *Journal of Experimental Analysis of Behavior* 9: 191–204.

5. Eisenberg, (1962). Studies on the behavior of *Peromyscus maniculatus gambelli* and *Peromyscus californicus parasiticus. Behaviour* 19: 177–207; E. C. Simmel and D. A. Walker (1970). Social priming for agonistic behavior in a "docile" mouse strain. *American Zoologist* 10: 486–487.

6. D. Zumpe and R. P. Michael. (1979). Relation between the hormonal status of the female and direct and redirected aggression by male rhesus monkeys (*Macaca mulatta*). *Hormones and Behavior* 12: 269–279.

7. F. Walther. (1984). *Communication and Expression in Hoofed Mammals.* Bloomington, IN: Indiana University Press.

8. C. J. Zabel, S. E. Glickman, L. G. Frank, Woodmansee, K. B., and Keppel, G. (1992). Coalition formation in a colony of prepubertal spotted hyenas. In: *Coalitions and Alliances in Humans and Other Animals* (ed. A. H. Harcourt and F. B. M. de Waal). Oxford, UK: Oxford University Press.

9. F. Aureli, H. C. Veenema, van Panthaleon van C. J. Eck, and van Hooff, J. A. R. A. M. (1993). Reconciliation, consolation, and redirection in Japanese macaques (*Macaca fuscata*). *Behaviour* 124: 1–21.

10. A. J. N. Kazem and F. Aureli. (2005). Redirection of aggression: Multiparty signaling within a network? In *Animal Communication Networks* (ed. P. K. McGregor). Cambridge, UK: Cambridge University Press.

11. D. K. J. Morgan, J. R. Waas, and J. Innes (2007). Can redirected aggression explain interspecific attacks by Australian magpies on other birds? *Behaviour* 144: 767–786.

12. Wil Cruz (2004). "Dog Could Be Returned: If Family Wants Her, Boxer Who Mauled Girl May Be Released." *Newsday* 8 Feb. Queens edition, pp. A16 ff.

13. A. Marder. (1999). "How to Keep Your Cat from Going Crazy!" *Prevention.* March, 167.

14. B. L. Chapman and V. L. Voith. (1990). Cat aggression redirected to people: 14 cases 1981–1987. *Journal of the American Veterinary Medical Association* 186: 947–950.

15. B. V. Beaver. (2004). Fractious cats and feline aggression. *Journal of Feline Medical Surgery* 6: 13–18.

16. A. J. N. Kazem and F. Aureli (2005). Redirection of aggression: Multiparty signaling within a network? In *Animal Communication Networks* (ed. P. K. McGregor). Cambridge, UK: Cambridge Univ. Press.

17. M. Bastock, D. Morris, and M. Moynihan (1953). Some comments on conflict and thwarting in animals. *Behaviour* 6: 66–84.

18. Niko Tinbergen (1953). *The Herring Gull.* London: Collins.

19. S. A. Buturlin. (1906). The breeding grounds of the Ross's Gull. *Ibis* 131–139.

20. A. C. Bent. (1938). Life histories of North American birds of prey. Smithsonian Institution Bulletin #170.

21. M. Bastock, D. Morris, and M. Moynihan, (1953).

22. M. L. Jensvold, A.-A. Field, J. Cranford, R. S. Fouts, and D. H. Fouts (2005). Incidence of wounding within a group of five signing chimpanzees (*Pan troglodytes*). *Laboratory Primate Newsletter* 44(1): 8–12.

23. N. Malone, L. Vaughan, and A. Fuentes (2000). The role of human caregivers in post-conflict interactions of captive chimpanzees (*Pan troglodytes*). *Laboratory Primate Newsletter*: 39(1): 2–7.

24. See, for example, F. Aureli and F. B. B. de Waal (eds.) (2000). *Natural Conflict Resolution.* Berkeley, CA: University of California Press.

25. See, e.g., Joan B. Silk (2002). The form and function of reconciliation in primates. *Annual Review of Anthropology* 31(2002): 21–44.

26. S. E. Koski, H. de Vries, S. W. van den Tweel, and E. H. M. Sterck (2007). What to do after a fight? The determinants and inter-dependency of post-conflict interactions in chimpanzees.

Behaviour 144: 529–556. R. M. Wittig and C. Boesch (2005). How to repair relationships— reconciliation in wild chimpanzees. *Ethology* 111: 736–763.

27. S. Scucchi, C. Cordishi, F. Aureli, and R. Cozzolino (1988). The use of redirection in a captive group of Japanese monkeys. *Primates* 29: 229–236.

28. M. Das, Z. Penke, and J. A. R. A. M. van Hooff, (1997). Affiliation between aggressors and third parties following conflicts in long-tailed macaques (*Macaca fascicularis*). *International Journal of Primatology* 18: 157–179.

29. D. L. Cheney and R. M. Seyfarth (1989). Redirected aggression and reconciliation among vervet monkeys, *Cercopithecus aethiops*. *Behaviour* 110: 258–275.

30. P. G. Judge. (1982). Redirection of aggression based on kinship in a captive group of pigtail macaques. *International Journal Primatology* 3: 301; F. Aureli and C. P. van Schaik (1991). Post-conflict behavior in long-tailed macaques (*Macaca fascicularis*): I. The social events. *Ethology* 89: 89–100. F. Aureli, R. Cozzolino, C. Cordischi, and S. Scucchi, (1992). Kin-oriented redirection among Japanese macaques: An expression of a revenge system? *Animal Behaviour* 44: 283–291.

31. I. D. Chase, C. Bartolomeo, and L. Dugatkin, (1994). Aggressive interactions and intercontest interval: How long do winners keep winning? *Animal Behaviour* 48: 393–400. I. D. Chase, C. Tovey, D. Spangler-Martin, and M. Manfredonia (2002). Individual differences versus social dynamics in the formation of animal dominance hierarchies. *Proceedings of the National Academy of Sciences* 99: 5744–5749.

32. M. Bekoff and L. A. Dugatkin. (2000). Winner and loser effects and the development of dominance relationships in young coyotes: An integration of data and theory. *Evolutionary Ecology Research* 2: 871–883.

33. Kazem and Aureli, (2005).

34. D. P. Watts (1995). Post-conflict social events in wild mountain gorillas (*Mammalia, Hominoidea*). I. Social interactions between opponents. *Ethology* 100: 139–157.

35. D. L. Castles and A. Whiten (1998). Post-conflict behavior of wild olive baboons. II. Stress and self-directed behaviour. *Ethology* 104: 148–160.

36. D. L. Cheney and R. M. Seyfarth. (1989). Redirected aggression and reconciliation among vervet monkeys, *Cercopithecus aethiops*. *Behavior* 110: 258–75.

37. P. K. McGregor (1993). Signalling in territorial systems: A context for individual identification, ranging and eavesdropping. *Philosophical Transactions of the Royal Society of London*, Series B, 340: 237–244. P. K. McGregor, T. M. Peake, and H. M. Lampe. (2001). Fighting fish, *Betta splendens*, extract relative information from apparent interactions: What happens when what you see is not what you get. *Animal Behaviour* 62: 1059–1065.

38. T. M. Peake (2005). Eavesdropping in communication networks. In *Animal Communication Networks* (ed. P. K. McGregor). Cambridge, UK: Cambridge Univ. Press.

39. R. F. Oliveira, P. K. McGregor, and C. Latruffe (1998). Know thine enemy: Fighting fish gather information from observing conspecific interactions. *Proceedings of the Royal Society of London*, Series B, 265, 1045–1049.

40. R. L. Earley, and L. A. Dugatkin (2002). Eavesdropping on visual cues in green swordtail (*Xiphophorus helleri*) fights: A case for networking. *Proceedings of the Royal Society of London*, Series B, 269: 943–952.

41. M.-E. Hogue, J. P. Beaugrand, and P. C. Lague (1996). Coherent use of information by hens observing their former dominant defeating or being defeated by a stranger. *Behavioural Processes* 38: 241–252.

42. T. M. Peake, A. M. R. Terry, P. K. McGregor, and T. Dabelsteen (2001). Male great tits eavesdrop on simulated male-to-male vocal interactions. *Proceedings of the Royal Society of London*, Series B, 268: 1183–1187.

43. Kazem and Aurelli, (2005).

44. A. Keddy Hector, R. M. Seyfarth, and M. J. Raleigh (1989). Male parental care, female choice, and the effect of an audience in vervet monkeys. *Animal Behaviour* 38: 262–271. D. L. Cheney and R. M. Seyfarth (1990). Attending to behavior versus attending to knowledge: Examining monkeys' attribution of mental states. *Animal Behaviour* 40: 742–753.

45. C. Doutrelant, P. K. McGregor, and R. F. Oliveira (2001). The effect of an audience on intra-sexual communication in male Siamese fighting fish, *Betta splendens*. *Behavioral Ecology* 12: 283–286.

46. D. J. Mennill, L. M. Ratcliffe and P. T. Boag (2002). Female eavesdropping on male song contests in songbirds. *Science*, 296: 873.

47. S. H. Kim, R. H. Smith, and N. L. Brigham. (1998). Effects of power imbalance and the presence of third parties on reactions to harm: Upward and downward revenge. *Personality and Social Psychology Bulletin* 24: 353–361. R. Kurzban, P. DeScioli, and E. O'Brien. (2007). Audience effects on moralistic punishment. *Evolution and Human Behavior* 28: 75–84.

48. R. B. Felson. (1982). Impression management and the escalation of aggression and violence. *Social Psychology Quarterly* 45: 245–254.

49. Amotz Zahavi, Avishag Zahavi, Amir Balaban, and Na'ama Ely. (1997). *The Handicap Principle: A Missing Piece of Darwin's Puzzle*. New York: Oxford University Press.

50. N. J. Emery, E. N. Lorincz, D. I. Perret, M. W. Oram, and C. I. Backer, (1997). Gaze following and joint attention in rhesus monkeys (*Macaca mulatta*). *Journal of Comparative Psychology* 111: 286–293. M. Tomasello, J. Call, and B. Hare (1998). Five primate species follow the visual gaze of conspecifics. *Animal Behaviour* 55: 1063–1069.

51. F. Aureli, and C. P. van Schaik, (1991). Post-conflict behavior in long-tailed macaques (*Macaca fascicularis*): I. The social events. *Ethology* 89: 89–100.

52. D. C. Blanchard, R. R. Sakai, B. McEwen, and R. J. Blanchard (1993). Subordination stress: Behavioral, brain and neuroendocrine correlates. *Behavioural Brain Research* 58: 113–121.

53. R. J. Blanchard, C. R. McKittrick, and D. C. Blanchard. (2001). Animal models of social stress: Effects on behavior and brain neurochemical systems. *Physiology of Behavior* 73(3): 261–71. M. P. Hardy, C. M. Sottas, R. Ge, C. R. McKittrick, K. L. Tamashiro, B. S. McEwen, S. G. Haider, C. M. Markham, R. J. Blanchard, D. C. Blanchard, R. R. Sakai. (2002). Trends of reproductive hormones in male rats during psychosocial stress: Role of glucocorticoid metabolism in behavioral dominance. *Biology of Reproduction* 67(6): 1750–1755. L. R. Lucas, Z. Celen, K. L. Tamashiro, R. J. Blanchard, D. C. Blanchard, C. Markham, R. R. Sakai, B. S. McEwen. (2004). Repeated exposure to social stress has long-term effects on indirect markers of dopaminergic activity in brain regions associated with motivated behavior. *Neuroscience*124(2): 449–57.

54. R. M. Sapolsky (2005). The influence of social hierarchy on primate health. *Science* 308: 648–652.

55. R. M. Sapolsky, L. Michael Romero, and Allan U. Munck. (2000). How do glucocorticoids influence stress responses? Integrating permissive, suppressive, stimulatory, and preparative actions. *Endocrine Reviews* 21: 55–89.

56. R. M. Sapolsky, and J. C. Ray (1989). Styles of dominance and their endocrine correlates among wild olive baboons (*Papio anubis*). *American Journal of Primatology* 18: 1–13. C. E. Virgin, Jr., and R. M. Sapolsky (1997). Styles of male social behavior and their endocrine correlates among low-ranking baboons. *American Journal of Primatology* 42: 25–39.

57. T. Schuurman (1980). Hormonal correlates of agonistic behavior in adult male rats. *Progress in Brain Research* 53: 415–520; R. P. Hannes, D. Franck, and F. Liemann (1984). Effects of rank order fights on body and blood concentrations of androgens and corticosteroids in the male swordtail (*Xiphophorus helleri*). *Zeitschrift für Tierpsychologie* 65: 53–65. Ø. Øverli, C. A. Harris, and S. Winberg (1999). Short-term effects of fights for social dominance and the establishment of dominant-subordinate relationship on brain monoamines and cortisol in rainbow trout. *Brain Behavior and Evolution* 54: 263–275. C. H. Summers, T. R. Summers, M. C. Moore, W. J. Korzan, S. K. Woodley, P. J. Ronan, E. Höglund, M. J. Watt, and N. Greenberg (2003). Temporal patterns of limbic monoamine and plasma corticosterone response during social stress. *Neuroscience* 116: 553–563.

58. D. A. Gust, T. P. Gordon, M. K. Hambright, and M. E. Wilson (1993). Relationship between social factors and pituitary-adrenocortical activity in female rhesus monkeys (*Macaca mulatta*). *Hormones and Behavior* 27: 318–331. D. C. Blanchard, R. R. Sakai, B. McEwen, and

R. J. Blanchard (1993). Subordination stress: Behavioral, brain and neuroendocrine correlates. *Behavioural Brain Research* 58: 113–121.

59. R. Knapp and M.C. Moore (1995). Hormonal responses to aggression vary in different types of agonistic encounters in male tree lizards, *Urosaurus ornatus*. *Hormones and Behavior* 29: 85–105. S. Winberg, A. A. Myrberg, and G. E. Nilsson (1996). Agonistic interactions affect brain serotonergic activity in an acanthopterygiian fish: the bicolor damselfish (*Pomacentrus partitus*). *Brain, Behavior and Evolution* 48: 213–220.

60. Y. Delville, R. H. Melloni, Jr., and C. F. Ferris (1998). Behavioral and neurobiological consequences of social subjugation during puberty in golden hamsters. *The Journal of Neuroscience* 18(7): 2667–2672.

61. R. M. Sapolsky and J. C. Ray (1989). Styles of dominance and their endocrine correlates among wild olive baboons (*Papio anubis*). *American Journal of Primatology* 18: 1–13.

62. R. M. Sapolsky (1998). *Why Zebras Don't Get Ulcers: An Updated Guide to Stress, Stress-Related Diseases, and Coping, 2nd ed*. New York: W.H. Freeman and Company.

3

Personal

Slings, Arrows, and Outrageous Scapegoating

No one is truly alone, as passing the pain makes so (painfully) obvious. It takes at least two to perform this troublesome tango: someone to inflict the initial pain and another to receive it. And then, not uncommonly, there is a third party who absorbs the victim's load of grief. When it comes to passing the pain along, therefore, the "personal" is actually plural. As we have seen, this is true in a deeper sense as well, in that lurking behind nearly every episode of pain-passing is a long evolutionary history, which seems to indicate that passing the pain along is altogether natural and—at least in the past—was also adaptive. There is "hardware" for the Three Rs: physiological and genetic adaptations to social challenges and stress. And there is also "software": social traditions, learning, and education. With physiological mechanisms and evolutionary pressures as well as social and cultural traditions all pushing in this same direction, pain-passing, when it breaks out, surprises no one even as it hurts nearly everyone.

The key cause, as we suggested in the preceding chapter, is stress, which comes from many sources. Some, such as heat, cold, fatigue, accident, illness, and so forth, are essentially nonsocial and impersonal. Others derive from competition or predation between species: there is no doubt, for example, that a zebra is stressed when attacked by lions. But for most social species, it is likely that the greatest stressor is society itself, the negative interpersonal consequences of living with others of your own kind. This is not to deny the upside of social living; indeed, it is because the upside beats the downside that social species are what they are, and not asocial. Our point is that along with the benefits of sociality come costs.

Among these, the most straightforward are direct, personal assaults that can cause injury—physical and emotional—and are aimed specifically at the victim. Although difficult enough to deal with, these are at least widely anticipated. Less obvious, but at least as frequent and possibly more troublesome, is the indirect pain that comes from others who are merely living as best they can. Regrettably, but unavoidably, much of life is a zero-sum game, in which the pursuit of normal, necessary life goals (e.g., food, mates, living space) often means less food, mates, living space for others. And, of course, there are questions of social status and threats of subordination, as discussed in the last chapter.

As a result, one person's gain is frequently another's pain. And this, in turn, means that no one is in control of his or her own distress: It can be imposed by the actions of others, even when those others are following their own life goals and not intending any harm. Moreover, pain-passing can become a self-fulfilling prophecy whereby individuals and groups, fearing the worst from others, bring it about. This chapter will review the social psychology of personal pain, how it occurs, and the payback that it generates.

* * *

People are vulnerable to all sorts of injuries, psychological no less than physical, notes Aaron Beck, the founder of cognitive therapy. "As part of our survival heritage," Beck writes,

> We are very much aware of events that could have a detrimental effect on our well-being and personal interests. We are sensitive to actions that suggest a put-down, imposition, or interference. We monitor other people's behavior so that we can mobilize our defenses against any apparently noxious actions or statements. We are inclined to attach adverse personal meanings to innocuous actions and exaggerate their actual significance to us. As a result, we are particularly prone to feel hurt and angry with other people.[1]

Beck also explains that, even though people tend to respond vigorously and often violently to pain, such responses are not guaranteed. They are typically modulated by the victim's awareness of circumstance. Therefore, we do not attack the dentist who might cause us pain, or the physician who gives us a shot, although a very young child might in fact be outraged by the same behavior. Intelligent, mature people generally have no trouble recognizing when pain is intended for their own benefit.

Nonetheless, our extraordinary sensitivity to humiliations, rejections, and criticisms (the list is almost endless) renders human beings vulnerable to a vast armada of genuinely painful sensations. There is, moreover, a deep similarity between psychological and physical pain:

> Whether threatened with physical pain from a cutting instrument or psychological pain from cutting words, the individual automatically prepares to cope with the attack. In the first instance, the pain is localized and circumscribed; in the second, it is unlocalized and amorphous. The common denominator of the assaults is the suffering the individual

experiences. Psychological "damage" can produce distress as intense as physical damage. The suffering is illustrated in our language itself in the numerous analogies to physical pain: a bruised ego, hurt pride, injured psyche. Because of the unpleasantness of physical pain, people go to great lengths to prevent physical damage and preserve their physical functions. Similarly, the importance of psychological pain is underscored by the extreme care people take to avoid being humiliated or rejected. The victim may retaliate physically or verbally or may withdraw and nurse the physical or psychological "wound."

Beck emphasizes that the diversity of psychological abuse can be seen in the great abundance of "negative evaluation words" in the English language. And when it comes to describing human interactions, the hurtful greatly outnumber the helpful. He lists, for example,

> distanced, rejected, abandoned, isolated, displaced, defrauded, robbed, cheated, dispossessed, disenfranchised, disabled, immobilized, tricked, weakened, trapped, manipulated, exploited, dominated, misled, thwarted, opposed, undermined, intimidated, imperiled, exposed, betrayed, threatened, assaulted, attacked, wounded, trapped, defeated, slighted, insulted. . . .

And this litany merely scratches the surface. We caution that it is not necessarily true that people actually treat others more hurtfully than helpfully; rather, human psychology seems to have evolved a far greater sensitivity to the former than to the latter. There can be no doubt that humans are remarkably vulnerable to feeling hurt.

In the pages to come, we will look at some of the presumed causes of these "hurts," first at the level of individual psychology; then, in the next chapter, among groups. Throughout, we will explore how these experiences are translated into retaliation, revenge, and redirected aggression.

* * *

Experimental social psychologists have actively researched the sources of interpersonal aggression, in the process revealing much about the Three Rs. The scientific literature about aggression, including social psychology and psychiatry, parallels a similar interest among ethologists. As with ethology, interesting theories and experiments in social psychology and psychiatry go back to the early and mid-twentieth century, but after that the topic seemed to lose traction. One of the oldest and most respected theories in social psychology, for example, posits a connection between frustration and aggression, claiming in particular that the former leads to the latter.[2] In the theory's initial formulation, the relationship was exaggerated, with the claim that frustration always generates aggression and, moreover, that aggression inevitably signals prior frustration. Like the old song "Love and Marriage," the "frustration theory" of aggression claimed that "you can't have one without the other." These days, of course, most people realize that you can have love without marriage, and marriage without love—and similarly, that frustration can occur without aggression, and vice versa.

Nevertheless, it is also clear that frustration can generate psychological pain. It hurts to be frustrated; that is, kept from achieving the satisfaction of an ongoing response. Give a hungry rat access to food, or expose a sexually aroused male rat to a receptive female, and then frustrate the animal: He is more aggressive as a result. The same holds true for a frustrated person. A now-classic research project compared participants in high- and low-frustration situations and found that the high-frustration subjects were, as predicted, more aggressive.[3]

In another study, subjects were mildly irritated—asked to speak to the experimenter despite loud, annoying music in the background—then insulted after writing an essay, which was criticized: "I would have thought a college student would have done better than this." Other subjects were not presented with the annoying music, and were also spared the insult. When both groups were given the opportunity of punishing a confederate with a blast of unpleasant noise if he or she failed a simple test, those previously provoked were more inclined to punish.[4]

In yet another bit of revealing—if not surprising—research,[5] subjects were deprived of certain payoffs because of the behavior of someone else, who was actually in cahoots with the experimenter (this is a common ploy in social psychology research). Immediately afterward, the subjects were given the opportunity to take advantage of the individual who had been responsible for their troubles. They generally did so, although without going so far as to hurt themselves—with one exception, however: The experimental subjects who were told, allegedly by observers, that they had looked like suckers were likely to seek additional retribution on their earlier tormentors, carrying it so far that the subjects willingly even punished themselves in the process. The researcher's conclusion: Not only are people likely to inflict pain on others if they have themselves been wounded, but they will do so even if it has "only" been pain to their self-esteem.

This is but a small sample. Social psychologists have been "all over" studies of human aggression in general, and—although to a much lesser extent—redirected aggression in particular, which they often call "displaced aggression." As a result, the details of redirected aggression have undergone considerable fine-tuning, identifying specifics, which, like redirected aggression itself, might seem obvious but repay exploration. For example, when redirected aggression occurs, it usually does not simply spill out, willy-nilly, onto any random passer-by.

Take road rage: A typical, even iconic, case of redirected aggression. Yet road rage is also *directed*, in each specific event, toward someone who is perceived to have transgressed somehow—honked a horn, driven too slowly or too fast, swerved in front of one's car, and so forth—but who then receives a barrage that exceeds what seems appropriate to the immediate provocation. The idea here is that the particular offense, perhaps small in itself, triggered a response *because* it had probably been primed by an earlier affront. The term of art in social psychology is *triggered displaced aggression*, or TDA. A common finding is that a "trigger," such as a mildly insulting statement, which would not normally evoke an aggressive response, does so when the subject has previously experienced a stronger, negative provocation.[6]

To some degree, this is basic common sense: Only rarely, perhaps never, is redirected aggression evoked in the complete absence of some sort of trigger, something that acts as a lightning rod for a victim's already accumulated "negative energy."

It is one thing, for example, to come home after having a bad day at work and kick your innocent dog, or, like James Joyce's Mr. Farrington, beat your helpless little boy. It is slightly different—but still basically the same thing—when you have had a bad day at work, come home and kick the dog "because" she has been barking repetitively. The point is that even after being agitated, upset, and emotionally or even physically injured by your bad day, you still might not have kicked that dog if she had not *also* annoyed you by barking; in this situation, your redirected aggression was evoked, at least in part, by a "triggering" stimulus provided by the dog. (Recall that in Joyce's story, Farrington's son had let the fire go out—hardly a justification for a beating, but enough to serve as a trigger.)

In either case, the stage is set by some sort of prior pain: The barking dog or a cold hearth simply pushed the initial victim over the edge. The earlier provocation had a kind of priming effect, like cocking a gun. One research report concluded, only partly in jest: "If a dog barks and its owner is angry, the dog is in trouble if it is ugly or smells bad."[7] When social psychologists point out that "prior priming might influence people to make the attribution that the triggering event is an intentional provocation," this is called "attributional distortion." In other words, it can be almost like a mild paranoia: if you are already upset (because of "prior priming"), you are more likely to think that—or mindlessly act as though—the next provocation is somehow connected to the whole sorry business.

Imagine a golfer who plays poorly, then goes into the clubhouse where he loudly berates the waiter for messing up his order.[8] Even a golfer disappointed and angry with his poor play would presumably have a hard time losing his temper if the meal service were impeccable, but if the duffer is already upset and frustrated, then a small additional annoyance may trigger a disproportionate response. This leads to what has been called the "multiplicative effect," whereby the response is some combination of the initial, priming provocation (golfing poorly) as well as the triggering stimulus (lousy meal service). We hesitate to suggest whether the intensity is literally multiplied in an arithmetic sense, or simply added, or involves some proportion of initial and triggering stimuli. Moreover, no one knows how to quantify these stimuli, although it seems generally true that even if the triggering stimulus is relatively weak, the response is liable to be quite powerful in proportion as the earlier, priming provocation was "robust." In fact, one surprising discovery—still awaiting a convincing explanation—is that the aggressive response is often *larger* if the triggering response is relatively mild.[9]

For additional fine-tuning, can anyone actually measure whether the intensity of redirected aggression has any consistent, predictable relationship to the intensity of the initial, priming event?[10] To that of the second, "triggering" one? Does the "ratio" of the two have any substantial impact on the redirected behavior? And what if our golfer was also inebriated? It turns out that if the triggering event is conspicuous—really lousy meal service in the clubhouse—then alcohol intensifies the redirected aggression.[11] On the other hand, if it is inconspicuous—a minor screw-up in the dining room—then an intoxicated person, even if distressed by his poor showing on the golf course, is less likely than his sober counterpart to notice, and thus, to respond. Going further: What if our hypothetical golfer is a woman? Rich? Poor? Young? Old? Tall? Short? College-educated? Lacking a high school diploma? And what about the characteristics of the triggering individual, and of the initial problem-causer (assuming the latter was a person, and not a "situation"). There would seem to be enough variables to occupy legions of future researchers.

Let's go back to our earlier example of knitting socks. There can be a pattern, and even specific instructions like what weight of wool and what caliber of needles to use, but it is the individual's "wetware" that creates interesting discrepancies in every knitter's socks. We can see patterns within patterns, and yet, it is virtually impossible to predict each individual act of violence. This is the troubling truth about Homeland Security and the quest to prevent terrorism or violent outbursts more generally such as at Columbine High School, Virginia Tech, or the next horrific event. Despite demographic profiling, electronic data mining, psychological testing, and all sorts of orange and red alerts, and regardless of the insights that we hope will be generated by widespread understanding of the Three Rs, human beings remain complex and, at a deep level, not entirely predictable.

* * *

For example, most people are likely to respond quite differently to another's irritating or hurtful behavior depending on whether they believe that the transgression occurred on purpose or by accident. In such cases, "attributions" are important: whether one attributes the provocation to someone's malign intent, or mere happenstance.[12] In other cases, painful ("aversive") stimuli lead to anger and possible aggression, first by stimulating "associative networks," after which higher-order mental processes may or may not get into the act. This, at least, is the so-called cognitive-neoassociationistic model elaborated by renowned social psychologist Leonard Berkowitz.[13] According to this model, negative experiences activate parts of a supposed aggression-prone network (whatever that may be, anatomically and chemically), involving various thoughts, memories, emotions, and physiological responses, which in turn makes aggression more likely.

Simple physical discomfort also makes redirected aggression more likely and more intense. Unusually hot weather makes for short fuses. However, it is not just the heat, but the corresponding discomfort that is responsible: Experimental subjects who agreed to immerse their hands in uncomfortably *cold* water were also more aggressively inclined.[14] Social psychologists have also examined, often in excruciating detail, the effect of similarity between initial provocateur and subject, between subject and target of redirected aggression; intensity of initial provocation; intensity of triggering provocation; "negativity" of the overall setting; and so forth.

Surprisingly, there can sometimes be a negative relationship between the intensity of initial provocation and the amount of subsequent redirected aggression—perhaps because of the "contrast effect," whereby when the initial provocation is severe, the person generating the second, triggered stimulus appears comparatively less bad or noxious. In any event, after a review of 49 research articles, a technical manuscript concluded that "those who are provoked and unable to retaliate reliably respond more aggressively toward an innocent Other than those not previously provoked."[15] And yet, interestingly, although this particular research paper was titled "Displaced Aggression Is Alive and Well," concluding that "the phenomenon is quite real," the authors also pointed out that it has thus far received scant attention in social psychology textbooks. This, we hope, will change.

Many people, perhaps most, experience annoying, frustrating provocations on a daily basis. The workplace victimization experienced by James Joyce's fictional Mr. Farrington occurs regularly to millions in the real world, where it has ramifications beyond mere personal distress. Thus, employees who report high levels of "abusive supervision" at work are especially likely to redirect aggression onto co-workers,[16] thereby further disrupting an already-tense work environment. Victims of workplace bullying also experience increased interpersonal conflicts[17] and are likely to bring their distress home, and unthinkingly target their own families.[18] Thus, work-related conflict is closely linked to domestic violence,[19] although it is worth noting that women (who are the most frequent victims of workplace bullying) sometimes react against this tendency by resolving to maintain their personal integrity by *not* "taking out" their negative experiences on their families.[20]

Road rage, or at least, a tendency to engage in it, is yet another daily event. Here the connection with triggering events seems to go in both directions: It is not simply that people are more likely to drive aggressively when they have been aggrieved in their non-driving life, but there is evidence that long, stressful commutes tend to generate heightened workplace aggression.[21]

Efforts by social psychologists to explain redirected aggression often have an unacknowledged overlap with classic psychoanalytic theory, probably because the two disciplines developed around the same period of history, the early and mid-twentieth century, when World Wars I and II (not to mention the Great Depression and the Cold War) made aggression a particularly hot topic in which everyone had a stake, from physicists and biologists to psychologists and psychiatrists. Thus, as we turn briefly to look at the Three Rs from a psychoanalytical perspective, we find that there is a lot of overlap, as well as vigorous dispute, which continues to the present day.

Sigmund Freud held that a person can purge herself or himself of repressed negative emotions by discharging the accumulated "energy" in some harmless way—finding catharsis in, say, hitting a punching bag. Freud accordingly included displacement in his original roster of "defense mechanisms." He saw it as the shifting of an action from one target to a substitute, when for some reason responding to the preferred one is not possible or wise (e.g., one's boss), or is intangible and thus unavailable (uncomfortable weather or a stomachache). For Freud, displacement is not tied to evolution or subordination stress; rather, it occurs when the id seeks to do something that the superego will not permit, whereupon the ego steps in and finds a "safe" way of releasing the accumulated psychic energy in a more acceptable manner. (Recall our discussion of the classic ethological "hydraulic model.") As was his habit, however, Freud went further, seeing displacement nearly everywhere: someone afraid of locomotives is actually acting out his displaced fear of his grandfather; a sexually frustrated religious fundamentalist becomes a compulsive overeater or animal abuser; or, less injuriously, repressed hopes, fears and hurts come out, for most normal people, in dreams.

As mentioned earlier, Freud considered depression to be anger turned inwards, so that suicide derives, at least in part, from the response of some people to their burden of pain. The psychoanalytical story thus goes that suicide results when, for whatever reasons, someone is unable or unwilling to engage in the traditional Three Rs and instead pathologically redirects his aggression toward himself or herself. Interestingly, physically abused children are nearly three times likelier to engage in self-destructive behavior (suicide attempts plus self-mutilation) than a comparable group of "merely" neglected but non-abused children, and six times likelier than a group of normal controls.[22]

Freud himself, seldom a shrinking violet when it came to making definitive statements, showed his customary certainty when he wrote that "no neurotic harbours thoughts of suicide which are not murderous impulses against others redirected upon himself."[23] According to traditional psychoanalytic theory, such redirection, in moderate quantities, is altogether healthy and normal, instrumental in formation of the superego as individuals employ the proscriptions and prescriptions of dominant individuals (especially the parents) to redirect aggression toward themselves, thereby controlling impulses that would otherwise be socially disadvantageous.[24]

Freud also developed the notion of "sublimation," by which unacceptable aggressive and sexual desires are shifted onto socially tolerable activities, such as chopping wood, playing sports, and so on. He also hypothesized the existence of "dramatic catharsis," by which people can relieve their aggressive inclinations by watching violent or aggressive events. Here, psychoanalytic theory has antecedents going back to Aristotle, who first theorized that tragic theater is compelling because it is emotionally cleansing.

Pop psychologists in the 1970s and 1980s specifically developed therapies (both group and individual) involving catharsis and redirection. It was common on psychiatric wards in the 1970s for patients to be taken to padded rooms and handed "bataka bats"—large, foam-padded clubs, developed for the express purpose of mock battles and beating walls and furniture to "get the anger out." Subsequently, there has been considerable debate among social psychologists over whether "venting anger" is advisable, or rather, dangerous, which is an especially relevant concern in a world of violent movies and video games, particularly since the latter extend passive witnessing to simulated participation. Although Freud had suggested that aggressive tendencies could be reduced by engaging in aggressive behavior, some research has pointed in precisely the opposite direction: just as, in general, people learn by doing, they may become more aggressive by being aggressive.[25] This led at least one highly regarded social psychologist, Albert Bandura, to call for a moratorium on so-called "venting therapy," fearing that it could actually amplify any violence-prone tendencies.[26] Nowadays, it is more common for violence-prone inpatients to be taught "mindfulness" and meditation rather than martial arts or mock battles, although we are not aware of data that compare the two strategies.

On the other hand, the following study suggests that agitation can be relieved, not necessarily by venting in general, but by directing aggression specifically toward one's tormentor: The experimenter initially heckled his experimental subjects while they were attempting to count backward from 100 as quickly as possible. Their blood pressure went up. Then, the irritated subjects were given the opportunity of giving a mild electric shock (more accurately, thinking they had done so) to one of two different "victims"—either a randomly chosen individual or the experimenter who had aggravated them in the first place.

The subjects' blood pressure stayed up when they thought they were hurting the random person, but went down when the chosen victim was the original provocateur.[27]

Freud once famously noted that "sometimes a cigar is just a cigar." Sometimes, it appears, "directed aggression" is just more direct.

* * *

Many have argued that pain begins even at birth, as William Blake suggested in his cynical poem, "Infant Sorrow," and as numerous psychoanalysts have subsequently claimed. Here is Blake:

> My mother groan'd! my father wept.
> Into the dangerous world I leapt:
> Helpless, naked, piping loud:
> Like a fiend hid in a cloud.
> Struggling in my father's hands,
> Striving against my swaddling bands,
> Bound and weary I thought best
> To sulk upon my mother's breast.[28]

Significantly, this poem is part of a group titled *Songs of Experience*. It is not only the experience of birth that inflicts trauma, but often that of living itself. Our ways, the poet laments, are often "filled with thorns,"* and the forests of the night are inhabited by fearful tigers, "burning bright."†

Echoing Blake, writer Andrew Schmookler notes that:

> We are born more helpless than virtually any other animal. Yet, according to psychologists, we emerge into consciousness with a feeling of omnipotence. We believe the cosmos is ruled by our thoughts and feelings. Tiny, quivering bundles of fears and desires, we enter the world with a boundless egocentrism: we are each the center of our universe. What a painful shock to learn of our true place in the order of things. We are small, and prey to hostile forces we cannot control. Other people, with power over us, may be indifferent to our needs. And the final insult: we learn that we are mortal.[29]

In her book *Prisoners of Childhood*, German psychoanalyst Alice Miller argued that everyone is the prisoner of his or her childhood experience; ergo, we all

---

* "Holy Thursday."
† "The Tyger."

need psychoanalysis to set ourselves free. Free from what? For Miller, childhood necessarily imposes a heavy burden of trauma, because child-rearing, at least as practiced in the West, is an exercise in cruelty and the infliction of pain. In *For Your Own Good: Hidden Cruelty in Child Rearing and the Roots of Violence*,[30] Miller went further, claiming that *every* adult has been victimized as a child and, moreover, that anyone who claims to have had a happy childhood is—by his or her denial—further demonstrating that he is either lying or has forgotten the painful truth.

She doth assert way too much. Nonetheless, Alice Miller makes a convincing case that there has long been much hidden cruelty in the way parents treat their children, something that has been sanctioned by presumably well-meaning "authorities" for literally hundreds of years, at least within the European tradition. Consider this, from Robert Cleaver and John Dowd's *A Godly Form of Household Government*, 1621:

> The young child which lieth in the cradle is both wayward and full of affections; and though his body be but small, yet he hath a reat wrong-doing heart, and is altogether inclined to evil. . . . Therefore parents must . . . correct and sharply reprove their children for saying or doing ill.

Or the following, from John Eliot's *The Harmony of the Gospels*, 1678:

> Withhold not correction from the child, for if thou beatest him with the rod he shall not die, thou shalt beat him with the rod and deliver his soul from hell.

And finally, J. G. Krüger's *Some Thoughts on the Education of Children*, 1752:

> Disobedience amounts to a declaration of war against you. Your son is trying to usurp your authority, and you are justified in answering force with force in order to insure his respect, without which you will be unable to train him. The blows you administer should not be merely playful ones but should convince him that you are his master.

Miller concludes that "The former practice of physically maiming, exploiting, and abusing children seems to have been gradually replaced in modern times by a form of mental cruelty that is masked by the honorific term child-rearing," and that:

> an enormous amount can be done to a child in the first two years: he or she can be molded, dominated, taught good habits, scolded, and

punished—without any repercussions for the person raising the child and without the child taking revenge. The child will overcome the serious consequences of the injustice he has suffered only if he succeeds in defending himself, i.e., if he is allowed to express his pain and anger. . . . If there is absolutely no possibility of reacting appropriately to hurt, humiliation, and coercion, then . . . the feelings they evoke are repressed, and the need to articulate them remains unsatisfied.

Insofar as victims have a need to "articulate" such feelings, it is not simply a matter of verbalizing them, but rather, acting upon them, often to the dismay of others. We disagree with Alice Miller. We do not believe that child-rearing equals child abuse and that every adult is therefore a trauma survivor, desperate to offload his or her painful burden onto someone else. And in fact, in a later chapter we shall show how certain behaviors, including parenting, can increase mental stability and reduce redirected aggression by training impulse-control, compassion for self and others, and an introductory course in "Reconciliation 101." But there is at least a modicum of truth in Miller's dire vision: As we have seen, some pain is unavoidable—perhaps more in childhood than later—and, moreover, when this occurs, it is liable to be even more hurtful and long-lasting than when experienced by adults. In addition, some people doubtless endure more than their share, and for them, the consequences may well be severe . . . not only for them, but for their subsequent victims as well.

The most dramatic cases are those in which victims subsequently become prominent victimizers. Not surprisingly, when philosopher/psychologist Erich Fromm undertook to dissect the anatomy of human destructiveness (in his book of that name),[31] he catalogued the public offenses of people who had been privately offended against. Without exonerating the culprits, Fromm's now-classic book documents how the early abuse suffered by Stalin and Hitler, for example, contributed to their "malignant aggression" in adulthood, with dire consequences for millions.

More often, pain experienced in childhood gives rise to myriad personal tragedies. It is thus at least possible that the oft-claimed "cycles of domestic abuse" might have their roots in redirected aggression, insofar as victims of childhood abuse might disproportionately grow up to become abusers themselves. And the same holds true, perhaps, for situations of domestic violence. Although families are expected to be refuges from an often hurtful outside world, the fact is that "we often hurt the ones we love," so that even healthy, loving relationships are frequently characterized by pain. This being so, how much more troublesome are "dysfunctional" families, those marked by anger, resentment, and the infliction of genuine—if often unintentional—hurt?

"Home is one of America's favorite hitting places," explains an expert on violence, echoing some of the unsettling points made by Alice Miller:

> It is an opportune ground for small slights and major insults, where grudges can quietly smolder and violently flare, a private arena in which a self-appointed family dictator may take command, a tavern of sorts in which excessive drinking and lowered restraint can set a stage for violence, and a sheltered island in which aggression can let loose with little fear of punishment. It is also a physical structure and space often jointly occupied by potential aggressors and (literally) near-at-hand targets.[32]

As it turns out, however, the evidence indicting redirected aggression as a cause of intergenerational abuse is somewhat mixed, and the situation is murky.[33] On one hand, some research supports the commonsense observation that victims are especially likely to become victimizers. But on the other, a considerable body of evidence suggests that, rather than growing up to be abusers, abused children are especially likely to end up *victimized* yet again, on the receiving end of their own adult abusive relationships.[34] According to one detailed review, "violence in the family of origin is probably the most widely accepted risk marker for the occurrence of partner violence".[35] Roughly one out of three adults who were previously abused as children end up maltreating their own offspring. Note, however, that this also means that two out of three do not.[36] Indeed, many abuse victims, painfully aware of what they experienced, consciously resolve to treat their own children quite differently.

"Being maltreated as a child puts one at risk for becoming abusive," according to one careful review of the research literature. "But the path between these two points is far from direct or inevitable".[37]

A key consideration seems to be the victims' repertoire of "coping strategies." Victims of childhood sexual abuse are generally more likely to develop posttraumatic stress disorder (PTSD), to subsequently use drugs or alcohol, to act out sexually, and to withdraw from other people. Moreover, those with poorer coping strategies and higher self-blame are especially likely to victimize others once they become adults.[38] Comparing adult alcoholic men who have been abused as children with a control group of non-abused alcoholics, it turns out that the former group have "significantly more legal difficulties, domestic violence, and violence against authority figures than the controls. They also have a higher incidence of serious suicide attempts, suicidal drinking, and an increased level of pervasive and situational anxiety".[39] A survey of nearly 700 children also found that childhood victimization was highly correlated with antisocial personality disorder later in life.[40] Not surprisingly, those who have been victimized

as children are consistently more likely to be aggressive toward others—
that is, to "revictimize"—than are people whose childhood experiences did not
include victimization.[41]

One explanatory "culprit" in all this appears to be that favorite of psychologists: social learning. In this case, victimized children learn their "social role".[42]
Another, related possibility is "modeling," whereby children who simply witness
adults behaving violently are more likely to copy what they have observed and
thus, to be violent themselves. Whatever the precise causes, however, it seems
clear that any experience of family abuse tends to predict future abuse, even if
the experience was limited to interactions between the parents and thus merely
witnessed rather than specifically directed toward the subject when a child.[43] But
there is this ray of hope, also administered via social learning: After spending
just a few months in a benevolent residential care, childhood victims and
witnesses of violence are less likely to engage, as adults, in their own abusive
relationships.[44]

Another, and more pointed question arises: Are sexually abused children
more likely to become sexual abusers, in their turn? The situation is complex,
and the answer seems to be no. Sexually abused children are likely to become
re-victimized, and some sexual perpetrators were sexually abused as children.
However, sexual predators seem to have more in common with those bearing
traits for antisocial personality disorder (sociopathy) than those suffering from
post-traumatic stress disorders. Sexual sadism—taking sexual pleasure in the
pain of others—is not necessarily the result of child abuse, and it would be
wrong to expect that the legions of people who have been sexually abused are
especially at risk of becoming abusers. For example, some studies conclude that
about 20% of women in the United States have been or will be the victims of
sexual abuse or rape[45]. To our knowledge, there are no reputable suggestions
that these women should be under observation for fear that they will become
rapists themselves. The pain that is passed along by sexual violence is often morphed by depression into neglect of self and others, social withdrawal, and loss of
the ability to experience sexual pleasure. What goes around comes around, but
not in a directly circular fashion.

* * *

Things are emotionally darker, yet conceptually clearer, when it comes to the
question of whether victims of violence are likely to be violent, not merely to
their own offspring, but toward society generally. "The violent criminals I have
known have been objects of violence from early childhood," writes Dr. James
Gilligan, medical director of the Bridgewater State Hospital for the Criminally
Insane and director of mental health for the prison system of Massachusetts.
Note that Dr. Gilligan said "objects" of violence, which is to say, victims,
not perpetrators. After working clinically with violent men for more than

25 years, during which time he also directed the Center for the Study of Violence at the Harvard Medical School, Gilligan wrote as follows.[46]

> In the course of my work with the most violent men in maximum secu-
> rity settings, not a day goes by that I do not hear reports—often con-
> firmed by independent sources—of how these men were victimized
> during childhood. Physical violence, neglect, abandonment, rejection,
> sexual exploitation and violation occurred on a scale so extreme, so
> bizarre, and so frequent that one cannot fail to see that the men who
> occupy the extreme end of the continuum of violent behavior in adult-
> hood occupied an equally extreme end of the continuum of violent child
> abuse earlier in life.
>
> They have seen their closest relatives—their fathers and mothers
> and sisters and brothers—murdered in front of their eyes, often by
> other family members. As children, these men were shot, axed, scalded,
> beaten, strangled, tortured, drugged, starved, suffocated, set on fire,
> thrown out of windows, raped, or prostituted by mothers who were
> their "pimps"; their bones have been broken; they have been locked in
> closets or attics for extended periods, and one man I know was deliber-
> ately locked by his parents in an empty icebox until he suffered brain
> damage from oxygen deprivation before he was let out.
>
> The face and body of one Massachusetts prison inmate I know are
> covered with grotesque scars, despite many plastic surgical procedures,
> from burns caused by scalding water his mother had thrown on him
> repeatedly. It was her method of discipline during his childhood.
> Another man, who brutally raped and murdered a young woman whose
> apartment he had broken into one day while she was napping, has bul-
> let-hole scars on his arms and legs. He said they were inflicted on him
> in childhood by his mother, whose idea of "spanking" him was to take
> out her pistol and shoot him. This same man also described in vivid
> detail seeing his father murdered in front of his eyes by two other
> relatives when he was a child. (His descriptions were confirmed by
> his brother, who was also in prison at the same time for his own
> violent crime.)

For our purposes, two considerations are especially relevant: First, the evidently high rate of pain and injury suffered by those who subsequently become
victimizers, and second, their awareness of it; that is, a powerful temptation to
see themselves as victims rather than perpetrators, despite the fact that they
may have committed horrific deeds. Researcher Jan Arriens accumulated
writings by prisoners on death rows throughout the United States. One wrote,
"I am the hunted, the caught, the prey, the victim of the crafty, the cunning, and

powerful."[47] It is easy to disparage such notions as the delusions of a paranoid personality; more troublesome, however, is the prospect that to some extent, violent perpetrators really are likely to be victims as well.

A notable study reported in the *American Journal of Public Health* examined 802 subjects with serious mental illness, looking for risk factors that might explain their repeated episodes of violence. Of the many factors examined, three turned out to be significant contributors: substance abuse, currently being exposed to violence, and having been a victim of violence during childhood. If none of these three factors were present, the predicted probability of becoming a violent offender was essentially zero; if any one, 2 percent; if two out of the three, 7 to 10 percent; if all three, 30 percent.[48] Out of 226 incarcerated juvenile offenders, 67% reported having been beaten with a belt or extension cord, 32% at least five times. Twenty percent had been threatened with a knife or gun, and 12% were actually assaulted with a knife or gun—and generally, the more violence they had experienced, the more violent were they crimes they had committed.[49]

Once apprehended and imprisoned, the pattern does not end; if anything, it intensifies. A study of prison bullying discovered that most bullies (71%) are also victims themselves.[50] Prisoners were categorized into four groups: (1) "Pure bullies" who only bully others; (2) "Pure victims" who have only been bullied; (3) "Bully-victims" who have both been bullied and have bullied; and (4) "Non-involved" who were neither bullied nor did so. The researchers found that "bully-victims" (group 3) behaved in a more hostile and angry manner and displayed more negative attitudes toward prison guards than did the other groups. Furthermore, targets of bullies were especially more likely to redirect their aggression by destroying objects, fantasizing about revenge, and displaying impulsive tendencies than those who had not been victimized.

Do not misunderstand: We are not proclaiming pity for the poor perpetrator, many of whom feel an inordinate inclination to blame others, or their circumstances, for their misdeeds—behavior for which, in the great majority of cases, they owe responsibility. There is a French saying, *Tout comprendre, c'est tout pardonner* ("to understand completely is to pardon completely"). For now, let us simply be satisfied with understanding, for its own sake, and maybe also in the hope of preventing such deplorable events as the school shootings in Columbine, Colorado; Paducah, Kentucky; Jonesboro, Arkansas; at Virginia Tech University; and who knows where next. The perpetrators in such cases were almost certainly responding out of their own pathology, and not simply from what we might call the "Officer Krupke syndrome," from the rollicking song in *West Side Story*, in which the young hooligans sing:

Dear kindly Sergeant Krupke,
You gotta understand,

It's just our bringin' up-ke
That gets us out of hand.
Our mothers all are junkies,
Our fathers all are drunks.
Golly Moses, natcherly we're punks!
Gee, Officer Krupke, we're very upset;
We never had the love that ev'ry child oughta get.
We ain't no delinquents,
We're misunderstood.
Deep down inside us there is good!*

Maybe so, but often there is also bad. Even then, however, just as it is worth understanding what can induce good people to do bad things, it also behooves us to comprehend what makes bad people even worse.

Take the case of rape. Like nearly everything, crime is multifactorial. So is rape, and indeed, in our opinion much of the traditional understanding of rape tends to ascribe too much motivation to "hatred of women" and not enough to pathological and frustrated male sexuality.[51] In his book *Men Who Rape: The Psychology of the Offender*, A. Nicholas Groth[52] identified several different psychological profiles for rapists, including "anger-retaliatory rape murder." Here is part of Groth's description, which randomly mixes retaliation, revenge, and redirected aggression, but is in fact a painfully acute account of the latter:

> Nettled by poor relationships with women, the aggressor distills his anguish and contempt into an explosive revenge on the victim. . . . it is often precipitated by a criticism or scolding from a woman with power over him. In an attempt to express revenge and retaliation for being disciplined, the aggressive killer will either direct his anger at that woman or redirect his anger to a substitute woman. Because the latter type of scapegoating retaliation does not eliminate the direct source of hate, it is likely that it will be episodically repeated to relieve internal stresses. . . . Inasmuch as the actual source of the killer's anger is a woman who belittles, humiliates, and rejects the subject, the fatal hostility may not be directed at a mother, wife, or female supervisor but at an unsuspecting substitute victim whom the killer has sought out . . . as

a symbolic vehicle for resolving his internal stresses. . . . Regardless of
whether the victim is alive or dead, the assault continues until the subject is emotionally satisfied. . . . When the subject views the sexual
assault and murder as a success, he often leaves the crime scene with a
feeling of having been cleansed and renewed. Because the subject transferred the blame of the murder onto the victim, he does not experience
any sense of guilt.

Interpersonal violence—whether sexual or not, directed or redirected, or
pretty much undirected—has long been associated with the dynamics of interpersonal pain, often closely intertwined with social status and prestige. In the
past, there have been such highly choreographed patterns as dueling; it is especially revealing that within the European tradition, high-status individuals long
felt that if they have been insulted, they required the opportunity to kill or injure
their tormentor. Significantly, this was described as a demand for "satisfaction."
And in current street-language, when someone has been "dissed," he (and it is
nearly always *he*) is likely to suffer not only a social decrement, but also certain
predictable physiological changes. This sets the stage for face-saving retaliation,
or, if this is not possible, for taking it out on someone else, in an effort to keep
up one's prestige—and also, not coincidentally, although also not consciously, to
keep *down* one's titer of stress hormones.

A recent study of street crime, for example, found that redirected aggression
typically accomplished one or more of three objectives: "sending a message"
(regaining reputation after having been "disrespected"), "loss recovery" (getting
back lost material or money), or "anger release" (restoring a disrupted neurochemical balance).[53] And it is worth noting that even young children tend to
redirect aggression to a third party immediately after conflict—although a hopeful sign can be found in the discovery that redirection is significantly less likely
if reconciliation occurs between the initial combatants.[54]

Reconciliation is much harder to achieve among gang members, Mafiosi, and
even street criminals; that is, adults who specialize in violence. In many cases,
such violence is doubtless "instrumental," directed toward achieving a designated objective: robbing a store, a bank, or a person, or competing with other
gangs. At the same time, organized criminal groups in particular are notoriously
sensitive about their reputations, notably their need to pass along any violence
to which they have been subjected. Most effective, of course, is to get back at
anyone who dares to victimize you; alternatively, find some way to show how
"dangerous" you really are, after all.

Here is testimony from a young African-American man, a heroin dealer in
St. Louis, given to a team of British sociologists who asked him to explain why
he decided to kill someone who had previously shot and robbed him. Note
that this individual was not simply angry, or seeking revenge for its own sake.

Rather, he was concerned with the practical necessity of saving face, thereby making it clear that he does not tolerate victimization:

> See, you have to realize if I didn't get back at him, you and him could say I'm a punk. . . . You need to let it be known you not gonna take no shit, you know what I'm saying? Fuck no, you would be out of business . . . because you would have people, little kids, coming up trying to rob you thinking that "he ain't gonna do nothing, he's a punk."[55]

This comports with our earlier suggestion that much aggression serves to signal to others, "I may be down, but I'm not out, so don't think you can mess with me further."

* * *

In our previous discussion of redirected aggression and the "I'm not a patsy" hypothesis, we tried to show that redirected aggression was widespread in the animal world. By the same token, it is widespread in human societies, too. The likelihood is very great, in fact, that through much of human evolution, individuals and groups known to insist on "getting even" were more likely to be left alone in the first place. Consider, by contrast, the sorry state of a lineage which may have lacked the family tradition of demanding an eye for an eye and a life for a life. Its women, children, and possessions might well have been easy marks, vulnerable to anyone with the will to take advantage of them.

As we noted earlier, anthropologist Napoleon Chagnon studied the Yanomamo people of northern South America, a society whose nearly Stone Age lifestyle is widely thought to approximate that of our early ancestors. Chagnon reported that among the Yanomamo, individuals who were especially "fierce" were relatively immune to attack; they also, not coincidentally, accumulated more wives and, thus, more children. Moreover, tribes with a reputation for ferocious retribution were less likely to be raided, whereas those known to be exploitable were in fact more liable to depredation by their neighbors:

> Groups that retaliate swiftly and demonstrate their resolve to avenge deaths acquire reputations for ferocity that deter the violent designs of their neighbors. The Yanomamo explain that a group with a reputation for swift retaliation is attacked less frequently and thus suffers a lower rate of mortality. They also note that other forms of predation, such as the abduction of women, are thwarted by adopting an aggressive stance. Aggressive groups coerce nubile females from less aggressive groups whenever the opportunity arises. Many appear to calculate the costs and benefits of forcibly appropriating or coercing females from groups that are perceived to be weak.[56]

Significantly, such attacks typically resulted in their women being carried off, a loss that italicizes the evolutionary—no less than social—consequences of being victimized in this way. Recall, as well, our earlier discussion of the likely adaptive significance of redirected aggression in particular: demonstrating that one is not a patsy. You are not altogether a pushover if, after being pushed over, you can still push back against someone else.

Among the Yanomamo, in proportion as a group carries on a tradition of vengeance—of passing not only pain but also death and destruction to anyone who "started it"—that group appears to have acquired a kind of security (at least in the short term). The point is that feuding, bloody-minded vengefulness, and indeed much of warfare, may be an extreme development of the human penchant for passing the pain along, a tendency that could have originated in behavior that functioned primitively as a kind of don't-tread-on-me deterrence. Moreover, "Even if someone else has succeeded in treading on me, just see what I can still do . . . to somebody, and therefore possibly to you."

* * *

In her classic book *Patterns of Culture*, anthropologist Ruth Benedict wrote that culture was "personality writ large." For some people, life is a prison writ small. They grow up experiencing ironfisted discipline, combined—if they are lucky—with rigidity, and if they are not, with outright brutality and abuse. Some people, because of their genetic makeup, may simply be predisposed to hurt others. Thus far, however, no evidence supports this contention, except for the case of sociopaths, who evidently are hardwired to lack basic empathy, and who, rather than becoming agitated in the face of violence and suffering, actually calm down.

On the other hand, even non-Freudians are likely to agree that when it comes to forming our adult selves, early experience plays a crucial role, for better or ill. Shortly after World War II, social philosopher Theodor Adorno and his associates launched a massive study to uncover the causes of anti-Semitism.[57] They interviewed large numbers of people, inquiring about their stands on a variety of social issues. The researchers found that anti-Semitic tendencies were closely linked to a number of different attitudes, which could be scored on what became known as the "F-Scale" (for fascist). Ranking on the F-Scale was determined by the extent of agreement or disagreement with such statements as:

> Most of our social problems would be solved if we could somehow get rid of the immoral, crooked, and feeble-minded people.
> People can be divided into two classes, the weak and the strong.
> Obedience and respect for authority are the most important virtues children should learn.
> What youth needs most is strict discipline, rugged determination and the will to work and fight for family and country.

Most readers can anticipate the kind of questions—and answers—that result in a high F-Scale ranking. In their now-famous (albeit subsequently criticized) research, Adorno and his colleagues found a consistent syndrome that linked such people: They had what became known as an "authoritarian personality." Intensive interviews with people at each end of the F-Scale—those whose personalities were especially authoritarian and those who were minimally so—revealed that a common denominator for the highly authoritarian types was the kind of parenting they had received in their youth. In particular, parents who were especially harsh and threatening, and who coerced obedience from their children by threatening to withdraw their love as a sign of disapproval, tended to produce children who, when they grew up, were rigidly authoritarian in their own attitudes.

The mechanism seems to be as follows. A child growing up in such homes tends to be insecure, frightened of his or her parents, and yet at the same time, highly dependent upon them. These children suffer pain—emotional, and sometimes physical as well—because of their parents, but owing to their family situations, they are inhibited about expressing or otherwise acting out their anger and resentment. In most cases, they are not even consciously aware of harboring these feelings, and would probably deny them in any case.

Such injured children grow up to be angry adults who—fearful and insecure as well—proceed to redirect their anger toward others: Jews, African-Americans, gays, hippies, unwed mothers, "welfare cheats," undocumented immigrants, and, post-9/11, anyone with a Muslim name, Muslim clothing or seeming 'Arab' features. (Nor is this a recent phenomenon: research conducted more than forty years ago found that adults who displayed a high degree of racial prejudice were especially likely to blame their personal problems on innocent individuals from a minority group.[58]) In our terms, they pass their pain along to others, especially those that are relatively powerless, just as the authoritarians, when young, had been powerless against their own parents.

According to psychiatrist Jerome Frank, correlations of this sort have often been found between personality traits and political attitudes. The usual finding is:

> an authoritarian character pattern whose dynamic core lies in repression of strong hostility originally aimed at parents and other severe but close authority figures. Those with this type of character pattern exaggerate the importance in human affairs of power, force, domination, and submission, and displace their own aggression to safer targets than authority figures at home.[59]

In short, when the aggressor is a parent, the victims may respond by victimizing others, who are safer targets.

Closely related to this process is one of the weirdest examples of pain-passing, long known to mental health specialists as "identification with the aggressor," or, in a more recent variant, the "Stockholm syndrome." During the 1930s, for example, Jewish parents in central Europe were horrified to witness their children mimicking Nazi storm-troopers and giving "Heil Hitler" salutes. Identification with the aggressor seems to grow out of the traumas of individuals and of larger populations; it may well operate during the genesis of "authoritarian personalities." In some cases, this peculiar phenomenon involves a kind of magical thinking, often unconscious, whereby the victim associates with the victimizer, thereby achieving—at least in his or her mind—the fantasy of protection. By psychologically impersonating the purveyor of pain rather than merely remaining a victim, a sufferer can magically transform himself from a position of weakness to one of power. According to M. Scott Peck,

> The builders of medieval cathedrals placed upon their buttresses the figures of gargoyles—themselves symbols of evil—in order to ward off the spirits of greater evil. Thus children may become evil in order to defend themselves against the onslaughts of parents who are evil. It is possible, therefore, to think of human evil—or some of it—as a kind of psychological gargoylism.[60]

Those who succumb to psychological gargoylism promote evil and pass along pain in the course of trying to protect themselves from both.

Describing their experiences in a Nazi concentration camp, Rudolf Vrba and Alan Bestic[61] tell about Yankel Meisel, a prisoner who had forgotten to sew some buttons onto his uniform, as he had been instructed, just before an inspection by Heinrich Himmler. As a result, while the entire camp was standing at attention, waiting for Himmler to arrive, Meisel was beaten to death by the guards. As the victim screamed and pleaded for mercy, Vrba and Bestic recount that "all hated Yankel Meisel, the little old Jew who was spoiling everything, who was causing trouble for us all with his long, lone, futile protest." To the inmates, at least during that gruesome incident, the enemy was not Himmler—who after all had orchestrated the entire bestial system—or the guards who carried out his orders. Rather, it was the old, doomed Jew, like themselves, one of the victims.

This brings us to scapegoating.

* * *

Perhaps the earliest account of a human scapegoat is the Old Testament tale of Jonah, a rather misanthropic prophet who was aboard a ship in danger of sinking during a terrible storm. After a hasty and desperate meeting, the crew decided that to placate the Deity, a sacrificial victim needed to be thrown overboard. Jonah was "it." (According to scripture, he was not quite selected at random; rather, God already had a bone to pick with Jonah for other reasons. Nonetheless, our concern here is not why Jonah became the anointed scapegoat and not someone else, but rather, why the crew felt it was necessary and appropriate to find a scapegoat at all.) We can conclude, in any event, that the decision was correct: The ocean calmed, after which Jonah was famously swallowed by a whale. With or without divine sanction, when the seas get angry, injured and frightened people look for something—most often some*one*—to toss overboard.

Jonah was fortunate, as these things go: he was later vomited up onto dry land. Most scapegoats aren't so lucky, although not all such victims literally lose their lives. Some merely serve as "whipping boys," a phrase that derives from a seventeenth and eighteenth-century custom in the English court, by which a designated child was kept in close association with each young prince; when the latter misbehaved, the former got whipped. This way, at least someone got punished, and the seas of righteousness calmed. One such whipping boy, William Murray, was eventually made an earl, at the insistence of his royal protector/ tormentor, Charles I.

Most often, however, scapegoats suffer mightily. Here is a selection from Herman Hesse's *Narcissus and Goldmund*, describing the plague in medieval central Europe. First comes an account of the horror:

> . . . the empty houses, the farm dogs starved on their chains and rotting, the scattered unburied corpses, the begging children, the death that is at the city gates were not the worst. The worst were the survivors, who seemed to have lost their eyes and souls under the weight of horror and the fear of death. Everywhere the wanderer came upon strange, dreadful things. Parents had abandoned their children, husbands their wives, when they had fallen ill. The ghouls reigned like hangmen; they pillaged the empty houses, left corpses unburied or, following their whims, tore the dying from their beds before they had breathed their last and tossed them on the death carts. Frightened fugitives wandered about alone, turned primitive, avoiding all contact with other people, hounded by fear of death.

And here is what that horror, in turn, brought about when it came to people interacting with each other:

> Worst of all, everybody looked for a scapegoat for his unbearable misery; everybody swore that he knew the criminal who had brought on the

disease, who had intentionally caused it. Grinning, evil people, they said, were bent on spreading death by extracting the disease poison from corpses and smearing it on walls and doorknobs, by poisoning wells and cattle with it. Whoever was suspected of these horrors was lost, unless he was warned and able to flee: either the law or the mob condemned him to death. The rich blamed the poor, or vice versa; both blamed the Jews, or the French, or the doctors. In one town, . . . the entire ghetto was burned house after house, with the howling mob standing around, driving screaming fugitives back into the fire with swords and clubs. In the insanity of fear and bitterness, innocent people were murdered, burned, and tortured everywhere.

Plagues are not unique in generating scapegoats. Bad weather can do it, as can anything that yields widespread suffering. Economist Emily Oster examined "witchcraft, weather and economic growth in Renaissance Europe,"[62] showing that after a lull of 70 years, there was an inexplicable resurgence in witch-burning during the fifteenth century, which coincides with an exceptionally steep temperature decline.

The Little Ice Age that afflicted fifteenth-century Europe led to harsh conditions, including poor crop yields that, in turn, left people hungry, desperate, and looking for others to blame and to punish—in short, to serve as scapegoats. Nor was this merely the inclination of the uncouth and uneducated: "It has indeed lately come to Our ears," wrote Pope Innocent VIII, in a papal bull of 1484, "that many persons . . . have blasted the produce of the earth, the grapes of the vine, the fruits of the trees." Others have suggested that the infamous Salem witch trials in the colonial United States two centuries later may have been prodded by another unusual stretch of bad weather, which in turn triggered the same basic bio-psychosocial process that had earlier energized the pope and his minions.

It is noteworthy that during the sixteenth and seventeenth centuries, while large-scale witch-hunts were still underway in Christian Europe, comparatively few took place in Spain. Were Spaniards at the time especially witch-friendly? Perhaps, but more likely they were particularly Jew-unfriendly. Throughout Europe, rulers including Phillip II, III, and IV in the Spanish Netherlands, who felt themselves threatened by internal subversion as well as foreign aggression, were not shy about encouraging witch hunts, whereas Spain itself managed to avoid most of the anti-witch craze. Some historians argue that instead of hunting witches, Spaniards were redirecting their "negative energy" toward their Jewish population.[63]

Anti-Semitic Spanish sentiment had been mounting as far back as the fourteenth century, increasingly directed toward so-called *conversos*, who had accepted Christianity under pressure and who, it was believed, could never become "true Christians." In 1460, an influential publication, *Fortalitium Fidei* ("Fortress of the Faith"), had named heretics, demons, Muslims, and Jews as the four chief enemies of Catholicism, and when it came to the latter, there were only "public Jews and secret Jews," both groups believed to be guilty of "profanation of the Host and the murder of Christian children."

As anti-Semitism expanded, the Spanish Inquisition actually seems to have ameliorated its treatment of witches, especially compared to the rest of Europe. Some historians speculate that by this time, continental Europe had already expelled, murdered, or ghettoized many of its Jews, who were therefore less available as convenient targets, whereas Spain had substantial regions populated by Jews or by people of Jewish descent.[64] Interestingly, the most strenuous persecution of witches on the Iberian Peninsula was in the Basque country— where Jews were rare.

To be sure, Jews were not the world's only scapegoats. Nor are they the only ones today. Chinese have served, for example, in Malaysia; Indians in East Africa; African-Americans in the United States; and so forth. In his book, *A Crack in the Edge of the World*, Simon Winchester[65] described the aftermath of the Lisbon earthquake of 1755, which killed 60,000 people: "Priests roved around the ruins, selecting at random those they believed guilty of heresy and thus to blame for annoying the Divine, who in turn had ordered up the disaster. The priests had them hanged on the spot." It is claimed, as well, that the eruption of Krakatoa in 1883 gave extra momentum to a new, extremist and violent brand of Islam, directed toward everyone else, including noncompliant sects; we have not been able to confirm this, however.

Now jump ahead 524 years from Innocent VII's papal pronouncement about the various "blasters" of nature's bounty to a statement that was predictive (and likely to be sadly accurate) as compared to the medieval pope's proscriptive— and clearly destructive—one. In April 2008, *New York Times* columnist Nicholas Kristof forecast "a particularly bizarre consequence of climate change: more executions of witches." In rural Tanzania, Kristof noted, it is common for elderly women to be murdered when there is either too much or too little rainfall. One of the currently unanticipated consequences of global warming, he warned, may therefore be an increase in the socially sanctioned murder of scapegoats— notably old women. Mr. Kristof reached this conclusion without mentioning redirected aggression, but no matter. That's what he was talking about.

It is altogether fitting and proper that he did so, for scapegoating is a modern scourge no less than a blot on history. Earlier, we referred to the now-classic research by Carl Hovland and Robert Sears, which revealed a correlation between lynchings and bad economic times in the American South. Although these findings have been supported by researchers using modern statistical techniques,[66] at least one other study, which sought to expand the approach by examining hate crimes generally—against Jews, blacks, gay men and lesbians, etc.—was not able to connect these occurrences to unemployment rates.[67] Maybe what researchers call the dependent variables ("hate crimes") are too general, or the independent variable (unemployment rate) is too specific. Or maybe, we must acknowledge, the connection between distress and redirected aggression is not so robust after all. Our strong suspicion, however, is otherwise: that the inclination to respond to pain and distress by seeking a scapegoat is undeniable and perhaps even unavoidable. At present, it is unclear whether scapegoats are more likely to be drawn from among those personally known to the aggressor, or from a more anonymous population.

In an important book published in 2008, Raymond Fisman (Columbia University) and Edward Miguel (University of California, Berkeley), reported these research results from rural Africa:

> A survey we conducted in sixty-seven Meatu villages shows that nearly all victims of witch attacks are older females, and most come from "poorer than average" households. These desperately poor households— those with the least land, cattle, and assets like radios or bicycles— would be those facing the impossible and agonizing resource arithmetic of many mouths and little food. These killings don't happen at random. Witch murders and attacks are overwhelmingly concentrated in years when bad weather and the resulting crop failure cause farm incomes to plummet. In normal rainfall years, a witch murder occurs in a village once every thirteen years on average. In years of drought or flood, that rate nearly doubles to one murder per village every seven years. In the merciless famine year of 1998, there were nearly three times as many witch murders as in 2000, when moderate rains nurtured farmers' fields. One old woman every seven years is a lot in a village of only four hundred households. It translates into a 2 in a 1000 chance each year that a woman over the age of fifty is killed or attacked as a witch— nearly four times Colombia's overall murder rate at the peak of the 1990's drug wars. . . .

The two economists go on:

> Witch killings are not unique to Tanzania. Attacks follow a similar pattern in northern Ghana, where thousands of accused witches have been attacked or driven from their villages in the past decade, often following struggles over household resources. Witch killings of elderly women have also been documented in Kenya, Mozambique, Uganda, and Zimbabwe, in rural India—specially in Bihar, India's poorest state—and in Bolivia. Over four hundred accused witches have been killed since 1985 in South Africa's poor Northern Province.[68]

The present book was written in the midst of the great recession of 2008/2010, at a time when economic pain was distressingly widespread. Although there have not been any reported cases of witch killings in the United States or Europe (so far), there has been no shortage of genuine villains: individuals whose malfeasance and plain old-fashioned greed helped bring about these particular hard times. At the same time, given the persistent historical connection between tough times and the persecution of bystanders, there is a genuine risk that innocent persons will yet suffer as a result, and that these innocents will not simply include those whose homes, livelihoods, and fundamental well-being has been directly and disastrously compromised, but also those constituting a kind of "collateral damage," scapegoats in a sense: innocent, incidental bystanders liable to be sacrificed to the pain of others.

In anticipation of such outcomes, an article in the highly respected British medical journal *The Lancet* examined how changes in national economies has impacted mortality rates in the past thirty years, considering 26 European Union countries from 1977 to 2007. The basic finding was that "every 1% in unemployment was associated with a 0.79% rise in suicides at ages younger than 65 years . . . and with a 0.79% rise in homicides."[69] In short, as Sears and Hovland discovered many decades ago, economic hardship does not simply cause pain to the immediate victims, it induces many of them to seek out further victims, sometimes including, in the case of suicide, themselves.

Of course, this tendency does not keep victims from redirecting their pain and anger toward prominent external targets, when possible. Here is *New York Times* reporter Sabrina Tavernise, writing about Saddam Hussein's execution in Iraq, on December 31, 2006, an event that—like its victim—was notable for its ugly violence and the glee with which "justice" was administered. "The new Iraq," writes Ms. Tavernise, "appears capable of inflicting only more of the abuse it suffered for so long, perpetuating it with overwhelming brutality." It may also be noteworthy that Saddam's execution occurred on the first day of the Islamic holiday of *Id al-Adha*, a feast of sacrifice that harks back to Abraham's willingness to sacrifice his son, Isaac. Reprieved at the last moment, Isaac sacrificed a goat instead—a scapegoat if ever there was one. And today, Muslims around the world slaughter goats, sheep, and even camels in commemoration.

Even as fallen leaders such as Saddam Hussein or Slobodan Milosevic can themselves fall victim to being scapegoated, such leaders—so long as they are in power and are sufficiently unscrupulous—are often particularly adroit at manipulating the anger and suffering of their populace. Here is Aaron Beck, commenting on one aspect of Adolf Hitler's appeal to his German audience:

> His speeches, which often lasted for hours, started by playing on the people's fear of the Jews, Communists, and other unfriendly countries. The litany of wrongs was designed not only to revive the pains over past

humiliations but also to arouse fears of future abuse. After upsetting his audience with tales of past persecutions and the diabolical portraits of the enemy, he empowered them by providing the solution: wreak revenge on this accursed people.

In 1940, Churchill described Hitler as "the repository and embodiment of many forms of soul-destroying hatred, this monstrous product of former wrongs and shame." And it was during the harsh economic conditions of the 1930s that Hitler's assaults against the Jews gained a considerable following, while a few years earlier (during a more prosperous era), those same ideas had largely been ignored.

Listen, next, to Jerry Falwell, immediately after the 9/11 attacks: "I really believe that the pagans, and the abortionists, and the feminists, and the gays and the lesbians who are actively trying to make that an alternative lifestyle, the ACLU, People For the American Way, all of them who have tried to secularize America. I point the finger in their face and say 'you helped this happen.'" We cannot know whether the Reverend Falwell was "honestly" scapegoating some of his personal *bêtes-noires*, or cynically seeking, like so many demagogues, to capitalize on a shared moment of public pain. But either way, he is not unique.

Shortly after President Vladimir Putin announced tightened requirements for welfare as well as a stepped up military draft, in 2005, Russian skinheads began threatening Jewish communities and synagogues.[70] Immigrant-bashing is a worldwide phenomenon, one that predictably grows in direct proportion as times are hard for any "native" population. Indeed, with the worldwide economic debacle that began in 2008, we gloomily predict a significant increase in attacks— physical and verbal—against scapegoats of any convenient race, religion, ethnic group, age, and so forth. Furthermore, we expect an increase in domestic violence, as some people, already on the edge emotionally, and increasingly frustrated, angry, and desperate, "take it out" on their own families.

* * *

Therapists have long recognized the phenomenon of within-family scapegoating. Among so-called dysfunctional families, in particular, it is very common for at least one member (typically a child) to emerge as the one who fails at school, uses drugs, gets in trouble with the law, becomes pregnant out of wedlock, or gets someone pregnant. In these or a host of other ways, the problem-person serves as lightning rod for the family pain. Therapists refer to "triangulation," whereby a third party—an innocent child, troublesome adolescent, underachieving brother-in-law—is scapegoated, for the short-term benefit of others. The scapegoat is typically younger, weaker, or otherwise less connected and thus, more vulnerable. In some families, there really is a "problem child." When there is not, it is often necessary to invent one.

Significantly, therapists frequently discover that if the family scapegoat gets help and stops being the recipient of such pain, then others in the family may subtly attempt to undercut his or her recovery. Should the scapegoat successfully cast off the onus and really stop being such a goat, other family problems—not uncommonly, the genuine, underlying ones—emerge at last.

Interestingly, scapegoated children in particular are not merely "sacrificial lambs." They often actively collude in their role, perhaps because they have been trained to do so, but also, on occasion, because of a recognition—presumably unconscious—that by drawing negative attention to themselves, they are establishing balance and relieving tension that might otherwise be too painful for the family system to bear.[71]

According to Robert Coles, professor of psychiatry and medical humanities at Harvard Medical School, scapegoating is not just a within-family or within-society problem, but "the need for scapegoats causes war." That was the title of an article Dr. Coles wrote in 1982 for the magazine *Psychology Today*. In it, he told the following story:

> I will never forget an interview I did in 1963 with a member of the Ku Klux Klan. A desperate, hateful man poured out his frustrations and bitterness, his lifelong resentments and failures. His language was full of obscenities and self-revealing (and self-debasing) cries for struggle and social upheaval—as if, then, he would have his much-wanted (and needed) second chance to show himself able to make something of himself in the world. He was urging, really, a war—a war of all against all. He was mad, I thought. Yet he was also an ordinary American working-man, having a fairly hard time making a living, and with lots of sickness in his family and little money to meet the growing stack of bills on his kitchen table. I told him, in a moment of exasperation, that he seemed to be arguing the desirability of one more world war; and that I doubted that human life on this planet would survive such an outcome. He looked at me sharply and long; I girded myself for still additional irrationalities, banalities, indecencies. Instead, this: "there's a side of everyone that's mean as can be. There's another side that's good, like my 7-year old daughter can be, most of the time. What makes the difference is how you live. If you've got a lousy life, the meanness wins. If you've got things pretty good, you have a better chance of being nice to others. The same goes with countries. . . ."

We will look more closely at the social side of the Three Rs in general and scapegoating in particular in the next chapter. Let us first note that pain-passing is not limited to now-outlawed "codes of honor," family dysfunction, or social pathology and the "criminal underclass." In fact, it is institutionalized in many apparently respectable forms, such as hazing in fraternities, boot camp, and medical internships, as well as the British "public school" system. And second, it isn't not all doom and gloom. Some scapegoats are fun to have, as Bill Maher comically acknowledged in his "New Rules" blog, just before the 2004 presidential election:

> Let Bush win! I'm sorry. I know it's terrible to say that. But like every other swing voter in America, I got to think about the issues that are important to me. And to me the most important issue is . . . having an erratic jackass in the White House!
>
> Rocky 3 isn't any good if he doesn't have Mr. T to fight with. A satirical tackling dummy like George Bush doesn't grow on trees. Without Bush, who will America's schoolchildren have to look down on? And folks, this isn't just me, you might ask yourselves, without George Bush around, where does the hate go?
>
> Folks, I see the catharsis in a live audience every time I ridicule our president. . . . A hate, like Bush, only comes once in a lifetime. And when it walks through the door, you grab it and hold on tight, and never let it go.[72]

Even as Mr. Maher celebrated the delights of having George W. Bush to kick around, Calvin Trillin noted Mr. Bush's penchant for kicking Iraq, post-9/11. Here is the first stanza of Trillin's hilarious but painfully accurate poem, "Everything George Bush Needs to Know He Learned on the Playground":

> Let's say that from the east while you look south
> An icy snowball hits you in the mouth.
> You see the kid who did it run, the wretch,
> But he proves quite impossible to catch.
> He's gone. So you, your anger quite unsated,
> Beat up another kid you've always hated.[73]

What we have, then, are two accounts, both by humorists, both involving then–President Bush, one describing the author's personal "need" for Bush as a target of his own anger—as well as his jokes—the other recounting Bush's personal animus toward Saddam Hussein, and how, redirected, it helped produce a war. In both cases, the actions of a single individual are at issue, but since that individual was the world's most prominent politician, the consequences were multiplied many times over.

There should, in principle, be a clear line between individual and group behavior; we all know the difference between a personal act and that of a family, mob, tribe, or nation. And yet, the reality is that one melds seamlessly into the other insofar as the behavior of groups is that of individuals, enhanced and multiplied.

Peace advocates ask "What if they had a war and nobody came?" But it is pre-cisely because people—each an individual, but lots of them together—show up that wars take place. This is true of the Three Rs, too, with individual penchants for retaliation, revenge, and redirected aggression expanded into the "behavior" of larger social units.

Following is some personal testimony from novelist Paul Auster. It shows with unusual clarity how the writer's need for redirected aggression, multiplied by others in the crowd, morphed into a group event. Auster is describing a rally he had attended 40 years earlier, at Columbia University in 1968, ostensibly to protest the construction of a gymnasium in New York City's Morningside Heights:

> I didn't attend the rally because of the gym. I went because I was crazy, crazy with the poison of Vietnam in my lungs, and the many hundreds of students who gathered around the sundial in the center of campus that afternoon were not there to protest the construction of the gym so much as to vent their craziness, to lash out at something, anything, and since we were all students at Columbia, why not throw bricks at Columbia, since it was engaged in lucrative research projects for military contractors and thus was contributing to the war effort in Vietnam?[74]

Auster was not alone at the time, nor is he now; we are all groupies. Turn the page—each of you, individually—to find more about groups in the next chapter.

References

1. Aaron T. Beck. (1999). *Prisoners of Hate*. New York: HarperCollins.
2. J. Dollard, L. W. Doob, N. E. Miller, O. H. Mowrer, and R. R. Sears. (1939). *Frustration and Aggression*. New Haven, CT: Yale University. Freer, (1939).
3. R. Epstein (1965). Authoritarianism, displaced aggression, and social status of the target. *Journal of Personality and Social Psychology* 2(4): 585–589.
4. W. Pedersen, B. J. Bushman, E. A. Vasquez, and N. Miller. (2008). Kicking the (barking) dog effect: The moderating role of target attributes on triggered displaced aggression. *Personality and Social Psychology Bulletin* 34: 1382–1397.
5. B. R. Brown (1968). The effects of need to maintain face in interpersonal bargaining. *Journal of Experimental Social Psychology* 4: 107–122.
6. W. C. Pedersen, C. Gonzales, and N. Miller. (2000). The moderating effect of trivial triggering provocation on displaced aggression. *Journal of Personality and Social Psychology* 78: 913–927.
7. W. Pedersen, B. J. Bushman, E. A. Vasquez, and N. Miller. (2008). Kicking the (barking) dog effect: The moderating role of target attributes on triggered displaced aggression. *Personality and Social Psychology Bulletin* 34: 1382–1397.
8. W. C. Pedersen, et al. (2002). Psychological experimentation on alcohol-induced human aggression. *Aggression and Violent Behavior* 7: 293–312.
9. E. A. Vasquez, T. F. Denson, W. C. Pedersen, D. M. Stenstrom, and N. Miller, (2005). The moderating effect of trigger intensity on triggered displaced aggression. *Journal of Experimental Social Psychology* 41 (1): 61–67.

10. Eduardo Vasquez, et al. (2004). The moderating effect of trigger intensity on triggered displaced aggression. *Journal of Experimental Social Psychology* 41: 61–67.

11. T. F. Denson, F. E. Aviles, V. E. Pollock, M. Earleywine, E. A. Vasquez, and N. Miller (2008). The effects of alcohol and the salience of aggressive cues on triggered displaced aggression. *Aggressive Behavior* 34 (1): 25.

12. William C. Pedersen (2006). The Impact of Attributional Processes on Triggered Displaced Aggression Motivation and Emotion, *Vol. 30*, No. 1: 75–83.

13. L. Berkowitz (1989). Frustration-aggression hypothesis: Examination and reformulation. *Psychological Bulletin* 106: 59–73. L. Berkowitz (1990). On the formation and regulation of anger and aggression: A cognitive neoassociationistic analysis. *American Psychologist* 45: 494–503. L. Berkowitz (1993). *Aggression: Its Causes, Consequences, and Control.* New York: McGraw-Hill.

14. L. Berkowitz and E. Harmon-Jones (2004). Toward an understanding of the determinants of anger. *Emotion* 4: 107–130.

15. Berkowitz, L., Cochran, S. T., and Embree, M. C. (1981). Physical pain and the goal of aversively stimulated aggression. Journal of Personality and Social Psychology, 40, 687–700.

16. A. Marcus-Newhall, W. C. Pedersen, M. Carlson, and N. Miller (2000). Displaced Aggression Is Alive and Well: A Meta-Analytic Review.

17. M. S. Mitchell, and M. L. Ambrose (2007). Research reports—Abusive supervision and workplace deviance and the moderating effects of negative reciprocity beliefs. *Journal of Applied Psychology* 92 (4): 1159.

18. K. Aquino and S. Thau (2009). Workplace victimization: Aggression from the target's perspective. *Annual Review of Psychology* 60: 717–741. J. Barling, K. E. Dupré, and E. K. Kelloway (2009). Predicting workplace aggression and violence. *Annual Review of Psychology* 60: 671–692. J. M. Hoobler and D. J. Brass (2006). Research reports—Abusive supervision and family undermining as displaced aggression. *Journal of Applied Psychology* 91 (5): 1125.

19. J. V. Trachtenberg (2007). Work-home conflict and domestic violence: A connection. Ph.D. thesis, University of Connecticut, Storrs, CT.

20. S. E. Lewis and J. Orford (2005). Women's experiences of workplace bullying: Changes in social relationships. *Journal of Community and Applied Social Psychology* 15 (1): 29–47.

21. D. Hennessy (2008). The impact of commuter stress on workplace aggression. *Journal of Applied Social Psychology* 38 (9): 2315–2335.

22. C. E. Climent and F. R. Ervin. (1972). Historical data in the evaluation of violent subjects: A hypothesis generating study. *American Journal of Psychiatry* 27: 621–624.

23. S. Freud (1917). Mourning and melancholia. In *Collected Papers, vol. 4* (ed. D. Jones.) London: Hogarth Press.

24. A. Freud (1936). The Ego and Mechanics of Defense. New York: International Universities Press.

25. B. J. Bushman, R. F. Baumeister, and A. D. Stack (1999). Catharsis, aggression, and persuasive influence: Self-fulfilling or self-defeating prophecies? *Journal of Personality and Social Psychology* 76: 367–376.

26. A. Bandura (1973). *Aggression: A social Learning Analysis.* New York: Random House. Also see: Brad J. Bushman (2002). Does venting anger feed or extinguish the flame? Catharsis, rumination, distraction, anger, and aggressive responding. *Society for Personality and Social Psychology* 28(6): 724–731.

27. S Gambaro and A. I. Rabin (1969). Diastolic blood pressure responses following direct and displaced aggression after anger arousal in high- and low-guilt subjects. *Journal of Personality and Social Psychology* 12 (1): 87–94.

28. William Blake (1946). "Infant Sorrow," *The Portable Blake.* New York: Viking.

29. Andrew Bard Schmookler (1988). *Out of Weakness.* New York: Bantam Books.

30. Alice Miller (1983). *For Your Own Good: Hidden Cruelty in Child-Rearing and the Roots of Violence.* New York: Farrar Straus & Giroux.

31. Erich Fromm. (1973). *The Anatomy of Human Destructiveness.* New York: Holt, Rinehart & Winston.

32. A. P. Goldstein (1996). *Violence in America.* Palo Alto, CA: Davies-Black Publishing.

33. C. S. Widom (1989). Does violence beget violence? A critical examination of the literature. *Psychological Bulletin* 106: 3–28.

34. Lynette M. Renner and Kristen Shook Slack. (2006). Intimate partner violence and child maltreatment: Understanding intra- and intergenerational connections. *Child Abuse and Neglect* 30: 599–617.

35. G. K. Kantor and J. L. Jasinski. (1998). Dynamics and risk factors in partner violence. In:. *Partner Violence: A Comprehensive Review of 20 Years of Research* (ed. J. L. Jasinski and L. M. Williams). Thousand Oaks, CA: Sage.

36. B. C. Wallace (1996). *Adult Children of Dysfunctional Families: Prevention, Intervention, and Treatment for Community Mental Health Promotion*. Westport, CT: Praeger Publishers.

37. J. Kaufman and E. Zigler. (1987). Do abused children become abusive parents? *American Journal of Orthopsychiatry* 57: 186–192.

38. H. H. Filipas and S. E. Ullman (2006). Child sexual abuse, coping responses, self-blame, post-traumatic stress disorder, and adult sexual revictimization. *Journal of Interpersonal Violence* 21 (5): 652–672.

39. P. D. Kroll, D. F. Stock, and M. E. James. (1985). The behavior of adult alcoholic men abused as children. *The Journal of Nervous and Mental Disease* 173 (11): 689–693.

40. B. K. Luntz and C. S. Widom (1994). Antisocial personality disorder in abused and neglected children grown up. *The American Journal of Psychiatry* 151 (5): 670–674.

41. C. S. Widom, S. J. Czaja, and M. A. Dutton. (2008). Childhood victimization and lifetime revictimization. *Child Abuse and Neglect* 32 (8): 785–796.

42. David M. Fergusson, Joseph M. Boden, and L. John Horwood. (2006). Examining the intergenerational transmission of violence in a New Zealand birth cohort. *Child Abuse and Neglect* 30: 89–108.

43. Marilyn J. Kwong, Kim Bartholomew, Antonia J. Z. Henderson, and Shanna J. Trinke. (2003). The intergenerational transmission of relationship violence. *Journal of Family Psychology* 17(3): 288–301.

44. J. C. Huefner, J. L. Ringle, M. B. Chmelka, and S. D. Ingram. (2007). Breaking the cycle of intergenerational abuse: The long-term impact of a residential care program. *Child Abuse and Neglect* 31: 187–199.

45. R. A. Prentky, et al. (1989). Developmental antecedents of sexual aggression. *Development and Psychopathology* 1: 153–169. R. A. Prentky and R. A. Knight, (1993). Age of onset of sexual assault: Criminal and life history correlates. In *Sexual Aggression: Issues in Etiology, Assessment, and Treatment*. Washington, D.C.: Taylor and Francis.

46. J. Gilligan. (1996). *Violence, Our Deadly Epidemic and Its Causes*. New York: Grosset/Putnam

47. Quoted in R. Baumeister (1997). *Evil*. New York: W. H. Freeman and Co.

48. Jeffrey W. Swanson, Marvin S. Swartz, Susan M. Essock, Fred C. Osher, H. Ryan Wagner, Lisa A. Goodman, Stanley D. Rosenberg, and Keith G. Meador. (2002). The social-environmental context of violent behavior in persons treated for severe mental illness. *American Journal of Public Health* 92(9): 1523–1531.

49. M. Geller and L. Ford-Somma. (1984). Violent homes, violent children. A study of violence in the families of juvenile offenders. Washington, D.C.: National Center on Child Abuse and Neglect.

50. Jane Ireland and John Archer. (2002). The perceived consequences of responding to bullying with aggression: A study of male and female adult prisoners. *Aggressive Behavior* 28 (4): 257–272.

51. Randy Thornhill and Craig Palmer. *The Natural History of Rape*. Cambridge, MS: MIT Press.

52. A. Nicholas Groth. (1980). *Men Who Rape: The Psychology of the Offender*. New York: Perseus.

53. B. Jaccobs (2004). A typology of street crime retaliation. *Journal of Research in Crime and Delinquency* 41: 295–323.

54. M. Butovskaya, A. Kozintsev (1999). Aggression, friendship, and reconciliation in Russian primary schoolchildren. *Aggressive Behavior* 25: 125–139.

55. V. Topalli, R. Wright, and R. Fornango. (2002). Drug dealers, robbery, and retaliation. *British Journal of Criminology* 42: 337–351.

56. N. Chagnon. (1988). Life histories, blood revenge and warfare in a tribal population. *Science* 239: 985–992.

57. Theodor Adorno, Else Frenkel-Brunswik, Daniel Levinson, and R. Nevitt Sanford (1950). *The Authoritarian Personality*. New York: Harper and Bros.

58. G. Stricker (1963). Scapegoating: An experimental investigation. *Journal of Abnormal and Social Psychology* 67: 125–131.

59. Jerome Frank (1982). *Sanity and Survival in the Nuclear Age*. New York: Random House.

60. M. Scott Peck. (1983). *People of the Lie*. New York: Simon and Schuster

61. Rudolf Vrba and Alan Bestic, *I Cannot Forgive*. Bellingham, WA: Star and Cross.

62. *Journal of Economic Perspectives* 18(1): 215–228.

63. See especially Stephen Haliczer (1991). The Jew as witch: Displaced aggression and the myth of the Santo Niño de La Guardia. In *Cultural Encounters: The Impact of the Inquisition in Spain and the New World* (ed. Mary Elizabeth Perry and Anne J. Cruz). Berkeley, CA: UC Press.

64. B. Netanyahu. (1995). *The Origins of The Inquisition in Fifteenth Century Spain*. New York: Random House.

65. Simon Winchester. (2005). *A Crack in the Edge of the World: America and the Great California Earthquake of 1906*. New York: HarperCollins.

66. J. T. Hepworth and S. G. West. (1988). Lynchings and the economy: A time-series reanalysis of Hovland and Sears (1940). *Journal of Personality and Social Psychology* 55(2): 239–247.

67. D. P. Green, J. Glaser, A. Rich (1998). From lynching to gay bashing: The elusive connection between economic conditions and hate crime (interpersonal relations and group processes). *Journal of Personality and Social Psychology* 75(1): 82–92.

68. Raymond Fisman and Edward Miguel (2008). *Economic Gangsters: Corruption, Violence, and the Poverty of Nations*. Princeton, NJ: Princeton University Press.

69. David Stuckler, Sanjay Basu, Marc Suhrcke, Adam Coutts, and Martin McKee (2009). The public health effect of economic crises and alternative policy responses in Europe: An empirical analysis. *The Lancet* 6736(09): 61124–61127.

70. Frank Brown (2005). Russian far right scapegoats Jews again. *The Jerusalem Report*. 21 Feb.

71. Vimala Pillari (1991). *Scapegoating in Families: Intergenerational Patterns of Physical and Emotional Abuse*. New York: Brunner/Mazel.

72. Available at http://www.hbo.com/billmaher/new_rules/(2004)(1015).html.

73. Excerpted from *Everything George Bush Needs to Know He Learned on the Playground* by Calvin Trillin. Poem originally appeared in *The Nation*. Copyright © (2003), (2004) by Calvin Trillin. Reprinted by permission of Lescher and Lescher, Ltd. All rights reserved.

74. P. Auster (2008). The accidental rebel. *The New York Times*, April 23.

4

Social

Revenge, Feuding, Rioting, Terrorism, War,
and Other Delights

Human beings, as any biologist can attest, are perfectly good mammals whose physiology, anatomy, embryology, and so forth are not uniquely separated from the rest of the world (except in the trivial sense that every species is special in its own way). At the same time, there is much in our behavior that is distinct, setting us apart from other living things. Among these discontinuities—quantitative and perhaps qualitative as well—is the extent to which the behavior of individuals can have large-scale social repercussions. And here, the Three Rs have their part to play.

In the previous chapter, we examined some aspects of pain-passing in the context of personal psychology. Next, we look at how payback magnifies and ramifies onto a larger, social canvas. But even as we pursue this inquiry and seek to further develop the case for taking the Three Rs seriously, please be aware that intellectual modesty is very much in order. It is said that for every complex question there is an answer that is simple, satisfying . . . and wrong. Aggression and violence, especially among human beings, are complex indeed, and retaliation, revenge, and redirected aggression depending on one's perspective, are sometimes simple and sometimes satisfying. More than sometimes, they are also wrong.

Just as there are many cases of individual aggression that do not involve the Three Rs, there are many instances of social violence that need to be understood as resulting from other factors; most (although certainly not all) of them dutifully illuminated by decades, even centuries of careful scholarship. War, in particular, has many, many causes; the same is true for ethnic conflict, feuding, and so forth. Despite our enthusiasm for our subject, we are not so blinkered or so ignorant of the complexity of human behavior as to presume that the Three Rs are the key to all of these various tightly-tied Gordian knots. They are just *a* key.

* * *

Let's start with revenge. After all, a lot does. Revenge has all the hallmarks of what anthropologists call a "cross-cultural universal." That is, it appears in one form or another in all human societies, and we can therefore be confident (or alarmed) that this aspect of pain-passing is deeply rooted in human nature. Early in the twentieth century, social scientist R. F. Barton studied a Filipino tribe, the Ifugao, looking at their social rules and how they settled disputes. In an account that has since become a classic in legal anthropology, Barton wrote that "the Ifugao has one general law, which with a few notable exceptions he applies to killings, be they killings in war, murders, or executions. . . . That law is: A life must be paid with a life."[1] Nearly 70 years later, psychologists Martin Daly and Margo Wilson laboriously went through reports for 60 different tribes, distributed throughout the world, to see whether the Ifugao were unusual. Their findings were unequivocal: 57 of the 60 held the same belief, that it was proper for a life to be exacted in precise retribution for any life that had been taken.

Sometimes this principle is "permissive"; that is, a relative or tribesman of the victim is *allowed* to retaliate. More often, it is obligatory: revenge is a duty, a sacred responsibility, required to wipe away the stain of dishonor and often to allow the victim's soul to rest in peace. The paradoxical reality, of course, is that such prescriptions generally yield something less than peace for the living. The ghost of the murdered King Hamlet, demanding vengeance for wrongdoing, does not only stalk the brooding castle of Elsinore, nor is it merely a phenomenon of tragic literature. It is found, in one form or another, throughout the real world.

Here is an account of the South American Jivaro tribe:

> His desire for revenge is an expression of his sense of justice. The soul of the murdered Jivaro requires that his relatives shall avenge his death. The errant spirit, which gets no rest, visits his sons, his brothers, his father, in dreams, and weeping conjures them not to let the slayer escape but to wreak vengeance upon him for the life he has taken. If they omit to fulfill this duty the anger of the vengeful spirit may turn against themselves. To avenge the blood of a murdered father, brother, or son, is therefore looked upon as one of the most sacred duties of a Jivaro Indian. . . . It may happen that a Jivaro keeps the thought of revenge in his mind for years, even for decades, waiting for the opportunity to carry it out, but he never gives it up.[2]

Listen next to this testimony from Milovan Djilas, who was born into a perpetually feuding Montenegrin clan, eventually rising to be vice president of Yugoslavia and one of the architects of twentieth-century Titoism. Djilas spanned the interval between tribalism and modernity in his nation, and his insights into revenge—written nearly 40 years ago—ominously foretell the stubborn enmity that subsequently devoured his unhappy land:

> Vengeance—this is a breath of life one shares from the cradle with one's fellow clansmen, in both good fortune and bad, vengeance from eternity. Vengeance was the debt we paid for the love and sacrifice our forebears and fellow clansmen bore for us. It was the defense of our honor and good name, and the guarantee of our maidens. It was our pride before others; our blood was not water that anyone could spill. It was, moreover, our pastures and springs—more beautiful than anyone else's—our family feasts and births. It was the glow in our eyes, the flame in our cheeks, the pounding in our temples, the word that turned to stone in our throats on our hearing that our blood had been shed. It was the sacred task transmitted in the hour of death to those who had just been conceived in our blood. It was centuries of manly pride and heroism, survival, a mother's milk and a sister's vow, bereaved parents and children in black, joy and songs turned into silence and wailing.[3]

Tit-for-tat killings are perhaps *the* defining feature of persistent feuds throughout the world. Deriving from past pain, they demand the infliction of yet more in the future, continuing the vicious cycle. It is entirely possible that such actions literally reduce the distress of the aggrieved party, if only briefly, as measured by physiological indices as well as personal report. To our knowledge, however, such research has not been seriously undertaken. But there can be no doubt that sequences of this sort are not only common, but, given the widespread internalization of "the need to get even," oddly understandable.

Here is one example among many. Throughout the 1980s and 1990s, tit-for-tat murders were commonplace in Northern Ireland. On October 23, 1993, an IRA assassin's bomb—intended for the headquarters of the Ulster Defense Association (Protestant)—exploded prematurely, killing nine Protestants, among them a seven-year-old girl. The result was a grisly series of random responses: Several hours after the bomb blast, Protestant paramilitaries killed a Catholic fast-food delivery person. Two days after that, a 72-year-old Catholic man was murdered, and the following day, two Catholic garbage collectors. Then, on Halloween, Protestant gunmen entered a pub in Graysteel, a Catholic village, and fired randomly with automatic weapons, killing seven people. Not to be outdone, IRA snipers began assassinating British soldiers, bombing homes in Protestant neighborhoods, and burning Protestant-owned stores . . . whereupon Protestant operatives killed a man and a teenager who had been quietly sitting in a taxi office.

Feuds generally involve an initial outrage followed by counter-outrages that occur over a span of days, sometimes weeks or even months. But because of the power of such events and the vivid historical memory of their participants, individuals have often been forced to bear not only their own immediate pain and enmity but also the weight of grudges accumulated by earlier generations. Russian anthropologist Sergei Arutiunov described the situation of many Georgians, Abkhasians, Armenians, and Azeris:

> Among the Caucasus highlanders, a man must know the names and some details of the lives and the locations of the tombstones of seven ancestors of his main line. People fight not only for arable land; they fight for the land where the tombstones of their ancestors are located. Revenge is not only for events today, but also for the atrocities from wars eight generations ago.[4]

In April, 1998, an article appeared in *The New York Times* headlined "Feuds Wrack Albania, Loosed From Communism," which began as follows:

> Beneath the snow-splashed escarpments that protect northern Albania from the outside world and have left life much as it was centuries ago, the Sylaj family have been cooped up on their homestead for months, too afraid to move. A blood feud, following precepts laid down in a medieval canon, hangs over the men of the household, including the patriarch Shaban Sylaj, 99, who welcomes visitors with a two-tooth grin, wisps of ash-colored hair poking out from under his skullcap. Mr. Sylaj's son, Chel, 38, shot and killed another Albanian man in January, and now the dead man's family have the right, under the still-flourishing code, to take revenge. Their target is one of the Sylaj men.[5]

In a sense, the Sylaj family was lucky. The news article goes on to recount how one Fatmir Haklaj recently resigned as police chief of the town of Tropojo to revenge the murder of his brother, who had been shot with nine bullets. Mr. Haklaj leads one of the most powerful clans in northern Albania, and had vowed to kill one man from the offending Hoxe clan for every bullet that struck his brother. He had one killing to go.

Revenge often merges into redirected aggression. Thus, according to anthropologist Ruth Benedict, as recounted in her immensely influential book *Patterns of Culture*, there was a recommended code of conduct among a certain tribe of head-hunters:

> When a chief's son died, the chief set out in a canoe. He was received in the house of a neighboring chief, and after the formalities he addressed his host, saying, "My prince has died today and you go with him." Then he killed him. In this, according to interpretation, he acted nobly because he had not been downed, but had struck back in return.

It must be noted, however, that in this case, the bereaved chief was not really "striking back" at all, since the neighboring chief was not responsible for his son's death. Rather, instead of retaliation or revenge, he was redirecting his own pain and anger, precisely consistent with our understanding of its relationship to subordination stress. His personal loss would have caused him to be "downed," but by inflicting pain on someone else, this distress was eased. And presumably, relatives of that now-deceased neighboring chief were motivated to strike back in turn. Recall the ethnic cleansing in Banja Luca, as described by Lawrence Weschler, in which atrocities were perpetrated by Serbs upon Bosnian Muslims "because" of war crimes committed by Croats . . . two generations earlier.

* * *

The preceding suggests a possible inconsistency, not so much on the part of those seeking revenge or redirection, but concerning our efforts to explain and understand them. Laboratory studies of the sort described in the previous chapter have conclusively shown that anger generated by a provocation dissipates pretty quickly: generally in less than ten minutes. And this includes not only the victim's subjective feelings but also physiological measurements such as blood pressure, respiration rate, pupillary dilation, and so forth.[6] Accordingly, isn't it stretching things to interpret revenge—especially those notable cases of long-standing, often multigenerational feuds—as organically related to the same mechanism that connects subordination stress to redirected aggression? After all, one thing that makes vengeance-seeking among Serbs, Montenegrins, Caucasus highlanders, and others so notable is the extraordinary time lag between the initial provocation and the subsequent "need" to respond. It is not realistic to think that whole generations of victims experience in real time the various concomitants of subordination stress that initially bedeviled their elders, not to mention their distant ancestors, leading them eventually to pass their pain to others.

Or is it?

Earlier, we considered some of the research by social psychologists that explored various arcane aspects of aggression in general, and of redirected aggression in particular. Among these details is one that might constitute a bridge between redirected aggression as a prompt response, and something extended over time. In a word: rumination.[7] It is well documented that when people respond disproportionately to a seemingly small provocation—or for no apparent reason at all—they have probably been ruminating about it, mulling it over, marinating in their anger, which intensifies all the while, or at least comes to permeate their psyches like a spice that ripens and deepens over time.

Continuing the culinary metaphor, recall the Sicilian saying that "revenge is a dish best served cold." And in fact, when in a laboratory study subjects were encouraged to ruminate about an earlier provocation, they were more likely to behave aggressively toward someone who had been responsible for a minor annoyance. The technical manuscript describing these findings was also suitably gustatory, titled "Chewing on it can chew you up: Effects of rumination on triggered displaced aggression."[8] This particular research showed that subjects who were exposed to an irritating trigger-event and then encouraged to think about what had happened to them were more likely to "take it out" on an innocent victim eight hours later than were "non-ruminating" subjects (who had been distracted or encouraged to think positively). In a similar study, subjects were annoyed by a confederate of the experimenter, after which they were divided into three groups. Some were asked to hit a punching bag while thinking about those who had irritated them (rumination); others were asked to think about being fit while punching the bag (distraction); while others did nothing. Later, when all three groups were given the opportunity to retaliate against the people who had annoyed them, the ruminators were the most angry and aggressive.[9]

A social psychologist had earlier proposed that when it comes to personal styles of dealing with pain, anger, and disappointment, there is a continuum between "dissipaters" and "ruminators," with dissipaters being more likely to "get over it," while the ruminators are inclined to get increasingly angry as they contemplate the injustice of what happened or the perfidy of the perpetrators.[10] More recently, other researchers have suggested a similar distinction, whereby redirected aggression can be "arousal based" or "ruminatively based"; the former occurring immediately after the initial provocation, the latter after stewing about it.[11]

There is also evidence, not surprisingly, that those more likely to engage in rumination over past wrongs are less likely to practice forgiveness,[12] and also that marital conflict in particular is made worse when the parties engage in overly long and detailed post-mortems, reviewing and, in the process, intensifying their sense of aggrievement.[13] It is one thing, apparently, to clear the air, "release the anger," "get in touch with what's bothering you," and so on, and quite another to hold a grudge so firmly as to nourish its growth and flowering.

Our suggestion is that cultural traditions are often the social equivalent of personal rumination, masterpieces of communal grudge-holding and resentment-gathering. Just think of the group, ethnic, and nationally oriented practices that regularly remind people of their anger, humiliation, and pain via songs, stories, plays, sayings, and so forth. In this regard, the United States may well be something of an exception, since American holidays and other nationally identified cultural events are overwhelmingly celebratory rather than bitter, almost certainly because, with the exception of the Vietnam War (and possibly the Iraq and Afghanistan Wars—time will tell), U.S. history has been one of uninterrupted national successes. For all its exploding firepower, even the July 4th holiday—which marks a successful War of Independence—is self-congratulatory and not typically an occasion to gloat about defeating the British. The only departure is

Memorial Day, which, when observed at all, is largely a time for thoughtfulness, gratitude, and respect, rather than anger, bitterness, and calls for getting even. But in the rest of the world, things are often quite different: The commemoration of one nation's triumph is often an opportunity to stick a collective finger in another's eye.

Since the nineteenth century, for example, Northern Irish Protestants ("Orangemen") have paraded to Drumcree each year on the Sunday preceding the 12th of July. Until the recent Good Friday Accords and its attendant reconciliation between Irish Catholics and Protestants, this parade along with others during the "marching season" generated predictable violence and huge attendant anxiety. What was it all about? In 1610, England enacted the "Articles of Plantation," by which the best land was confiscated from the native Irish and given to Crown loyalists, nearly all of them Protestant Scottish and English. In 1641, the displaced Irish rebelled and slaughtered thousands of loyalists, after which, in 1649, the English, led by Oliver Cromwell, massacred thousands of Irish. Further Irish rebellions ensued, until eventually the English king, William of Orange, defeated the Irish resistance at the Battle of the Boyne in 1690. It is this victory, four centuries ago, that loyalists persisted in celebrating by their annual marches. Moreover, for decades they went out of their way—literally— to route the victory parades through Catholic communities.

It should be clear that the practice of gloating over victories and thus forcing others to mull over past defeats, embarrassments, pain, and anger is not limited to seemingly benighted inhabitants of the Balkans and Caucasus, or exotic and "primitive" hunter-gatherers. Often, victorious gloating is not even needed; left to themselves, losers are often predisposed to relive their pain. Following France's ignominious defeat in the Franco-Prussian War (1871), for example, the newly minted German state annexed the previously French province of Alsace and most of Lorraine. For decades thereafter, the return of these two regions became a French national obsession, with schoolchildren beginning their day by regularly reciting pledges to achieve this goal. Eventually they did, with the "help" of World War I.

Indeed, it was the French yearning for payback against the Germans that led to the pre–World War I Franco-Russian alliance in support of Serbia against Germany, after the assassination of the Austrian Archduke in 1914. And this, in turn, emboldened Russia to stand firm against Germany, which contributed mightily to dragging Europe into that horribly destructive and unnecessary war. And that isn't the end of pain's progression in twentieth-century Europe.

After its defeat, Germany's national distress exceeded what France had experienced more than four decades earlier. Germans chafed mightily from the humiliations inflicted by the Treaty of Versailles, now recognized as one of the great blunders of international diplomacy. Under its terms, Germany was labeled solely responsible for World War I, forced to pay substantial reparations, to surrender considerable territory as well as its colonies, and excluded from membership in the League of Nations. British Prime Minister David Lloyd George had recognized what was about to happen (although evidently he did not feel strongly enough at the time to prevent it). In his *Fontainbleau Memorandum*, Lloyd George was prescient: "You may strip Germany of her colonies, reduce her armaments to a mere police force and her navy to that of a fifth-rate power; all the same in the end if she feels that she has been unjustly treated in the peace of 1919 she will find means of exacting retribution from her conquerors."

Sure enough, Adolf Hitler played with virtuosity on German pain and anger over that nation's defeat in World War I and the national "stab in the back" suffered at Versailles. There is no consensus as to whether World War II would have happened in the absence of a mesmerizing and sociopathic *Fuhrer*, but as things transpired, there is also no doubt that Hitler's political and military agenda profited greatly from the shame, rage, and suffering of the German people following the First World War. These feelings were readily transformed into yet another assault on much of the outside world. Rumination indeed—with a vengeance.

* * *

The most troublesome national struggles are those that have been going on for a long time. To some extent, this is self-evident: If a dispute is not especially troublesome, it is unlikely to be especially persistent. But there is deeper meaning here as well. The existence of long-held animosity, with its deeply felt pain, is not simply a statement of how things were and long have been, but a cause of how they *are*. Israelis mourn the Holocaust, vowing that it will happen "never again," while Palestinians regularly and painfully remind themselves about *Al-Naqba* ("the Catastrophe") of Israel's founding and the subsequent departure (whether forced or voluntary) of 750,000 Palestinians from their homes in 1948. In short, historical experience matters, not simply as facts from the past but because such experience, especially when painful, generates passions and animosities as well as a felt need for revenge and restitution in the present:

> For Israel's Jewish population, this includes displacement, persecution, the life of the ghetto, and the horrors of the Holocaust; and the long, frustrated quest for a normal, recognized and accepted homeland. There is a craving for a future that will not echo the past and for the kind of ordinary security—the unquestioned acceptance of a Jewish presence in the region—that even overwhelming military superiority cannot guarantee.... For Palestinians, the most primal demands relate to addressing and redressing a historical experience of dispossession, expulsion, dispersal, massacres, occupation, discrimination, denial of dignity, persistent killing off of their leaders, and the relentless fracturing of their national polity.[14]

There can be no doubt that groups and nations often ruminate over past wrongs, reminding themselves of their need to respond, vigorously and violently, some day. We suspect that to some extent this is simply a tendency that naturally wells up among abused, angry, and victimized peoples, just as it does among individuals. But it is also true that leaders are often eager to manipulate this inclination for their own ends. In the last chapter, we briefly considered Hitler's manipulative scapegoating of Jews in particular, which he employed in large part as a cynical means of controlling the populace. But it is also true that such tactics would not have worked if the German people were not receptive to appeals to redirection as a way of satisfying their preexisting needs, based—at least in part—on their sense of having been victimized following their defeat in World War I (widely viewed in Germany as resulting from a "stab in the back" from their own politicians), the one-sided Treaty of Versailles, and by the postwar economic disasters of hyperinflation and the Great Depression.

Many Serbs, for another example, express genuine outrage about what befell them in the past, claiming—with some accuracy—that these wrongs fueled their violent treatment of Bosnian Muslims in particular. This doesn't merely apply to the "ethnic cleansing" in Banja Luca during the 1990s, so vividly described by Lawrence Weschler. If you think the Irish-English memory for grudge-keeping is overdeveloped, consider the history of Serbian aggrievement against Turkish Muslims. In 1989, Slobodan Milosevic, then leader of Yugoslavia, announced to an increasingly agitated gathering of Serbs, "No one will ever dare beat you again!" *Again*? It was not lost on Milosevic's audience that he was speaking on the precise 600th anniversary of the "Battle of the Blackbirds," near Pristina, the present-day capital of Kosovo. The year had been 1389, when invading armies of Ottoman Turks defeated Serb forces. *Six hundred years later*, Milosevic, standing on the exact same battlefield, set in motion the violent oppression of Kosovars—who, incidentally, were overwhelmingly Albanian and not Turkish. This wasn't simply a case of Milosevic reminding his listeners of past pain, but of literally reviving it within them.

Christians honor the suffering of Jesus, and in the past at least, the holiday of Easter was especially associated with outbreaks of anti-Jewish violence. The holiest day of the Shiite Muslim calendar is Ashura, which marks the martyrdom of Hussein, grandson of the Prophet Mohammed, who was killed in A.D. 680, near Karbala in today's Iraq. Today, blood flows abundantly as Shiites "celebrate" this event by flagellating themselves with chains and self-mutilating with swords. In modern Iraq, it is also a major opportunity for Sunnis to murder Shiites, and vice versa.

The strong likelihood is that in such cases the murderers feel little or no guilt for their actions; indeed, they almost certainly consider themselves heroes, their violent acts legitimized by a deep sense of past injustice inflicted on them or the group with which they identify. A fascinating study, conducted over the Internet, recently examined this phenomenon among Canadians and Americans, looking specifically at the role of "historical victimization" in justifying current victimization of others.[15] In one part of the research, Jewish Canadians were evaluated as to the degree that they felt personally guilty for hurtful Israeli actions toward Palestinians. The subjects who were first reminded of previous Jewish victimization—the Holocaust—felt considerably less guilt about victimizing Palestinians, even though Palestinians were not responsible for the Holocaust. It might be argued that simply being reminded of past horrors, regardless of who was the victim and who the victimizer, is likely to raise the threshold of current outrage, via a kind of habituation to violence. However, when the same subjects were told, in detail, about the genocide experienced by Cambodians under the regime of Pol Pot, this did not influence their responses. The key appears to be whether *one's own group* had suffered.

When Christian Americans were assessed as to their shared sense of guilt involving damage done to Iraqi citizens as part of the 2003 invasion, those who had been reminded of either the 1941 Japanese attack on Pearl Harbor or the terrorist attacks of 9/11 were less inclined to feel guilt or responsibility for destructive U.S. actions in Iraq. The researchers concluded that "feelings of collective guilt for harm to a current adversary are lessened when one's own group's history of victimization is salient," and that "one means of lessening feelings of collective guilt for current harm to another group is by referencing the in-group's own past victimization."

Social scientists have long been aware of a powerful worldwide inclination toward "in-group amity, out-group enmity,"[16] a phenomenon that accords with evolutionists' recognition of kin selection and the biologically potent tendency to favor genetic relatives while disfavoring those who are different. It appears that shared pain, like shared genes, provides not only a degree of social glue but also social repulsion toward the out-group, especially when the strangers not only are not part of the charmed circle of shared, collective distress, but are also identifiable, however tenuously, as connected to its original cause.

Thus, in what is probably the longest-lasting revenge epic of all times, Jews have been blamed, for two thousand years, for the killing of Christ. This "blood libel" is at least in part an excuse for anti-Semitism that derives from other sources—intolerance toward "the other," jealousy of cultural success, the deep and widespread search for scapegoats—but it also carries its own momentum, conjuring as it does the potency of group-sanctioned revenge.

It is notable that in the above Internet study, the Holocaust reminder was only effective for Jewish participants; it did not influence the perception of Christian subjects as to the legitimacy of Israeli harshness toward Palestinians. Similarly, reminders of historical victimization of Americans (Pearl Harbor or the 9/11 attacks) had a strong effect on American participants but not on Canadians.

Recall that Americans were more likely to perceive the American-led invasion of Iraq as justified when they were reminded of 9/11 *or* of Pearl Harbor.

The "9/11 effect" can be understood, at least in the case of some experimental subjects (presumably, the more gullible ones), as resulting from the Bush Administration's insistence that there was a connection between Iraq and 9/11. But Pearl Harbor? Clearly, there is no meaningful link between that "day of infamy" on December 7, 1941, and the other one on September 11, 2001. Something else is going on, namely a tendency to respond to pain—in this case, the memory of pain that was not even directly experienced by the subjects in question—by justifying in their minds the infliction of pain on others, who were in no way responsible for the events.

Our point is simply this: One of the most pernicious effects of certain cultural practices is to keep ancient grudges alive, and, in the process, to legitimize violence toward others—with those "others" not necessarily limited to the initial perpetrators. Rumination happens, and not just to individuals. Indeed, it does not merely "happen" passively; rather, it is frequently urged upon whole populations, by unscrupulous individuals (Hitler, Milosevic . . . George W. Bush?), and by cultural and religious traditions. This effectively blurs the distinction between "arousal-based" and "ruminatively based" redirected aggression, with the latter leading to the former, making past outrages a source of current pain and thereby keeping the Three Rs up to date.

* * *

Thus far in this chapter, we have tried to make the case that a solid line—based on the Three Rs—runs through revenge to feuding, through the personal to the social, often mediated by the behavior of unscrupulous leaders and abetted by the poisonous effects of culturally sanctioned rumination. But what happens when rumination becomes action? Take the case of ethnic rioting.

Certainly, to experience a riot is to undergo a high level of arousal. Participants, surfing on a wave of anger, adrenaline, and agitation, are overwhelmingly "in the moment" and not prone to rumination. But especially when it carries a strong ethnic flavor—with one group pitted against another—such events commonly emit more than a whiff of ruminative, redirected aggression, often fanned by unscrupulous, self-seeking leaders. For some examples, we turn to a bit of mid-twentieth-century history, events that are for the most part unfamiliar to the majority of Americans but which, precisely for that reason, are likely to be valuable because they offer the kind of clarity that comes with distance.

In 1949, riots broke out in the city of Durban, South Africa, in response to an electoral victory by the ultra-rightwing Nationalist party, which to most citizens signaled a forthcoming dramatic decline in the circumstances of black Africans.* In the resulting communal violence, interestingly, not a single white European,

---

* This supposition was correct, since the rigid apartheid laws of South Africa were instituted shortly afterward, in the 1950s.

neither British nor Boer, was attacked, presumably because they were considered too powerful. Instead, black African violence was directed—actually, redirected—toward South Africans of Indian descent. It is worth noting, at the same time, that redirected aggression was not the only underlying cause of the Durban riots: native Zulus and Xhosa had ongoing grievances against the Indian-Africans, whose entrepreneurial culture rendered them not only economically more successful on balance than their black African counterparts, but also direct targets of envy.[17]

Before the Durban riots came the equally instructive Burmese riots of 1938. Here, once again, ethnic Indians were lightning rods for accumulated anti-colonial pain and anger that were in fact more "honestly" and universally felt against white Europeans—notably, the imperial British occupiers of Burma—and that had earlier surfaced during the so-called Saya San rebellion of 1930–1931. However, the military power of the occupying British Indian Army had made these efforts futile, so[†] the hostility of the indigenous Burmese was redirected toward the economically successful but socially vulnerable Indo-Burmese.

The Burmese riots began when a book written by an Indian Muslim presented an unflattering image of the Buddha. Protesters demonstrating against this book turned and attacked Indo-Burmese citizens, whereupon British police forcibly quelled the near-riot. The next day, several Burmese newspapers printed a largely apocryphal story in which British police had brutalized innocent monks leading a peaceful protest. Clearly, it was the British, rather than the local Indian population, that warranted wrath.

Nonetheless, a few days later, Burmese mobs throughout the country stormed into local villages, where they proceeded to target, not British colonialists, but Indo-Burmese residents. For reasons that are unclear, however, and that in turn suggest that factors other than "simple" redirected aggression were operating, Indian Muslims were targeted more often than were Indian Hindus. Another little noted but intriguing fact is that a decade or so later, as violence increased between Hindus and Muslims in British-occupied India, the frequency of comparable violence directed at the British colonizers went into proportionate *decline*.[18] Perhaps it was simply too demanding for the Hindu and Muslim population to engage in a "two-front war" against the British as well as each other. So they chose the latter.

Yet another example of ethnically oriented rioting with distinct implications for culturally inspired redirected aggression are a series of attacks against the Fulani people by native Guineans during the mid-1950s. In this case, violence

---

[†] Note how this tiny, two-letter word is heavily freighted with implications; notably, the unspoken presumption that pain and anger, when it cannot be directed at the victimizer, will "naturally" be redirected toward someone else.

broke out once again as a consequence of mounting indigenous hostility toward their hated French colonial occupiers, who had exhibited a clear preference for the Fulani. A similar pattern occurred 40 years later, when Hutus massacred hundreds of thousands of Tutsis in Rwanda; much of this animosity derived, not surprisingly, from Hutu fury at their European colonial overlords, who, generations before, had favored the somewhat taller, more aquiline-featured (and thus, European-looking) Tutsis.[19]

Examining these and earlier cases of ethnically oriented communal rioting, political scientist Donald Horowitz came to an interesting conclusion: In such conflicts, it is rare for the "superior" class to be targeted. More often, a "parallel" group is victimized. Moreover, according to Horowitz, even when actual violence is not involved, "communal tensions tend to mitigate hierarchical strains," resulting in a "progression from vertical to horizontal conflict." At the same time, the parties involved are predictable, as opposed to random lashing-out. Who-attacks-whom is in part a result of preceding conflicts and accumulated antipathy between the groups. We must acknowledge, therefore, that direct aggression, and not just its redirected counterpart, is also relevant.

For a final and more recent case of ethnic violence, we turn to Kenya, where horribly violent events unfolded in February of 2008, following a hotly contested election. Kenya's intertribal conflict was, once again, less a matter of immediate cause-and-effect than a consequence of accumulated wrongs and their resulting pain and anger.[†]

Kenya had been colonized in the late nineteenth century by the British, who quickly populated the fertile uplands of the Rift Valley around Mount Kenya, displacing the Kikuyu people who had lived and farmed there for generations. This area, which became known as the "White Highlands," emerged during the 1950s as the primary setting for the famous Mau Mau rebellion, in which angry Kikuyu villagers struck back at British farms, settlers, and officials.

In 1963, after much political and military struggle, Kenya achieved independence from British rule. As with many African nations, such abrupt freedom from the colonial power left Kenyans with a struggling economy, a fledgling infrastructure, and a tiny cadre of educated elite to govern the disenfranchised and oppressed masses. Jomo Kenyatta, an activist in the years leading up to independence, became the first president. He was a member of the Kikuyu tribe, the most populous in Kenya, followed by the Kalenjins and the Luo (Barack Obama's father, incidentally, was a Kenyan Luo). One of Kenyatta's first acts as president was to buy up the lands of white settlers from the Rift Valley, who began leaving the area after decolonization. Kenyatta then sold their land

---

[†] The following account owes much to Katherine Apfel, a University of Washington student who spent several months in Kenya shortly after the violence.

cheaply back to the Kikuyu, who had been the ones most often displaced during those first colonial settlements. He also appointed exclusively Kikuyu as ministers and high officials.

Over the ensuing years, the presidency changed hands several times, although power stayed in the hands of the Kikuyu and Kalenjin elite, while people from other ethnic groups watched in growing dismay as members of the Kikuyu in particular received plum positions over equally qualified applicants from other tribes. Tension and resentment increased as the Kikuyu upper class became increasingly entrenched and economic and political power became less a function of personal qualities than of tribal affiliation. The majority of Kenyans came to feel overlooked, under-represented, and certainly not cared for by "their" government. Daniel Arap Moi—president of Kenya for 24 years—became a frightening embodiment of this, exercising dictatorial leadership that ignored human rights, stole votes to win elections, and used torture to eliminate political opposition.

In 2002, Mwai Kibaki, another Kikuyu, defeated Daniel Arap Moi's chosen successor in a presidential election. In his campaign, Kibaki had promised to be accountable to all the people—not just fellow Kikuyu—and to choose officials based on merit and not tribal affiliation, as well as to end the corruption of the Moi regime. But he proved to be almost as bad as his predecessor, surrounding himself largely with Kikuyu ministers and officials, ignoring others who had stood by him during his campaign.

By 2005, a new constitution was long overdue, since the old colonial version was still formally in place. A government committee solicited hundreds of thousands of opinions, aiming—it was claimed—to write a "people-driven constitution." One can only imagine the excitement and hope when, as the overlooked majority, the various non-Kikuyu tribes of Kenya were asked how *they* wanted to be governed. A new constitution was duly drafted, but before a vote could be taken, Kibaki and his supporters doctored it to fit their wishes.

Non-Kikuyus increasingly began to blame the Kikuyu as a tribe—alleging an innate Kikuyu propensity for greed and corruption. Amid growing anti-Kikuyu anger and frustration, a new political party emerged, headed by a rising Luo star, Raila Odinga, widely seen as a strong favorite to win the presidency. Odinga won the presidential primary over five other provincial leaders, whereupon the five losing candidates agreed to support his candidacy, a strategic move designed to prevent a third candidate from splitting the anti-Kibaki, anti-Kikuyu vote in the final presidential election. Odinga emerged increasingly as the clear candidate of the Kenyan masses.

Presidential elections took place in late 2007, with morale especially high among Odinga supporters. As the results came in, Odinga was ahead by 1.2 million votes and victory seemed assured . . . until mysterious new ballots began turning up for Kibaki, who was quickly declared the winner just as the media were beginning to report on the shady vote count. A recount was initiated, but the chairman of the electoral commission arbitrarily pronounced Kibaki the victor.

Kibaki was sworn in as president on the same day as his "electoral victory" was announced—an unprecedented and irregular procedure. Confusion and outrage erupted immediately, with violence beginning on December 30, 2007. Simple protest soon changed to rioting, the rioting to burning and looting, and then physical attacks, mostly centered around the cities of Nairobi, Mombasa, and Kisumu. To no one's great surprise, the violence was initially directed at the Kikuyu people, against whom simmering resentment had been building for generations.

For anyone "on the ground" in Kenya, the motivation of these attacks is no mystery. Frustrated, angry people who had begun to hope, for the first time in years, that something might change, that government corruption might cease, that life might be fair after all, felt that the rug had been pulled from under them. It was the last straw when they saw their candidate win, only to be told that he had lost, and as a result frustrated mobs struck, not at the men who had wronged them—Kibaki and his officials—but at his tribe, those who represented the favoritism and nepotism of the last fifty years. After all, as with most situations of redirected aggression, the initial provoker, Kibaki, was inaccessible, whereas members of his tribe were targetable; although the Kikuyu are the largest single ethnic group in Kenya, they are themselves a minority, representing little more than 20% of the population.

The violence, however, did not stay simple for long. Soon, Luo and Kalenjin were targeting Kikuyu, Kisii were killing Luo, and Kikuyu were fighting back, also initiating attacks of their own. The government began using police to "restore order" by killing non-Kikuyus, essentially at random, in revenge for any Kikuyu killed in the Rift Valley. And in the city of Kisumu, "President" Kibaki brought in Ugandan armed forces, giving them permission to use live ammunition to kill *anyone*. Millicent Onyango, a Luo woman from the isolated Rabuor Village, was contacted by relatives to go pick up her sister's son from Kisumu. She saw a woman walking down the road shot by a policeman, who then shot her baby as well; police had been heard to say that they were "helping" children by killing them along with their parents. In one especially infamous episode, fifty Kikuyu, including women and children, were burned alive while seeking refuge in a church in the city of Eldoret.

The violence finally came to an end on February 28th, 2008, when, following mediation efforts by former UN Secretary-General Kofi Annan, Kibaki agreed to sign a power-sharing agreement with Odinga, creating a "coalition government" with the latter as prime minister. The initial violence and rage seemed finally to have burned itself out, although tensions were still palpable more than 18 months later.

It appears that Africa has been especially prone to events such as these, in part perhaps because poverty renders its people especially vulnerable to pain,[§] while the diversity of distinct ethnicities, combined with the artificial borders resulting from European colonialism, provides the opportunity for suffering people to vent their distress upon others: in-group amity, out-group enmity. Take Darfur: from August 1984 to November 1985—two decades before the much-lamented genocide—a famine in that part of Sudan caused an estimated 95,000 deaths out of a population of about 3.1 million. This famine forced historically settled ethnic groups to migrate in search of food, which in turn generated violent clashes as various populations became increasingly intolerant of each other—not so much due to anything these people actually did to one another but because of the distress generated by the famine itself.[20] The "moral geography" of the region had been lethally altered, with black Africans and Arabs pitted against each other with a special intensity that derived at least as much from their shared, in-group distress as from any direct provocations on the part of the out-group.

* * *

If we are right and the Three Rs are implicated in some of the most notably unpleasant cases of intergroup violence, then terrorism should be no exception. Sure enough, it isn't.

We have already suggested that the post-9/11 pain of most Americans was exploited by the Bush administration to help motivate the disastrous invasion of Iraq in 2003. This action in turn unleashed a catastrophic flood of violence and counter-violence, pain and the passing along of yet more pain, in which rumination doubtless played—and continues to play—a significant role, as it does when it comes to terrorism itself in the same manner as previously shown for feuding and ethnic rioting. Nor is this connection limited to Iraq.

A Palestinian suicide bomber blew himself up—accidentally, it appears—in December 2001, in front of a Jewish-owned hotel in Jerusalem. No one else was killed, and in a sense, this seemingly isolated event was barely noticed or remembered in the wider world. But it was part of a continuing pattern of tit-for-tat killings that have long bedeviled Israel and the occupied Palestinian territories. Here is an account of the true-life prequel to that particular small-scale tragedy:

> Four days before the explosion . . . three Hamas suicide bombers killed twenty-five people—ten, all of them teen-agers, at a café-lined pedestrian mall in Jerusalem, and fifteen on a bus in Haifa. Three days before

[§] Which includes, in addition to political unrest, such "objective hazards" as drought, malaria, sleeping sickness, and so forth.

then, a suicide bomber killed three Israelis on a bus near Hadera, Israeli soldiers killed two Palestinians at one checkpoint, and a Palestinian killed an Israeli soldier at another. Two days before that, two Palestinian gunmen killed two Israelis at a bus station before being killed themselves. Four days before that, Israeli soldiers killed a fifteen-year-old Palestinian boy in a clash after the funeral of five Palestinian schoolboys who had been killed when a bomb planted by Israeli soldiers went off in Gaza. The same day, Mahmoud Abu Hanoud, the senior Hamas military commander in the West Bank, was killed as part of Israel's policy of trying to prevent terrorism via selection assassination. (To judge how well that policy has worked, see above.)[21]

A strong case can be made that, paradoxically, terrorists themselves often rely on their avowed enemies (typically, governments in power) to advance their own cause. Certainly they gain recruits in proportion as governments act in a manner that inflicts pain on large segments of the population. It is widely and plausibly claimed that the grotesqueries of Abu Ghraib along with the excesses of Guantanamo and the Bush administration's use of torture on detainees has served as a "recruiting tool" for al Qaeda. Terrorist organizations themselves have long been aware, as well, that they can enlist enemy governments as their chief benefactor, often by provoking the authorities via some sort of violent assault, thereby inducing them to retaliate, the more hurtfully the better. The resulting pain, felt by much of the population, typically brings additional members into the terrorist organization.

The use of unmanned drones and other error-prone bombing tactics against the Taliban in Afghanistan appears to have generated more anti-NATO and anti-American fighters than it has eliminated. And as this book was being written, the government of Pakistan responded to its own growing Taliban insurgency by displacing literally millions of rural residents, killing many (as "collateral damage"), and in the process, creating a risk that the Taliban, previously very unpopular within Pakistan, will gain adherents and rapidly become a serious threat to the country's stability.

Here is another exemplary case. ETA, the violent Basque separatist group, refers to the "action-reprisal-action cycle," something that has served ETA well. Thus, in 1973, ETA operatives were responsible for assassinating the premier of Spain, Luis Carrero Blanco. The Spanish government, under the dictator, Francisco Franco, responded with a very heavy hand, which, in turn, sparked what virtually became a civil war. The terrorists' operative technique was pain: ETA caused pain to the Spanish government, counting on the fact that the government would respond in kind . . . and then some. They were not disappointed. Outraged at the violent repression done to them by Spanish soldiers, many Basques—who had not previously shown much interest in Basque separatism or in ETA, which was barely noticeable at the time on the Spanish political horizon—committed themselves to ETA and its vision of anti-government violence.

In Sri Lanka, the Tamil Tigers were politically and militarily insignificant until they killed 13 government soldiers in 1983. This, by itself, would not have made the Tigers major players in Sri Lanka, except that the government responded with a volley of severe anti-Tamil reprisals, which succeeded (from the Tigers' perspective) in igniting what became a bloody civil war.

When Muslim extremists, quite likely sponsored and supported by the Pakistani government, attacked the Indian parliament on December 13, 2001, their intent—almost certainly—was not simply to kill some Indian government officials, but to reprise the ETA strategy: Induce so much pain and anger that violent retaliation would ensue, which could be counted on to generate more hatred of the Hindu-dominated Indian government on the part of infuriated Pakistanis and Indian Muslims. Similar considerations likely drove the terrorist assault on Mumbai in November 2008. But the Indian government has defied expectation and showed remarkable restraint, doubtless disappointing the Pakistani Islamist extremists who apparently orchestrated the event. Thus far, the government in New Delhi has refused to fan the flames by retaliating, which shows that at least some people, some of the time, are capable of behaving with intelligence and dignity, and rising above the Three Rs (see Chapter 7). More often, the opposite is true, and beleaguered governments act out their own anger and pain, in a manner similar to the terrorists they oppose. Writing about the Israeli/Palestinian cycle of outrage and retaliation, journalist Nichole Argo reported that

> I observed plenty of funeral rallies that had a common catalyst: In the night, the Israel Defense Forces entered with tanks and helicopters, attempting to seize a militant or two. (The legitimacy of the mission was irrelevant to what came to pass.) Shaken from sleep, families hid in their homes if they could. If the sounds of violence came close, they often ran terrified through the streets, trying to get away from the army. Inevitably, somebody fell or was shot. He could be a militant; she could be unarmed. Usually friends and family stopped to aid. But bent, black shadows appeared threatening to young soldiers, who had little choice but to shoot again. Daylight rose in a blur of green flags (the signature color of Hamas), the drone of a loudspeaker, and throngs of people circling another mark on the ground. Through the megaphone came ardent words: "The enemy will feel our pain."[22]

In the words of a supporter of suicide bombings, "If we don't fight, we will suffer. If we do fight, we will suffer, but so will they."[23] And this apparently makes the slaughter of innocents not only okay, but also justified. According to Robert Pape, whose book *Dying to Win: The Strategic Logic of Suicide Terrorism* offers an exceptionally perceptive window onto its subject, suicide terrorism is not simply a matter of Islamic fundamentalism, or of psychopathology. After analyzing 315 attacks around the world from 1980 to 2003, Pape concluded that the common denominator was not religious fundamentalism, but perceived injustice, in which people's dreams were stymied by dictators, often with the support of the United States.

Similar conclusions have been reached in several other carefully researched books, including *Making Sense of Suicide Missions*, edited by Diego Gambetta,[24] Mia Bloom's *Dying to Kill: The Allure of Suicide Terrorism*,[25] and *The Road to Martyr's Square: A Journey into the World of the Suicide Bomber*, edited by Anne Marie Oliver.[26] Over and over, the pattern is clear: From their own perspectives and that of their communities, suicide bombers are largely seen as heroes, and—ironically—as altruists. As Nichole Argo concluded, "If self-sacrifice was viewed as the only way to make the enemy feel their pain, it was offered out of a sense of duty."

As president, George W. Bush claimed that the United States was attacked on 9/11 because it is rich, modern, open, powerful, pluralistic, democratic, secular, and so forth, that the United States is hated by many people for what it *is*. But it is clearly worth asking whether those who hate America are not also acting in response to what they perceive the United States has *done* . . . more specifically, to injure them, their self-esteem, their beliefs and their group's. Although it may have been convenient to label terrorists as simply crazy or the "embodiment of evil," it is more helpful to inquire whether, in their determination to cause pain to the United States, they too are responding, at least in part, to their own pain, born of resentment, anger, and humiliation.

In most cases, that pain has not been caused by the United States directly. The overwhelming likelihood is that failures of Middle Eastern countries to provide a decent standard of living for their people despite their oil wealth, the decline of Islamic empires from their fifteenth century grandeur, humiliation of Muslims in other countries from Kashmir to Israel, and other psychological insults have helped generate redirected aggression against the United States, even though the United States clearly has not been the sole or even the primary perpetrator of these insults.

After analyzing what he calls "the staircase to terrorism," psychologist Fathali Moghaddam concluded that a major factor is "displacement of aggression."[27] By encouraging virulently anti-Western *madrassas* (Islamic religious schools), for example, to displace aggression onto "out-groups," notably the United States, Middle Eastern governments sponsor fanaticism and violent "us-versus-them" thinking. Moghaddam points out that this is not simply a matter of personal psychology, with individuals acting out of their anger and pain. It also derives from a "complex relationship between some movements and leaders in Asia and Africa who are supported by the United States and other Western powers and who at the same time directly and indirectly use anti-Americanism to bolster their own positions." Such demagoguery is used to deflect resentment otherwise directed at their own governments—even though, paradoxically, without support from the United States, these same governments (e.g., Saudi Arabia, Egypt, Pakistan) would probably collapse. When popular passions are redirected, the powers-that-be are to some extent let off the hook.

Not only is there nothing inherently "Islamic" about all this, but Islam has in fact served as a convenient outlet for redirected aggression in the Western tradition. Thus, in Shakespeare's *Henry IV, Part 2*, the dying King Henry obsesses over the fact that he obtained the crown of England by forcing the abdication of the previous king, Richard II. Feeling guilty and insecure, Henry tells his son, the young Prince Harry, that he had planned

> To lead out many to the Holy Land,
> Lest rest and lying still might make them look
> Too near unto my state.

In other words, he intended to lead a crusade to distract his people, getting them to redirect their aggression toward the Muslim "infidels," lest they turn against his own regime. He then offers the following advice:

> Therefore, my Harry,
> Be it thy course to busy giddy minds
> With foreign quarrels; that action, hence borne out,
> May waste the memory of the former days.

In the United States, this became popularly known as the "wag the dog" phenomenon, after a popular movie by that title. It depicted how an American president (modeled on Bill Clinton), suffering serious political criticism and plummeting popularity at home, responds by ginning up an unnecessary war. Does this sound familiar?

* * *

War, in a broad sense, does not really exist. Rather, there are specific wars, each with its unique causes, historical background, and participants. By the same token, each case of "feuding," "rioting," or "terrorism" must be considered in its individual particularity. The same holds true for aggression as a whole, and indeed, for every claimed manifestation of any one of retaliation, revenge, and redirecting aggression, from a defeated monkey who threatens a bush to a threatened Bush who invades Iraq. There is, nonetheless, value in looking for general causative principles; after all, this is what distinguishes scientific explanations from anecdotal accounts. And there is probably no human phenomenon more in need of explanation—scientific and otherwise—than war. Here, too, the Three Rs are illuminating.

The twentieth century was characterized not just by specific wars, but also by debate about the legitimacy of war in general. It is widely agreed that World War II, for example, was "just." Historians acknowledge, by contrast, that World War I was not (or at least, there were no easily identifiable "bad guys"). By most accounts, in fact, the "Great War" was preventable, since the nations of Western Europe slid into terrible bloodletting without clearly defined reasons; that is, *without the legitimizing pain of prior provocation.* For some other cases: People dispute whether the Vietnam War was just, although most agree that the genocide in Rwanda involving the Hutus and Tutsis was not, whereas the initial U.S. incursion into Afghanistan may have been.

Henry IV was on to something. It is not uncommon for the leader of a "frustrated" country to guide his or her nation's collective anger toward neighboring countries in order to prevent the population's negative sentiment from turning inward. In fact the technique of leaders turning such feelings against weaker forces in order to divert attention from themselves has long been employed, not just in Shakespeare's fictional account, but by genuine historical figures.

After the defeat and humiliation of the Ottoman Empire (the former "sick man of Europe"), early in the twentieth century, the "Young Turks" under Kemal Ataturk achieved unity by promising to "purify the nation" by destroying various traitors, notably the Armenians, especially after the Turkish army was badly mauled by the Russians during the winter of 1914. The resulting genocide became one of the ugliest chapters of modern history.

In 1982, Argentina's General Galtieri, threatened by growing domestic opposition, orchestrated an attack on the Falkland Islands; this ploy failed utterly, but not because Galtieri and his military junta underestimated the powerful unifying impulse of redirected aggression—rather, because the Argentineans underestimated Britain's military strength and willingness to fight back.

Given the above, and informed by a perspective that looks for preexisting pain as a causative factor when nations go to war, peace would seem to be more readily attained during times of good fortune, when pain is mild. Conversely, one might predict that war will occur more frequently during periods of social and economic strife. It deserves note, however, that redirected aggression serves more as a mechanism that leaders employ to ally people against a common enemy, rather than as an actual precipitator of wars. Recall that the American people initially rallied round and supported the Iraq War. And for its part, the Bush Administration doubtless anticipated precisely this response, and indeed may well have initiated the war in order to gain political advantage as a result. The *actual causes* of that war, by contrast, probably lay elsewhere.

We strongly suspect that in the run-up to the U.S. invasion of Iraq in 2003, the Bush Administration neocons (including, but not limited to Dick Cheney, Donald Rumsfeld, and Paul Wolfowitz), were not especially motivated by a heavy dose of their own personal redirected aggression as such, although it is likely that they were confident that as a result of 9/11, such a war would be favorably perceived by the American public. In other circumstances, however, especially in the emotionally fraught context of a war that is already ongoing, it is quite likely that the temptation to redirect their own sentiments has influenced the decisions of high government officials. For example, in 1972, during the Vietnam War, civilians in Laos and Cambodia were killed in large numbers during what became known as the "Christmas bombing" campaign, which was publicly justified at the time as part of an effort to interdict the flow of weapons and soldiers from North Vietnam. Perhaps to some extent this was the genuine motivation. But one cannot help wondering whether it was not also a case of redirected aggression, in which a frustrated and angry Nixon Administration, bloodied politically by the peace movement at home just as the military had been bloodied on the battlefield by the forces of Ho Chi Minh, found it psychologically soothing to inflict pain on others, mostly civilians in Laos and Cambodia, who could be attacked and killed with impunity.

By the same token, it is clear that the first Gulf War, following Iraq's invasion of Kuwait, was an embarrassing and painful defeat for Saddam Hussein. And it was probably no coincidence that immediately afterwards, Saddam attacked the Kurds with special brutality and violence. If so, this exemplifies not only redirected aggression but also its face-saving "I'm not a patsy" underpinnings, a consideration that might be especially important in the ever-fraught Middle East. "I may have been beaten by the U.S.," Saddam would have been saying—to his own citizens as well as his not-terribly-friendly neighbors—"but don't get any silly ideas." Indeed, this fear of losing face and thus becoming yet more vulnerable (especially to his archrival, Iran) may well have motivated Saddam's curious refusal, in the days leading up to the second Gulf War, to acknowledge how militarily weak he actually was.

Redirected aggression is especially significant when it operates upon national leaders, since its effects are then multiplied so dramatically. But just as it applies in complex ways to domestic behavior (as discussed in the last chapter), it can range from entire nations down to individual soldiers, whose military training often purposely provokes feelings of frustration and anger, which is then focused upon the chosen enemy. Modern-day drill sergeants, for example, evoke not only subordination on the part of military recruits but also outright antagonism, their goal being to energize *esprit de corps* and within-group unity in the face of an "enemy"—the sergeant himself—that will eventually be transferred to the external enemy on the other side of the battlefield. This technique may also aid in distracting soldiers from possibly "taking out" their anger against the political regime that has pulled them away from home and family.

During an interview with a U.S. intelligence officer during the Nuremberg war crimes trials, in 1946, Herman Goering—the third-highest Nazi official captured at the end of World War II—made this now-famous observation:

> Why, of course, the people don't want war. Why would some poor slob on a farm want to risk his life in a war when the best that he can get out of it is to come back to his farm in one piece? Naturally, the common people don't want war; neither in Russia nor in England nor in America, nor for that matter in Germany. That is understood. But, after all, it is the leaders of the country who determine the policy and it is always a simple matter to drag the people along, whether it is a democracy or a fascist dictatorship or a Parliament or a Communist dictatorship . . . the people can always be brought to the bidding of the leaders. That is easy. All you have to do is tell them they are being attacked and denounce the pacifists for lack of patriotism and exposing the country to danger. It works the same way in any country.

It is also possible that the tendency to respond to fear and pain is so great that there is an urge, on the part of the victims, to assume that they must have done something to deserve it. This peculiarly self-destructive, self-blaming phenomenon is well known in the therapeutic community as a frequent response by victims of domestic violence to their own abuse: Instead of blaming the perpetrators, they may conclude that they must have done something to warrant their own victimization. Interestingly, wars, too, have occasionally been thought (at least in the European tradition) to be chastisement for a population's inequities. At the outbreak of World War II, for example, newspaper letters to the editor in England announced that the war was due to the hedonism that had prevailed during the 1920s and 1930s, and which had offended God.

* * *

Warfare against civilians is not only counter to the laws of war, it is nearly always counterproductive to military and political goals, because it induces the victims to rebel against their victimizers, to pass their pain along to those who initiated it. This is the take-home message of Caleb Carr's short, brilliant book, *The Lessons of Terror*, written in the immediate aftermath of 9/11.[28] Echoing our earlier argument that the infliction of pain on the part of governments typically serves to enhance the stock of terrorism, Carr writes that a similar process occurs when civilians are victimized during war:

> Warfare against civilians, whether inspired by hatred, revenge, greed, or political and psychological insecurity, has been one of the most ultimately self-defeating tactics in all of military history—indeed, it would

be difficult to think of one more inimical to its various practitioners' causes. And yet those same imperatives—hatred, revenge, greed, and insecurity—have driven nations and factions both great and small to the strategy of terror and the tactic of waging war on civilians time and time again. Some parts of the world, in fact, have become so locked into the cycle of outrages and reprisals against civilians that their histories comprise little else.

Later, Carr emphasizes that warfare against civilians does not merely generate eventual retaliation in kind, but it typically perpetuates a "cycle of revenge and outrage" that can persist for generations. Therefore, he notes, "it should be avoided in both its forms—initial and reactive—for, again, those nations and peoples who indulge in warfare against civilians to the greatest extent will ultimately see their people and their interests suffer to a similar degree."

Among other things, such awareness ought to foster commanders' insistence on strict discipline among soldiers, especially when it comes to their treatment of noncombatants, because otherwise the growing burden of pain, anger and resentment accumulated by civilians is ultimately likely to be redirected against those authorities associated with the initial victimization. Hence, the outrage among Iraqis following revelations about civilian massacres committed by the private security contractor, Blackwater, as well as the blessedly rare but nonetheless shocking cases of lethal misbehavior by U.S. and other coalition troops.

In May 2009, General David Petraeus—no shrinking violet when it comes to the use of violence—warned in an interview with National Public Radio of the dangerous temptation to achieve "short-term tactical advantage" via Predator drones and aerial bombardment in the struggle against the Afghan Taliban, but at the cost of "long-term strategic losses" when it comes to winning over the population.

The phenomenon is not new. During the seventeenth and eighteenth centuries, Louis XIV, oblivious to the long-term consequences, sought to establish a *cordon sanitaire* around France: "In the Rhineland, in Catalonia, and in Piedmont, French troops burned farms, killed and raped civilians, destroyed cultivated fields and livestock, and stole what little remained in order to create a wide swath of land around France that would be a dead zone to hostile armies." But as a result, "The rulers and citizens of the countries ravaged by Louis's troops were only steeled [in their animosity] by the severity of the French."

In his masterpiece *The Law of Nations* (1758), Emmerich de Vattel, generalizing perhaps from the earlier French experience, warned that:

If you once open a door for continual accusation of outrageous excess in hostilities, you will only augment the number of complaints, and influence the minds of the contending parties with increasing animosity; fresh injuries will be perpetually springing up; and the sword will never be sheathed till one of the parties be utterly destroyed.

Nor was this pattern limited to Western Europe:

Like Rome, the Ottoman and Mughal were empires that did not reach dizzying heights *because* of their brutality; they reached them *despite* it, and their eventual decay and collapse was hastened in no small measure because of their identification as ruthless, repressive regimes, and because of the vengeful willingness of many of their own citizens to participate in their toppling.

The gratuitous destruction visited upon the Confederacy toward the end of the Civil War had similarly predictable and tragic consequences, once again italicizing how trauma inflicted on a civilian population generates a powerful tendency to inflict subsequent trauma, in return:

Its long-term effect was the creation of endless resentment and hatred among the defeated people of the South, who subsequently vented their murderous rage through such home-grown terrorist groups as the Ku Klux Klan. And these groups did not direct their violence against federal troops but against victims over whom they had much more physical and political power: those blacks who were left behind when the federal army went home.

During the Second World War, Nazi atrocities against the defeated populations of Eastern Europe were especially intense and frequent. As one historian put it, "Everywhere in the lands they [the German Army] occupied, the oppressors raped women, tormented old men, tortured POW's, and abused innocent children." Then, when the tide turned and the Red Army pushed Hitler's forces back to Berlin,

Now was the time for Russian soldiers to restore their manhood, to overcome their sense of impotence arising from the Nazi's barbarous treatment of their wives, mothers, fathers and children. Now was the time for the Germans to pay for their racial arrogance and ruthless exploitation. Within a few weeks, almost a hundred thousand Berlin women sought medical attention for rape.[29]

Revenge? Perhaps. Redirected aggression? Almost certainly.

References

1. Roy Franklin Barton (1919). *Ifugao Law*. Berkeley: University of California Press.
2. Christopher Boehm (1986). *Blood Revenge: The Enactment and Management of Conflict in Montenegro and Other Tribal Societies*. Philadelphia: University of Pennsylvania Press.
3. Milovan Djilas (1972). *Land Without Justice*. Boston: Mariner Books.
4. Sergei Arutiunov (1995). Ethnic Conflict and Russian Intervention in the Caucasus. Institute on Global Conflict and Cooperation, IGCC Policy Papers, #16.
5. April 14 (1998), by Jane Perlez. Pg. A3.
6. P. D. Tyson (1998). Physiological arousal, reactive aggression and the induction of an incompatible relaxation response. *Aggression and Violent Behavior* 3: 143–158.
7. N. Miller, W. C. Pedersen, M. Earleywine, and V. E. Pollock (2003). A theoretical model of triggered displaced aggression. *Personality and Social Psychology Review* 7: 75–97.
8. B. J. Bushman, A. M. Bonacci, W. C. Pedersen, E. A. Vasquez, and N. Miller (2005). Chewing on it can chew you up: Effects of rumination on triggered displaced aggression. *Journal of Personality and Social Psychology* 88: 969–983.
9. B. J. Bushman (2002). Does venting anger feed or extinguish the flame? Catharsis, rumination, distraction, anger, and aggressive responding *Personality and Social Psychology Bulletin* 28: 724–731.
10. G. V. Caprara (1986). Indicators of aggression: The Dissipation-Rumination Scale. *Personality and Individual Differences* 6: 665–674.
11. N. Miller, W. C. Pedersen, M. Earleywine, and V. E. Pollock (2003). A theoretical model of triggered displaced aggression. *Personality and Social Psychology Review* 7: 75–97.
12. J. W. Berry, E. L. Worthington, L. Parrott, L. E. O'Connor, and N. G. Wade (2005). Forgivingness, vengeful rumination, and affective traits. *Journal of Personality* 73: 183–225.
13. L. K. Kachadourian, F. Fincham, and R. Davila (2005). Attitudinal ambivalence, rumination, and forgiveness of partner transgressions in marriage. *Personality and Social Psychology Bulletin* 31: 334–342.
14. H. Agha and R. Malley (2009). Obama and the Middle East. *The New York Review of Books* Vol. LVI, (10): 67–69.
15. Michael J. A. Wohl and Nyla R. Branscombe (2007). Remembering historical victimization: Collective guilt for current in-group transgressions. *Journal of Personality and Social Psychology* 94: 988–1006.
16. Arthur Keith (1949). *A New Theory of Human Evolution*. New York: Philosophical Library.
17. Donald L. Horowitz (1973). Direct, displaced, and cumulative ethnic aggression. *Comparative Politics* 6(1): 1–16.
18. Richard Lambert (1951). Hindu-Muslim Riots (Ph.D. dissertation, University of Pennsylvania)–cited in Horowitz (1973), but not independently verified.
19. Mahmood Mamdani (2002). *When Victims Become Killers: Colonialism, Nativism, and the Genocide in Rwanda*. Princeton, NJ: Princeton University Press.
20. Gerardo Prunier (2008). *Darfur: A 21st Century Genocide, 3rd ed*. Ithaca, NY: Cornell University Press.
21. *The New Yorker*, The Talk of the Town. Dec. 17, 2001.
22. Nichole Argo (2006). The role of social context in terrorist attacks. *The Chronicle of Higher Education* Feb. 3: B15–16.
23. Quoted in Robert A. Pape (2005). *Dying to Win: The Strategic Logic of Suicide Terrorism*. New York: Random House.
24. Oxford University Press, 2005.
25. Columbia University Press, 2005.
26. Anne Marie Oliver (2005). New York: Oxford University Press.

27. F. M. Moghaddam (2005). The staircase to terrorism: A psychological exploration. *American Psychologist*, 60(2): 161–169.
28. Caleb Carr (2002). *The Lessons of Terror*. New York: Random House.
29. Melvyn P. Leffler (2007). *For the Soul of Mankind: The United States, the Soviet Union and the Cold War*. New York: Hill and Wang.

5

Stories

Pain-Passing in Myth and Literature

Violence, as everyone knows, can produce injury. Our point thus far has been that the process also works in reverse: *Injury produces violence.* Moreover, since retaliation, revenge, and redirected aggression are so deeply inscribed upon the human psyche, it seems reasonable to expect them to be reflected in works of the human imagination, since, like imagination itself, they embody a deep truth about the nature of *Homo sapiens.* The stigmata of pain-passing, in short, should be evident not only in overt behavior but also in the stories we tell ourselves.

Interestingly, retaliation—a prompt response to being attacked, aimed exclusively at the perpetrator—does not figure prominently in literature, probably because it is so automatic and "natural" as to be unremarkable and thus, literally not worth remarking upon. Revenge and redirected aggression, however, are different "takes" on the universal story, whereby victims are impelled to pass their pain in less obvious ways: either after a delay and with intensification (revenge), or to a third party (redirected aggression). Yet these too are "natural," something that any injured rat or baboon—and even many fish— might understand.

As Mark Twain once noted, "The difference between fiction and nonfiction is that fiction must be real." It is simply not true that in the realm of fiction, "anything goes." For a story to have human resonance, it must reflect our inchoate sense of the nature of human nature, so that even bad guys must be portrayed as having some comprehensible motivation, nearly always deriving in some way from their own pain and hurt. Otherwise, their bad actions are not the stuff of story, but rather, cartoonish caricatures with a deservedly short shelf life.

Admittedly there are exceptions to this rule, such as recent arch-villains like The Joker in the movie *The Dark Knight* or Anton Chigurh in Cormac McCarthy's *No Country for Old Men.* Perhaps in the post-9/11, post-Iraq and Afghan War world, where violence seems so senseless and random, Americans in particular are experiencing a renewed cultural interest in pure sociopathy.[*]

In the late–twentieth century, initial victimization powered the notably unsettling movie *Natural Born Killers*, a narrative about a killing spree akin to that of Bonnie and Clyde, in which the female lead is clearly a victim of severe domestic violence and abuse. In the early twenty-first century, Quentin Tarantino's parodic revenge saga, *Kill Bill*, is just as bloody. "Don't get mad, get even," might be the second-most-honored plotline in Hollywood, barely behind "Boy meets girl, boy loses girl, boy gets girl." The revenge theme, however, has a much older pedigree. We therefore predict that in the realm of literature no less than in life, the most bloody-minded actions—if they are to seem in any way believable—are traceable to prior injury. (On occasion, revenge is the driving force behind a tale that is not so much dark and bloody as rollicking good fun; we are thinking here of *The Count of Monte Cristo*. But this is an exception, and indeed, for all its reading pleasure, Dumas's classic children's story is mostly just that, a children's story.)

Shakespeare, not surprisingly, is a model practitioner of serious revenge fiction. Even Othello's bane, that *über*-villain Iago—who, according to Coleridge, demonstrated a "blind, motiveless malignity"—was not entirely lacking in motivation. We learn that Iago had been passed over by Othello in favor of his rival, Cassio. Another archfiend, Richard III, complained of the "hideous deformity" that rendered him unsuitable for love. The lethal nastiness of Edmund, illegitimate son of Gloucester in *King Lear*, may similarly bespeak redirected aggression as well as revenge, as Edmund responds homicidally to his social opprobrium suffered as a bastard, in addition to his father's ill-considered taunts. What is certain is that neither Iago, nor Richard III, nor Edmund is unique; all are part of a pattern that speaks to our deeper selves and how people respond to pain and injury.

* * *

Revenge is not only one of the signature themes of literature, but also perhaps the oldest. It is most convincingly depicted in *The Oresteia*, a series of bloody tales from the House of Atreus, presented in all its horror and violence 2,500 years ago by the first great Greek tragedian, Aeschylus. True to expectation, this particular cycle of violence was set in motion by an initial infliction of pain: ten years before the action depicted in Aeschylus's classic trilogy, Agamemnon, commander of the Greek armies sailing for Troy, had sacrificed his daughter, Iphigenia, in order to propitiate the gods and obtain a favorable wind

---

[*] On the other hand, Ian Fleming didn't feel a need to invent sympathetic or humanizing life stories for the many perfectly evil, pre-9/11 characters who populated his James Bond novels.

for his fleet. News of Agamemnon's deed enraged his wife—Iphigenia's mother, Clytemnestra—who eventually exacted her revenge by murdering Agamemnon when he returned from Troy.

The pattern of vengeful comeuppance did not end here, as we will soon see. It did not even begin with Agamemnon's killing of Iphigenia. A generation earlier, Atreus (Agamemnon's father) had slaughtered the children of his competitor, Thyestes, serving them for dinner to their unwitting father. Thus, the tragedy of the House of Atreus began with a suitably lethal deed.[†] Atreus, in turn, had two sons, Menelaus and Agamemnon, the former becoming the cuckolded husband of Helen (she of Troy), and the latter chosen to lead the Greek army against that city, and who, in the process, presided over the death of his own daughter. When Agamemnon returned home after the Trojan War, he was murdered by the infuriated Clytemnestra, who had been plotting bloody revenge along with her lover, Aegisthus. If this seems complicated, it is about to get more so, although it remains noteworthy that all this complexity merely italicizes its underlying simplicity: When it comes to revenge, pain is paid for, eventually, with yet more pain. Aegisthus (Clytemnestra's lover and co-conspirator in Agamemnon's murder) turned out to be the sole surviving son of Thyestes, the one who was deceived into eating his own children, after they had been slaughtered by Agamemnon's father. Accordingly, Aegisthus, too—and not just Clytemnestra— had a bone or two to pick with the clan of Atreus.

After Agamemnon's murder, Aegisthus struts on stage and exults over the dead body:

> O happy day, when Justice comes into her own!
> Now I believe that gods, who dwell above the earth,
> See what men suffer, and award a recompense:
> Here, tangled in a net the avenging Furies wove,
> He lies, a sight to warm my heart; and pays his blood
> In full atonement for his father's treacherous crime.[1]

The Chorus nearly gets into a brawl with Aegisthus and his followers, whereupon Clytemnestra intervenes, imploring—with considerable (albeit self-serving) wisdom, given her recent actions—"There is pain enough already. Let us not be bloody now." At this point, it is not only those in the audience familiar with the myth of *The Oresteia* who know that there will be yet more pain and more blood before the cycle can end. The biosocial metabolism of pain demands it.

[†] And which was itself motivated by revenge, since Thyestes had ostensibly been sleeping with Atreus's wife.

Agamemnon is the first of Aeschylus's three monumental tragedies. In part two, *The Libation Bearers*, Orestes—son of the murderess, Clytemnestra, and the murdered murderer, Agamemnon—is incited by his sister Electra to avenge their father by killing both Clytemnestra and Aegisthus. Then, in part three, *The Eumenides*, Orestes is in turn pursued by the aptly named Eumenides ("Furies"), in furtherance of "justice," by which perpetrators of lethal violence must themselves be made to suffer. In an especially haunting scene, the Furies close in on Orestes by smelling the blood of Clytemnestra, his slain mother. And of course, committing matricide has rendered Orestes, too, irretrievably bloody (the associated Aegisthus-cide seems to slip by unnoticed, perhaps because there do not appear to be any surviving members of Thyestes's clan).

At the end of the play, the Chorus chants this paean to an all-too-human penchant, filtered through poetry that transfixes modern sensibility as a recognizable *cri de coeur*, although fully two and a half millennia old: "Even in our sleep, pain that cannot forget falls drop by drop upon the heart, and in our own despair, against our will, comes wisdom to us by the awful grace of God."

Notably, part of this "wisdom" involves a switch from passion and personal revenge to something administered by society (more on this in Chapter 6). Equally notable: The classical world seems to have been quite taken with revenge, nearly always portraying it as necessitated by the repetitive cycling and recycling of pain. Despite the significant recognition in *The Eumenides* that socially sanctioned justice is on a "higher" plane than the primitive Furies, the sad truth is that only rarely is legal, impersonal, socially sanctioned justice permitted to run its course.

In *Medea*, for example, the later Greek tragedian Euripedes gives us the horrifying tale of a woman's vengeance against her philandering hero-husband, Jason. When Jason announces his intention to leave her for another woman, Medea does not serve divorce papers or take him to court. She proceeds not only to kill the other woman, but also her own children, as a way of punishing Jason to satisfy her need for vengeful pain-passing. If the act itself seems "over the top," as a plot device it is highly effective, calling shocking attention to Medea's fury and despair. Her need for revenge is so great that Medea not only kills her female rival but even targets her own offspring in order to get at her tormentor, Jason. (It is also possible that by killing her children, Medea was simultaneously redirecting her aggression.)

The classic account of tragedy and its powerful impact was developed by Aristotle, who pointed to the capacity of certain stories to evoke pain and awe, and then, as the audience witnesses the cleansing effects of a tragic outcome, to experience a healing "catharsis." Clearly, Aristotle was unaware of subordination stress and the physiological basis of retaliation, revenge, and redirected aggression, just as he was necessarily naïve about the likely evolutionary underpinnings of the Three Rs. His analysis nonetheless translates remarkably well into our modern scientific understanding, while also helping illuminate why the basic parameters of pain-passing have remained so compelling and relatively unchanged for millennia.

If the literature of revenge began, at least in the Western tradition, with the Greeks, it certainly did not end there. So-called revenge tragedies have loomed especially large in the history of theater; of these, one of the most influential was a play titled *The Spanish Tragedy* by Thomas Kyd, a contemporary of Shakespeare's. In it, a Spanish gentleman named Hieronimo is driven nearly insane by the murder of his son. He exacts his revenge upon the culprits by including them in a play-within-the-play, in the course of which he kills them in turn, during the *faux* theatrical.

Perhaps the most famous tragedy of all, Shakespeare's *Hamlet*, is also essentially a tale of revenge, given added spice by the difficulty that Hamlet, the wronged party, experiences in bringing himself to accept the situation and to settle upon his course of action. Today's audience, no less than Shakespeare's Elizabethan one, knows deep in its bones (more correctly, in its cultural tradition, nervous system, physiology, and evolutionary history) that Hamlet simply has to do something. Moreover, that "something" must involve the infliction of pain.

Hamlet's tragedy is that he was not up to the violent retribution—the passing of pain—that was demanded of him as the son of a murdered father. For all the profound human insight contained in the play, and beyond Hamlet's lengthy agonizing about his "duty," nowhere in Shakespeare's masterpiece is there a serious examination of why revenge should be called for in the first place, and whether it is in any way ethical or even useful. Those things we take for granted are often the most revealing.

Return for a moment to *Othello*: The tragedy herein is widely seen to lie in the fact that our eponymous hero was tricked by Iago into thinking that Desdemona had been adulterous when actually she was innocent . . . not that Othello ended up killing her. Thus, Othello's tragedy is not considered to be his thirst for revenge or his act of violence per se, *but the fact that it was misguided*. Feeling immense pain at what he took to be Desdemona's behavior, Othello felt the need to strike at her, to seek expiation of this pain by inflicting some of it on her, to wipe off his sense of dishonor by wiping Desdemona from the earth. This much we understand, even if as a logical proposition it makes no sense.

Sometimes the paybacks for prior injury are not just senseless but downright bizarre, as in the case of Edgar Allen Poe's dark story "The Cask of Amontillado." In this classic of gothic horror, Montressor, the deranged protagonist, responds to some unspecified insult from Fortunato and resolves to avenge himself: "The thousand injuries of Fortunato I had borne as I best could, but when he ventured upon insult I vowed revenge. You, who so well know the nature of my soul, will not suppose, however, that I gave utterance to a threat. At *length* I would be avenged; this was a point definitively settled. . . ."

Montressor's revenge is chilling: The promise of a rare Amontillado wine is used to lure Fortunato deep into a basement, where he is chained and left to plead for mercy while Montressor very deliberately constructs a brick wall behind which his victim will die of thirst and starvation. Particularly notable is that, although the details vary from run-of-the mill to weirdly idiosyncratic, the underlying theme of returning pain for pain is *not* perceived as bizarre at all. Over and over, injured parties – fictional no less than real – insist on paying pain for pain, responding hurtfully toward those who have injured them. And no one seriously questions the connection.

There are a few exceptions, however, when vengeance itself is explicitly justi-fied. Shylock, in *The Merchant of Venice*, explains his demand for a pound of flesh as a response to past wrongs: "If you prick us, do we not bleed? If you tickle us, do we not laugh? If you poison us, do we not die? And if you wrong us, shall we not revenge?" But even here, the issue is less a rationalization of revenge itself than an affirmation that since Jews are human—they bleed, laugh, and die, like everyone else—then it makes perfect sense that they, like everyone else, will seek revenge if wronged.

Revenge-taking is not merely a phenomenon of Old World stories: It powers some of the greatest works of American literature, including Nathaniel Hawthorne's *The Scarlet Letter*, a tale of the relentless pursuit of the Reverend Dimmesdale by cuckolded husband Roger Chillingworth. The latter's grim and ultimately lethal persistence is chilling indeed, but nonetheless understandable once we grasp the need for the injured to achieve "redress" by injuring, if possi-ble, the original perpetrator.

The boundary between personal and group revenge is necessarily vague: the former is an individual act, and the latter, the stuff of feuds. Of course, the behavior of a single person—especially considering that he or she is a member of a family—shades directly into that of groups once someone's experience is taken up by others. Connecting the two is the curious glue of demanded retribu-tion. At one point in *The Adventures of Huckleberry Finn*, young Huck stumbles into the middle of an ongoing feud between the Grangerfords and the Shepherdsons. He is befriended by Buck Grangerford (after convincing the Grangerford family that he is not a Shepherdson, thereby barely avoiding getting his head blown off). When the two boys are out walking and Buck shoots at a Shepherdson boy, Huck asks why he has just tried to kill someone he doesn't know and who has done him no harm, whereupon Buck explains the fine points of feuding:

> "Well," says Buck, "a feud is this way: A man has a quarrel with another man, and kills him; then that other man's brother kills *him*; then the other brothers on both sides goes for one another; then the *cousins* chip in—and by and by everybody's killed off and there ain't no more feud. But it's kind of slow and takes a long time."

"Has this one been going on long, Buck?"

"Well, I should *reckon*! It started thirty years ago, or som'ers along there. There was trouble 'bout something and then a lawsuit to settle it, and the suit went agin one of the men and so he up and shot the man that won the suit—which he would naturally do, of course. Anybody would."

"What was the trouble about, Buck? —Land?"

"I reckon maybe—I don't know."

"Well, who done the shooting? Was it a Grangerford or a Shepherdson?"

"Laws, how do *I* know? It was so long ago."

"Don't anybody know?"

"Oh, yes, pa knows, I reckon, and some of the other old people; but they don't know now what the row was about in the first place."

We get to redirected aggression shortly, but first let's examine what is probably the most memorable case of vengefulness in American letters, and perhaps in all of literature. It's a feud of sorts, but with only one (human) participant.

* * *

Captain Ahab is the central character in what is widely judged the greatest American novel, one often criticized for its excessive realism, at least in its peculiarly detailed account of how to kill and "process" a whale. On the other hand, Ahab's single-minded pursuit of Moby Dick seems more than a little "over the top," and thus unrealistic in the extreme. Ahab himself has become synonymous with obsession, specifically an absurd, unyielding, irrational insistence on bringing down one's opponent. Ahab's intensity has made the captain a notorious icon of commitment so heedless and extreme that it destroys oneself. Indeed, even as Ahab has become identified with monomaniacal pursuit, famously striving to penetrate "the mask" whereby the inchoate hides behind the merely corporeal, it is easy to lose track of what Captain Ahab is monomaniacal about: revenge.

He is the paradigmatic example of someone with a demonic need to pass along his pain. All the same, there is something oddly genuine about Ahab's quest, something that touches each of us so deeply that we can hear the harmonic vibrations of underlying needs. What is Ahab without his nemesis, Moby Dick? Just an old man, unusually bitter we might assume, but empty without his pursuit of the white whale. Ahab was filled with his hatred of Moby Dick and his need for vengeance. This is not simply to say that he was well-stocked with hatred as well as his own pain. Rather, he was almost literally inflated by his animosity, like a pillow by its feathers or a balloon by air. Remove the stuffing, and the pillow or the balloon or the man shrinks and shrivels. One does not exist without the other. He is defined by his pain, and, more to the point, by his need to pass it along.

Can we imagine Ahab healthy and whole—aside from the fact that he lost a leg to the white whale—having let go of his obsession and the source of his pain? To some extent, of course, this question is a straw-man, since Ahab never really existed. He is a fictional device, a creation of Herman Melville, designed to depict such a pain-filled and revenge-obsessed character. But that is also the point: Ahab succeeds brilliantly precisely because he is so effectively characterized— albeit caricatured—by his need for revenge, something that has resonated as "real" with generations of readers.

By seeing Melville's creation through the lens of human pain-passing, Ahab becomes intelligible not only as a participant in symbolic struggles against evil, or alternatively, against nature, God, or the "ghastly" and "appalling whiteness of the whale," but also as a human being who embodies a recognizable—if excessive—response to overwhelming pain.

In Ahab's case, the source of his agony is straightforward and physical: the loss of his leg. When we meet him in *Moby Dick*, the Captain had already been "dismasted" by the great whale. It was this mutilation, we are told, that evoked Ahab's vindictive fury. Indeed, just as it is impossible to imagine Ahab without his whale, it is equally impossible to imagine him behaving as he does if he had *not* been dismembered by Moby Dick. Maybe the young Ahab was already inclined to harbor grudges, to be rigid in his goals and bitter when crossed, but it is significant that his behavior only became remarkable after he had been severely injured. Then, his pain—mental no less than physical—gradually filled his being as Ahab came to connect Moby Dick with all his hurts, frustrations, and disappointments:

> Ever since that almost fatal encounter, Ahab had cherished a wild vin-dictiveness against the whale, all the more fell for that in his frantic morbidness he at last came to identify with him, not only all his bodily woes, but all his intellectual and spiritual exasperations. The White Whale swam before him as the monomaniac incarnation of all those malicious agencies which some deep men feel eating in them, till they are left living on with half a heart and half a lung. . . . He pitted himself, all mutilated, against it. All that most maddens and torments; all that stirs up the lees of things, all truth with malice in it; all that cracks the sinews and cakes the brain; all the subtle demonisms of life and thought; all evil, to crazy Ahab, were visibly personified, and made practically assailable in Moby Dick. He piled upon the whale's white hump the sum of all the general rage and hate felt by his whole race from Adam down; and then, as if his chest had been a mortar, he burst his hot heart's shell upon it.

As Melville tells it, Ahab's fury became his sole nourishment, feeding malignantly upon itself: "As the grizzly bear burying himself in the hollow of a tree, lived out the winter there, sucking his own paws, so, in his inclement, howling old age, Ahab's soul, shut up in the caved trunk of his body, there fed upon the sullen paws of its gloom."

Malignancy is in fact the appropriate term, since Ahab's quest for revenge almost literally devoured him, just as a cancer might have done. To be sure, he had been partly eaten by the whale, but in a deeper sense Ahab was consumed from within. "Beware thyself, old man" warns the prescient first mate, Starbuck, who later expostulates (in vain), "Moby Dick seeks thee not. It is thou, thou, that madly seekest him!"

Pioneering psychoanalyst Karen Horney puts it this way: "In simplest terms the vindictive person does not only inflict suffering on others but even more so on himself. His vindictiveness makes him isolated, egocentric, absorbs his energies, makes him psychically sterile, and, above all, closes the gate to his further growth."[2]

Even before being pulled to his lamentable end, lashed to Moby Dick, Ahab has already gone overboard. His determined pursuit of revenge left him with no capacity for life, much less growth. There is simply no additional room in the human personality structure once it is occupied by so fulsome a determination. As Ahab himself recognizes, his insistence has vanquished his own freedom of action: "The path to my fixed purpose is laid with iron rails, whereon my soul is grooved to run. Over unsounded gorges, through the rifled hearts of mountains, under torrents' beds, unerringly I rush! Naught's an obstacle, naught's an angle to the iron way!"

There we have it, the iron way of vengeance, of unending insistence upon "getting even," getting an eye for an eye—and then some—whatever the cost, whatever the outcome. It is not surprising that we shrink from it with true fear and loathing: There is something inhuman about so demonic an insistence on passing along one's pain. But at the same time, there is nothing "unnatural" about it: There are numerous perfectly natural but nonetheless pathological situations—autoimmune diseases, for example—that involve healthy immune responses run amuck, in which the body misfires and causes distress, debility, or even death. Most evolutionary strategies are successful for most of their population; that is how they have persisted. But sometimes even adaptive responses (especially if excessive) can function poorly in particular instances, as with Ahab. Thus, there is something about Ahab's "iron way" of revenge that human beings shrink from, even as they know it all too well.

* * *

Ahab is one of two great pursuit-obsessed characters in Western literature. The other is Inspector Javert of Victor Hugo's *Les Miserables*. Just as Ahab exudes a superhuman determination, so does Javert: "He was one of those people who, even glimpsed, make an immediate impression; there was an intensity about him that was almost a threat. His name was Javert and he belonged to the police."

Just as Ahab hunts Moby Dick, Javert hunts escaped convict Jean Valjean, who had committed the crime of stealing a loaf of bread to feed his starving sister and her family. Although Valjean has long since reformed and is leading a more-than-exemplary life, Javert is obsessed with his task. As with Ahab, Javert's life is given meaning by his commitment to pursue and destroy his prey.

And when it comes to rigidity, Javert yields nothing to Ahab:

> His mental attitude was compounded of two very simple principles, admirable in themselves but which, by carrying them to extremes, he made almost evil—respect for authority and hatred of revolt against it. . . . His eyes were cold and piercing as a gimlet. His whole life was contained in two words, wakefulness and watchfulness. He drew a straight line through all that is most tortuous in this world. . . . He would have arrested his own father escaping from prison and denounced his mother for breaking parole, and he would have done it with a glow of conscious rectitude. His life was one of rigorous austerity, isolation, self-denial and chastity without distractions; a life of unswerving duty. . . .

Inspector Javert, about to make an arrest, is as arrogantly self-assured and self-righteous, as utterly bereft of any doubt or introspection as Ahab poised to destroy a whale. And Javert's prey—in the case described below, a poor woman named Fantine—is as undeserving of his violence as any free-living, innocent leviathan is of Ahab's lance. But nonetheless, closing in on the guiltless Fantine,

> Javert was in heaven. . . . He was the guardian of order, the lightning of justice, the vengeance of society, the mailed fist of the absolute, and he was bathed in glory. There was in his victory a vestige of defiance and conflict. Upright, arrogant and resplendent, he stood like the embodiment in a clear sky of the superhuman ferocity of the destroying angel, and the deed he was performing seemed to invest his clenched fist with the gleam of a fiery sword. He was setting his foot in righteous indignation upon crime, vice and rebellion, damnation, and hell, and was smiling with satisfaction as he did.

Ahab had been physically injured, and his commitment to destroying Moby Dick grew from the anguish of his injury. Javert had also been maimed by life, not physically but emotionally:

> He had been born in prison, the son of a fortune teller whose husband was in the galleys. As he grew older he came to believe that he was

outside society with no prospect of ever entering it. But he noted that there were two classes of men whom society keeps inexorably at arm's length—those who prey upon it, and those who protect it. The only choice open to him was between those two. At the same time, he was a man with a profound instinct for correctitude, regularity, and probity, and with a consuming hatred for the vagabond order to which he himself belonged. He joined the police.

Great writers such as Melville and Hugo, just like Shakespeare before and James Joyce after, have long recognized the human tendency to pass the pain along, and how in extreme cases the results can be deforming and tragic. But whereas Melville's great whale can respond only with dumb rage to Ahab's persecutions, Hugo's Jean Valjean responds with an almost saintly compassion and forgiveness: Granted the opportunity to kill Javert, Valjean frees him instead. And thus, near the end of *Les Miserables*, when Javert has finally gotten his target in his grasp, Javert finds himself utterly undone by his own triumph. Ahab gets his vengeance, and is killed in the process. Javert gets the opportunity to achieve his, but cannot bring himself to do it; tormented by the prospect of having to arrest the man who had saved his life, he drowns himself in the River Seine. Inhibited from passing along his pain, Javert absorbs it into himself, finds the burden intolerable, and chooses death instead.

Both Ahab and Javert are tragic figures, but Javert is by far the more sympathetic character. He refrained from destroying his enemy, after which, unable to contain his own torment at the impossible bind in which his conscience and his "duty" had entrapped him, he had no choice but to destroy himself:

> The man of action had lost his way. He was forced to admit that infalli-
> bility is not always infallible, that there may be error in dogma, that
> society is not perfect, that a flaw in the unalterable is possible, that
> judges are men and even the law may do wrong. What was happening to
> Javert resembled the derailing of a train. . . .

For our purposes, however, the similarities between *Moby Dick* and *Les Miserables* are more important than the differences. Both are psychologically compelling portraits of people being destroyed by their need to pass along their pain, a need which—although demonic in its excess—is at the same time recognizably human and thus, believable.

As limiting and distorting as it is, the Ahab syndrome nonetheless has a kind of grandeur. We may pity or despise and often avoid the Ahabs of this world, but we are nonetheless inclined to view them with a degree of wonder, if only because most of us are not guided by so potent a will, nor do we bear such immense burdens:

> Captain Ahab stood erect, looking straight out beyond the ship's ever-pitching prow. There was an infinity of firmest fortitude, a determinate, insurrenderable willfulness, in the fixed and fearless, forward dedication of that glance. Not a word he spoke; nor did his officers say aught to him; though by all their minutest gestures and expressions, they plainly showed the uneasy, if not painful, consciousness of being under a troubled master-eye. And not only that, but moody stricken Ahab stood before them with a crucifixion in his face; in all the nameless regal overbearing dignity of some mighty woe.

But despite their power and the awe they often evoke, the fact remains that Ahabs are miserably unhappy. Toward the end of *Moby Dick*, Ahab encounters the ship's blacksmith, who is repairing a steel implement that had become "seamed and dented" from hard use:

> "And can'st thou make it all smooth again, blacksmith, after such hard usage as it had?"
>
> "I think so, Sir."
>
> "And I suppose thou can'st smoothe almost any seams and dents; never mind how hard the metal, blacksmith?"
>
> "Aye, Sir, I think I can; all seams and dents but one."
>
> "Look ye here, then," cried Ahab, passionately advancing, and leaning with both hands on Perth's shoulders; "look ye here—*here*—can ye smoothe out a seam like this, blacksmith," sweeping one hand across his ribbed brows, "if you could'st, blacksmith, glad enough I lay my head upon thy anvil, and feel thy heaviest hammer between my eyes. Answer! Can'st thou smoothe this seam?"
>
> "Oh! that is the one, Sir! Said I not all seams and dents but one?"
>
> "Aye, blacksmith, it is the one; aye, man, it is unsmoothable; for though thou only see'st it here in my flesh, it has worked down into the bone of my skull—that is all wrinkles!"

Such people are dangerous, to themselves and those around them. Generations have been riveted by the story of Ahab's obsession with his own personal revenge. In so doing, they often lose sight of the fact that Ahab brings ruin and tragedy not only upon himself, but upon his ship and the entire crew. He does so because his own personality is so powerful and overwhelming that he is able to enlist the crew's emotions and commitment on behalf of his own needs. Only Starbuck, the grim and pessimistic first mate, remains critical of Ahab's undertaking. Yet even he is unable to change the old man's mind, and unwilling to disobey his orders.

* * *

The biblical Israelites who wrote the first accounts of scapegoating were not strangers to anger or vengeance. Consider their exultation at the drowning of the Pharaoh and his armies in the Red Sea. Or the enthusiasm with which they carried out Yahweh's many Old Testament injunctions to kill their—that is, His—enemies, often sparing neither women nor children. And yet, they were also called upon to show compassion. "Ye know the heart of the stranger," the Israelites repeatedly admonished themselves, "for ye were strangers in the land of Egypt." (This warning is still regularly repeated in Passover services.) Do we not similarly know the heart of those who feel pain and respond "accordingly" because there is something of the same within our own hearts?

In some cases, that pain is in dreadful excess. People thus stricken are often simultaneously buoyed up as well as dragged down by it. They surf on their pain and anger, riding the waves of its energy, propelled by its heady surge of momentum and power. These are the Ahabs among us, people whose personal pain—and the retributive motivation it generates—becomes a consuming passion, a reason for living as much as for dying. And killing.

If "Vengeance is mine, said the Lord," it was not to validate revenge, but to restrain it. Once relegated to God's bailiwick, it is taken out of human hands; that is, "Vengeance is *mine*, you jerk, not yours!" As with the Ten Commandments prohibiting murder, adultery, and so forth, presumably there would be no need to lay divine claim upon vengeance if people were not otherwise inclined to partake of it themselves.

The search for revenge appears to be as old as recorded human history, well documented in the most ancient writings, from Homeric epics and tragic Greek plays to the Old Testament and *The Mahabharata* of ancient India. Still, polite society recoils from the raw emotion, as well as from the haters and the seekers of vengeance, who—as we shall see—are expected to couch their quest in softer, more acceptable terms such as "recompense," "fairness," or "justice." Yes indeed, we know the heart of the hater, and we shun it. Maybe we simply fear the intensity of the hate-obsessed, for the same reason that we do not like bad tidings, or its bearers. As Terrence Des Pres, chronicler of concentration camp survivors, puts it,

> Refusal to acknowledge extremity is built into the structure of existence as we, the lucky ones, know it. More perhaps than we care to admit, spiritual well-being has depended on systems of mediation which transcend or otherwise deflect the sources of dread. . . . Too close

a knowledge of vulnerability, of evil, of human insufficiency is felt to be ruinous.[3]

People who manifest such extremity, as Des Pres noted, are often rejected. And surely it is no coincidence that such individuals—having suffered greatly—are often pain-filled and vengeance-obsessed, modern-day Ahabs whose very presence generates discomfort among the rest of us, even as we acknowledge the regrettable "humanness" of their emotions. Such rejection is not altogether misplaced. After all, Captain Ahab and his ilk have an intensity and monomania that is not only eerily familiar but that also—as the ancient Greeks well knew—often forebodes tragedy. Frequently, it causes disasters, and not only for their intended victims. This may be why the ability of concentration camp survivors Elie Wiesel and Victor Frankl to transform their pain into something creative and loving is admired by so many.

Obsessive pain-passing can only result in trouble, partly because excess in anything is liable to be unhealthy. Tragedy is therefore likely for the overwrought pain-passer no less than for his or her target, because such a posture, whether directed toward a white whale, an ideology, another person, or a larger group, is bound to deform any human being. And whatever the magnitude of their vengefulness, people are only human, after all.

Erich Fromm relates the following story, a telling one for our purposes.[4] A fascist Spanish general, Millan Astray, had been maimed in battle. His ironic motto was *Viva la muerte* ("Long live death"). When Astray gave a speech at the University of Salamanca in 1936, shortly before the bloodletting of the Spanish Civil War was to begin, one of his supporters shouted "*Viva la muerte!*" In response, writer and philosopher Jugo Miguel de Unamuno, then rector of the University and in the last year of his own long and productive life, rose and denounced Astray's poisonous obsession with suffering and death: "This outlandish paradox is repellent to me. General Millan Astray is a cripple. Let it be said without any slighting undertone. He is a war invalid. So was Cervantes. Unfortunately there are too many cripples in Spain just now. And soon there will be even more of them if God does not come to our aid."

There can be no doubt that the obsessed pain-passers among us need help, whether from blacksmiths, psychotherapists, spiritual teachers, or God. And so do the rest of us, lest we wind up caught in the carnage of future Spanish Civil Wars, or in the same boat as the *Pequod's* crew.

Near the climax of *Moby Dick*, once the epic battle between man and whale has been joined, Captain Ahab allows himself to fantasize—if only briefly—about victory. He imagines Moby Dick's carcass lashed to the side of his ship. But the thought is only fleeting. No surprise here; just as one cannot imagine Captain Ahab without his nemesis, Moby Dick, it is equally outlandish to picture a victorious Ahab, calm and peaceful in his triumph, made whole by his revenge.

The point is not simply that killing his enemy can never restore Ahab's leg. It is that—as we often say but rarely believe—two wrongs really do not make a right . . . neither in fiction nor reality.

Let us try rewriting the ending of *Moby Dick*: After a lengthy struggle—or, worse yet for the Captain, perhaps one that is all too easy—Moby Dick spouts his last. He lies there, literally dead in the water, huge rivers of blood making an estuary where it joins the salty foam, his great bulk utterly insensate, no longer lashing its mighty tail, incapable of even the slightest twitch. Ahab gives a great shout of triumph. Balancing uneasily with his ivory leg upon the sloping, slippery back of his vanquished foe, he thrusts his harpoon again and again, while his crew cheer and then, after a time—embarrassed, perhaps, by their captain's excess—avert their eyes. Then begins the time-consuming process of butchering the whale, and eventually sailing home to Nantucket. But what of Ahab all this time? Does he dance a jig in Moby Dick's intestines? Drink his blood? Bathe triumphantly in his rendered blubber? Make a hundred artificial legs out of the creature's jaw-bone? Is he happy at last? Is he finally at ease? Or, having achieved his all-consuming goal, does he feel just a wee bit deflated, still mangled in body and no more peaceful in mind?[†]

* * *

Like revenge, redirected aggression inhabits the literary world no less than the real one. This is not surprising, since as already noted, literature must conform to certain basic principles of human nature in order to be believable and thus enduring. And as we have seen, when pain has been inflicted in the real world, it nearly always generates more of itself, either immediately (retaliation), after a delay and often with amplification (revenge), or, perhaps most often, through redirected aggression.

George Bernard Shaw famously quipped that those who can, do, and those who can't, teach—a calumny against a noble profession, but a useful statement of how violence frequently operates. Those who can, either retaliate or take revenge, while those who can't, redirect their aggression. "The tyrant grinds down his slaves and they don't turn against him," observes Heathcliff in Emily Brontë's *Wuthering Heights*. "They crush those beneath *them*."

Sometimes, even when retaliation or revenge is feasible, they just aren't satisfying, especially if the former is too quick and easy, or if the latter, paradoxically, takes too long or is too difficult and therefore unattainable. Redirected aggression may also prove additionally useful to the initial victim, because once the door is opened to attacking anyone, regardless of actual guilt, there is no end to

---

[†] Or maybe he would decide that the dead whale really was not Moby Dick after all, so he must continue his quest.

the universe of prospective targets. Using twenty-first century war-fighting jargon, redirected aggression generates a "target-rich" environment.

To see this in the "real world" of great fiction, lets look at *The Iliad*, which begins with these lines:

> Sing, O goddess, the anger of Achilles son of Peleus,
> that brought countless ills upon the Achaeans.

Actually, *The Iliad*'s very first word in the original Greek is *menin* ("anger" or "wrath"), and scholars agree that Homer's masterpiece revolves around Achilles' anger, beginning with the pain and humiliation inflicted upon him by Agamemnon, who had taken Achilles' beautiful slave and war-prize, Briseis. As Achilles famously sulks in his tent, and the Greeks are temporarily bested on the battlefield by the Trojans, Agamemnon tries to get Achilles to join the fray. He even offers to return Briseis, along with an immense dowry. But Achilles is unmoved, declaring at one point, "Not if his gifts outnumbered the sea sands, or all the dust grains in the world could Agamemnon ever appease me. Not till he pays me back full measure, dishonor for dishonor, pain for pain."

What, then, finally moves Achilles to action? Not Agamemnon's promises of wealth, or any other such inducements, but rather the loss of Achilles' friend and lover Patrocles; which is to say, the infliction of more pain, which can only be erased by Achilles' offloading his burden onto others. Our hero accordingly responds by revenging himself on Hector, the Trojan who slew Patrocles. But that is not enough; Achilles must also redirect his pain, passing it onto other Trojans. Thus, Achilles vows to the dead Patrocles, "I will not give you burial, Patrocles, until I carry back the gear and head of him who killed you, noble friend. Before your funeral pyre I'll cut the throats of twelve resplendent children of the Trojans. That is my murdering fury at your death."

Although Achilles avenges Patrocles by killing Hector, and then, for good measure, dishonoring his body, he proceeds to murder those dozen "resplendent"—and *innocent*—young Trojans on Patrocles's funeral pyre. Even that, however, does not suffice, because Achilles also slaughters additional Trojans left and right, until the river Xanthus runs "red with blood" and is so choked with bodies that the river god complains to the Olympian deities. Only then does Achilles finally cease the massacre.

In Milton's *Paradise Lost*, the devil explains and seeks to justify his vendetta against human beings as resulting from his having been bested by God: "Should I at your harmless innocence / Melt, as I do, yet public reason just . . . compels me now to do what else, though damned, I should abhor." In short, revenge and redirected aggression made him do it! Its all God's fault: "Thank him who puts me, loath, to this revenge / On you, who wrong me not . . ." This is, at least, an advance over Achilles, who showed no awareness that his behavior called for even the slightest explanation.

Achilles' anger and the Devil's compulsion were both clearly of mythic proportions, although both were based on more than a whiff of genuine human inclination. Figures from Homeric Greece and the Bible have long been the superheroes (and villains) of the Western world, and although our focus in this chapter is on "classical" stories, we cannot help noting that retaliation, revenge, and redirected aggression also loom large in today's pop-culture world of action superheroes. Batman, for example, is said to have witnessed the murder of his parents, which powered his subsequent quest for justice and the apprehending of wrongdoers. In fact, nearly every superhero who populates today's comic books and movie screens is depicted as carrying out some sort of vendetta or pain-passing—on the side of righteousness, to be sure, but there seems to be a kind of psycho-biological righteousness at work here as well. The result is that even though their superpowers demand more than the usual "suspension of disbelief," the personal motivations of twenty-first-century superheroes remain fundamentally believable.

As a general rule, literary figures, like their real-life counterparts, are less oversized than demi-gods such as Achilles or Batman. Likewise is their hunger for violent payback: They often settle for redirected aggression, although that can be bad enough. Recall the regrettable Mr. Farrington, of James Joyce's "Counterparts." Had he been Achilles, Farrington presumably would have slaughtered his unpleasant boss and then caved in the skull of that young upstart who bested him at the pub, before divesting himself of any leftover pain by eradicating half of Dublin. But Farrington represents something more disturbing: a distressingly accurate "slice of life." Achilles is like Godzilla or King Kong, too oversized to be taken seriously; Farrington, by contrast, is more like the axe-murderer next door—just real enough to be genuinely frightening.

For another fundamentally human albeit grotesque case of redirected aggression, here is Victor Hugo's account of Quasimodo, the misshapen Hunchback of Notre Dame: "From his first intercourse with men, he had felt and seen himself despised, scorned, repulsed. To him, human speech meant nothing but mockery or curses. As he grew up, he encountered nothing but hate. He caught the infection. He acquired the universal malevolence. He adopted the weapon with which he had been wounded."

The Hunchback is best known for his bizarre appearance. Equally important for the story, however, although less celebrated, was Quasimodo's initial attitude toward others: nasty, aggressive, and altogether unpleasant. And Hugo's description makes it clear how Quasimodo came to be this way. It is not simply a matter of an ugly man having a correspondingly ugly personality; rather, his deformity caused the world to treat him badly, whereupon Quasimodo, in turn, treated others in a like manner. In short, he passed his pain along, redirecting aggression toward the citizens of Paris, not unlike Sweeney Todd's engagement with his London clientele.

Quasimodo's malevolence was generalized, and (re)directed toward nearly everyone, excepting only the lovely Esméralda. Another "realistic" literary theme involves redirected aggression that is personalized, whereby a victim aims his or her venom at a specific individual . . . although once again, this person is not the original wrongdoer, but rather, "collateral damage." We find this, for example, in *Notes from the Underground*, by Fyodor Dostoyevsky. The "Underground Man"— literature's first notable antihero—has just been deeply embarrassed in front of his friends. He visits a prostitute, whom he humiliates in turn: "To avenge my wounded pride on someone," the Underground Man says to her, "To get my own back, I vented my spite on you and I laughed at you. I had been humiliated, so I too wanted to humiliate someone; they wiped the floor with me, so I too wanted to show my power by hurting you."

In his book *Trauma and Mastery in Life and Art*, Gilbert J. Rose describes a deeply painful experience that Dostoevsky was supposed to have had at age 15 when he witnessed a courier beat a watchman, who in turn whipped a horse.[5] This memory seems to have been part of a chain of abuses that Dostoevsky observed, including his father's tyranny over his mother, masters over serfs, authorities over prisoners, and the violent responses, often toward innocents, that followed. They notably reappeared in several of Dostoevsky's works—*Crime and Punishment, The Peasant Marey,* and *The Double*—in addition to *Notes from the Underground.*

Not surprisingly, children are especially likely to be victimized, in fiction as in real life. In Charles Dickens's *Oliver Twist*, young Oliver has been apprenticed to a coffin-maker, where his immediate superior is a young fellow named Noah Claypole.[5] Noah was especially unkind to Oliver, and Dickens explains why:

> Noah was a charity-boy, but not a workhouse orphan. . . . The shop-boys in the neighborhood had long been in the habit of branding Noah, in the public streets, with ignominious epithets . . . and Noah had borne them without reply. But, now that fortune had cast in his way a nameless orphan, at whom even the meanest could point the finger of scorn, he retorted on him with interest.

[5] Since modern movie audiences often outnumber readers, it may well be that more people are familiar with *Oliver* and *Les Miz* than with the books *Oliver Twist* or *Les Miserables*. If so, then sadly, the nuance of a Noah Claypole and Inspector Javert is often missed.

Dickens then adds, with no small sarcasm, "This affords charming food for contemplation. It shows us what a beautiful thing human nature may be made to be."

A century and a half later, Toni Morrison also shows how behavior borne of abuse can be destructive, not only to others, but to oneself. In *The Bluest Eye*, the black residents of Lorain, Ohio, make an innocent young girl into a scapegoat for their own insecurities and angers, boosting their sense of worth by diminishing hers. Pecola is a small black child, inconspicuous in her community, just as countless young, uneducated, and quiet black children are ignored today. She is known only for her overwhelming ugliness, and is therefore celebrated by the people around her—as a way to release their own anger and frustration. One character, Chick, recognizes that "Pecola represents the self-hatred of the entire community," which flourishes on her degradation. As Claudia, the story's narrator, explains:

> All of us—all who knew her—felt so wholesome after we cleansed ourselves on her. We were so beautiful when we stood astride her ugliness. Her simplicity decorated us, her guilt sanctified us, her pain made us glow with health, her awkwardness made us think we had a sense of humor [. . .] Even her waking dreams we used—to silence our own night-mares. [. . .] We honed our egos on her, padded our characters with her frailty, and yawned in the fantasy of our strength.

Being the recipient of such undeserved emotional violence causes Pecola to disintegrate into madness and insanity, so that conversations with herself become her only recourse. Pecola "spent her days, her tendril, sap-green days, walking up and down, up and down, her head jerking to the beat of a drummer so distant only she could hear."

Redirected aggression can be visited upon inanimate objects, too, not unlike African-American violence against Korean-owned grocery stores in real-life South-Central Los Angeles.[1] Thus, Morrison's *Sula* depicts townspeople joyfully destroying a tunnel that both symbolizes their oppression and becomes a convenient scapegoat. The white town government had decided to build a road but refused to employ African-American laborers, instead hiring "thin-armed white boys from the Virginia hills and bull-necked Greeks and Italians." For almost ten years, people of "The Bottom" swallowed their aggravation, their "chest pains unattended, school shoes unbought, rush-stuffed mattresses, broken toilets . . ." until one day when the community was out on a kind of parade, which passed by the tunnel site. They passed "the place where their hope [for money and jobs]

---

[1] These stores, in turn, are typically stand-ins for their Korean owners.

had lain since 1927," unattended by the white bosses, and proceeded to "smash the bricks they would never fire in yawning kilns, split the sacks of limestone they had not mixed or even been allowed to haul," seeking to "kill, as best they could, the tunnel they were forbidden to build."

Morrison's *Song of Solomon* gives us a vision of some human casualties as well. Here, a secret society called "The Seven Days" responds to any unpunished murder of an African-American by randomly killing a white person. Guitar, "spokesperson" for this group, explains that "the judge, the jury, the court, are legally bound to ignore anything a Negro has to say [. . .] If there was anything like or near justice or courts when a cracker kills a Negro, there wouldn't have to be no Seven Days. But there ain't; so we are." Members of the Seven Days not only kill, but are destroyed in the process.

* * *

It is important, maybe even revelatory, that there is such a potent confluence between literature and biology (as well as anthropology, history, psychology, and a variety of other disciplines) when it comes to one of the root causes of violence. But at the same time, human beings are not necessarily captives of retaliation, revenge, and redirected aggression. The tale we have to tell— reflected in the tales people actually recount—is not simply one of despair and the inevitable passing along of pain and injury. Within our exploration also lie the seeds of transformation, because not all stories end with death, murder, or mayhem.

Unlike fish, birds, rats, or baboons, people—at least some people, or perhaps all people on occasion—are capable of rising above their more "biological," pain-passing inclinations. And these better angels of our nature, no less than our more obnoxious ones, are also depicted, at least sometimes, in literature.

Take, for instance, the heroic attorney Atticus Finch, whom we meet in Harper Lee's *To Kill a Mockingbird*. Toward the novel's end, Bob Ewell, a likely murderer who also physically abused his own family, has just been humiliated by Atticus in court. Ewell responds by spitting in the attorney's face and threatening his life. Atticus is savvy enough to know that Ewell feels the need to redirect his pain onto innocent parties. When asked how he could tolerate Ewell's behavior without retaliating, Atticus answers: "See if you can stand in Bob Ewell's shoes for a minute. I destroyed his last shred of credibility at that trial, if he had any to begin with. The man had to have some kind of come-back. His kind always does."

But the farseeing Mr. Finch shows not only an intuitive insight into redirected aggression, but also some admirable high-mindedness: "So, if spitting in my face and threatening me saved Mae Ella Ewell one extra beating, that's something I'll gladly take. He had to take it out on somebody and I'd rather it be me than that house full of children out there. You understand?"

Most of us do in fact understand. Literature is inextricably connected to life, part of which includes a deep-seated demand to "get even" by passing along one's pain. This makes people like Atticus Finch, who refuse to play along, especially notable and—one might hope—not limited to fiction.

References

1. Aeschylus (1959). *Agamemnon* (translated by P. Vellacott). Harmondsworth, UK: Penguin.
2. Karen Horney (1948). The value of vindictiveness. *American Journal of Psychoanalysis* 8: 3–12.
3. Terrence Des Pres (1977). *The Survivor*. New York: Pocket Books.
4. Erich Fromm. (1973). *The Anatomy of Human Destructiveness*. New York: Holt, Rinehart & Winston.
5. Gilbert J. Rose (1987). *Trauma and Mastery in Life and Art*. New Haven: Yale University Press.

6

Justice

Not Revenge?

The story goes like this: In a small, isolated village in Switzerland, during the early nineteenth century, a prominent farmer was found dead, the back of his head caved in by a heavy object. There was little doubt that the blacksmith was the murderer; the two had recently had a bitter falling out, and there was blood and hair on the smith's iron tools. After a fair trial, the blacksmith was found guilty—but since this was an agricultural community, the sentence was easier to pronounce than to carry out. The local economy depended on its horses; hence, on its blacksmith. And in the entire village, he was the only one.

But as luck would have it, there were seven tailors, so one of them (the least skillful) was hanged instead.

An apocryphal tale? Probably. But the point is clear enough: When people are outraged and suffering, whether in body or spirit, something within them cries out for redress, or at least a response. In such cases, it is more seemly (at least in recent times and in much of the Western world) to demand "justice" rather than revenge. But given the potency of pain-passing as a biosocial universal, it is only fair to wonder to what extent the latter masquerades as the former, leading us to ask what "justice" really means.

Specialists in the field of peace studies make a distinction between "negative peace"—the prevention of war—and "positive peace," which is even more complex and difficult: how society ought to function in the absence of war. "Negative peace" sounds like war, but it is not; rather, it means the *prevention* of war.

To achieve negative peace, one considers such matters as negotiations, arms control and disarmament, international law, and so forth; and various ways of avoiding or terminating war, and of course, war is something that most people *do not* want. In pursuit of positive peace, one must wrestle with such things as economic fairness, human rights, and environmental sustainability, with the goal of achieving what most people presumably *do* want; namely, a world at peace that involves more than the "mere" absence of war.

Justice is a bit like peace. For positive peace, substitute "distributive justice"—a blueprint for how things ought to be, in the absence of war, if society is to be "just." For negative peace, substitute "retributive justice"—the specification of how things ought to be, following the civil equivalent of war; namely, unacceptable acts of violence. The two aspects of justice are deeply connected, as are positive and negative peace, and not merely because both involve "justice," with its implication of fairness. Demands for distributive justice are often accompanied by insistence on retributive justice, too. Consider the immediate aftermath of the French and Russian revolutions, when the din of inequity included popular demands that someone had to pay for the misery that came before. (It may be of more than historical significance that the words "pay" and "peace" derive from the same Latin root: it has often been necessary to pay— with one's life or, literally, with money—in order to restore peace.)

Interestingly, however, the civic current is less likely to flow the other way, at least in the West: retributive justice, in the form of criminal law, is meted out all the time with typically no thought about the appropriate society-wide distribution of money, or other resources, except for the chimera of "equality before the law."* A crucial function of law, we submit, is to provide for equality, not so much before the law as *after* a violation: equality of pain and suffering, or at least, a healing semblance of its equitable distribution. And this, in turn, poses a big problem for that lady wearing the blindfolds: Justice must be blind as to the guilt or innocence of those being weighed, but it cannot be blind to the suffering that provoked the weighing in the first place, which is to say, to the need for victims to deal with their losses and suffering.

When it comes to the punishments meted out by criminal law, there is no doubt that the intention of a perpetrator is critical: hence, the difference between murder (intentional) and manslaughter (unintentional). But it is also clear that the damage done—the amount of pain inflicted on a victim—also counts heavily, even if the perpetrator performs identical acts, as long as the outcomes are different. For example, imagine that a drunk driver runs a red light but does no direct harm; now, imagine that the same driver, equally intoxicated, goes through the identical red light and then runs over a child: The same actions, very different results, and, you can be sure, very different punishments. The only distinction is that in the latter case, great pain has been caused to the victim, the victim's friends and family, society at large, and so forth. In the former, there was no victim, no pain, and therefore not nearly as much blame or punishment. When it comes to the meting out of justice, pain matters.

---

* Tort law provides an interesting exception: When it is a question of civil penalty rather than criminal offense, it is readily assumed that an exchange of money can—in a revealing turn of phrase—make the injured party "whole."

In his essay "On Anger," the Roman philosopher and statesman Seneca wrote that "Retribution is an admission of pain." We add that this, in turn, is an admission that many will dispute, claiming instead that it (if not "retribution" then "justice") is loftier than that: a recognition of misdeeds by a malefactor, and the search for a suitable remedy.

To be sure, the relationship between punishment and pain is not simple. The two words derive, however, from the same root, the Latin *poena* or "punishment, penalty." In fact, the phrase "on pain of death" originally referred specifically to the use of death as a punishment. At the same time, even within the United States, which is currently the most incarceration-prone and juridically punitive of all Western democracies (as well as the only one to retain an institutionalized death penalty), the means of execution have "progressed" from firing squad, hanging, electric chair, and gas chamber to lethal injection, all in a presumed effort to minimize pain to the condemned person while still retaining capital punishment. Thus, there appears to be some movement from the intentional causing of pain to treating the about-to-be executed criminal as a subject of medical solicitude, albeit closer to euthanasia than to healing. At this writing, the use of lethal injection continues to be legally contested, via the claim that it causes undue pain.

It must nonetheless be acknowledged that by definition as well as common practice, punishment is deliberately inflicted pain. Moreover, some would object that a painless execution, if achievable, would not be desirable anyway because it would be "too good" for the criminal. For many people, the equation of punishment with pain is itself a painful and maybe even a punishing admission. By a similar token, according to so-called just war theory, war in the Christian tradition is necessarily a somber endeavor, to be undertaken only as a last resort, and even then with a tinge of regret; ideally, the Christian goes to war with sorrow no less than determination. Similarly for criminal punishment: Given Christ's seemingly clear-cut injunction to forgive one's enemies and turn the other cheek, the confining of someone against her will, not to mention possibly taking her life, is not to be undertaken lightly, and certainly not with good cheer.

This, in turn, has evoked efforts to rationalize punishment (capital and otherwise), not unlike "Christian realism" applied to just war theory, which is to say, to breaches of negative peace. Some of these ethical gyrations have been quite creative, following their own peculiar logic. For example, a novel suggestion was made by philosopher Herbert Morris: that punishment is necessary because otherwise, a malefactor is being denied his human dignity, his "fundamental human right to be treated as a person."[1] Instead of the old bromide, "This hurts me more than it hurts you," substitute "I am doing this to you because I respect your personhood."†

---

† Anyone who has ever tried to train a dog by "correcting" his misbehavior knows that doing so does not enhance his "doghood," which, at least from the perpetrator's perspective, would more likely be achieved by chewing on a bone or chasing a car.

Just as genuine peace, however, is more than simply the absence of war, for crime victims and for society at large, genuine justice—whatever it may be—is more than simply a response to the infliction of pain. But just as "negative peace" is a legitimate undertaking in itself, retributive justice (or something that recognizes the pain of victims and, in turn, satisfies their needs for a response) is not only psychologically, socially, and even biologically sponsored, but perhaps even necessary. According to the late philosopher Robert C. Solomon, "Justice begins with compassion and caring . . . but it also involves, right from the start, such 'negative' emotions as envy, jealousy, indignation, anger, and resentment, a keen sense of having been personally cheated or neglected, and the desire to get even."[2] It is payback with a purpose. In large measure, the quest for justice emerges from the pain of injustice. Or as Elizabeth Hankins Wolgast puts it, injustice "grammatically" precedes justice.[3] By the same token, negative peace precedes positive peace, as a matter of practice as well as grammar, in that basic security—the absence of ongoing violence—is a prerequisite for anything resembling a positively peaceful society.

Nobel Prize–winning economist Amartya Sen begins his epochal book *The Idea of Justice*[4] by quoting Pip, the young hero of Charles Dickens's *Great Expectations*: "In the little world in which children have their existence, there is nothing so finely perceived and finely felt, as injustice." To which we add that such perceptions are not limited to children and their "little world."† Professor Sen hastens to note that "the identification of redressable injustice is not only what animates us to think about justice and injustice, it is also central" to any viable theory of justice more generally.

Some see punishment as the embodiment of justice itself, not social expediency or some sort of bio-psycho-necessity; hence, to justify the punitive impulse as serving deterrence, enhancing social safety, or responding to evolutionary influences is to demean with trite practicality an act that is ethically pure and valid in itself. Under this view, crime *requires* punishment, and justice *is* the punishment of injustice. In his classic *Utilitarianism*, for example, John Stuart Mill wrote that "we do not call anything wrong unless we mean to imply that a person ought to be punished in some way or other for doing it."

Contributing to this yearning to connect punishment with wrongdoing in particular is a parallel inclination associated with pain in general, one that appears to be no less deep and widespread than the Three Rs themselves: when bad things happen, even good people look for a specific cause—if possible, a malefactor. "Why did this happen to me?" they demand, often satisfying themselves by pinning the blame, or at least the causation, on someone's negligence

---

† Dickens himself was notably sensitive to injustice, a passion that animates much of his fiction.

or malign intent.[5] People deal poorly with randomness. Maybe this is a reflection of species-wide narcissism, the often-unspoken assumption that the cosmos has somehow been organized with each subjective individual specifically in mind. And this may help explain the presumption—and we believe it really is extraordinarily presumptuous—that there is a "purpose" to each person's life, that he or she was "put here" for a reason rather than having emerged as a result of physical and biological processes that play themselves out somewhat differently in each individual case, without evolution, a god, or the universe especially caring about the outcome. Hence, we look for meaning in things where there is none, like straining to see the man in the moon. This process may be both a cause and effect of religion, which often teaches that what we get is somehow our due, because we were insufficiently righteous or indelibly suffused with original sin.

Whether the above speculation proves fruitful, it is clear that for most people, most of the time, causation is a presumption to be reckoned with, so that every event implies a causal agent, typically one possessing intentionality. For some people, pain implies a pain-cause, just as injustice, wrongdoing, and suffering are proof of the existence of unjust systems and felonious individuals, which, in turn, legitimizes punishment. More than that, it requires it.

In suggesting a connection between justice and retaliation, revenge, and redirected aggression, we are not claiming that the former is nothing but the latter three, dressed up in civilized clothes. Not every victim is a version of Baboon B, having been injured by Baboon A and therefore seeking to respond, or, failing that, to "take it out" on Baboon C. Nor is every victim of personal injustice necessarily yearning to prove that he may be down but is not beaten. Certainly, forgiveness, too, is real (more on that in the next chapter); and, moreover, although many a victim feels angry and vengeful, often such sentiments are held privately, with no particular yearning to achieve public validation in the manner we have described for redirected aggression generally.[¶]

And yet, the fact that such motivations are often suppressed or themselves "redirected" does not mean that they do not still linger near the heart of the retributive impulse. Once instilled by natural selection, and unless "selected out" because of associated disadvantages, they could readily have become part of the individual human psyche, somewhat disconnected from its original adaptive function and its likely social context.

It is not merely tragic, but downright ludicrous—as well as unjust—to insist upon the "legal" killing of an innocent person, such as the unfortunate (and, we

---

[5] Not surprisingly, people are considerably more inclined to attribute any good fortune to their own merits.

[¶] And as we have pointed out, there is also positive justice, just as there is positive peace.

hope, mythic) Swiss tailor. Yet this is also something that most people can intuitively understand. Can it be that, in the aftermath of violence, the crucial thing is less that the guilty party be punished than that *someone* experience the collective wrath of the community—especially the pain of those most directly connected to the victim? As we have seen, there are powerful forces urging that only the pain of others can allay our own distress. Only someone else's suffering can soak up our blood. (In the story of the blacksmith and the tailor, the Swiss, true to their vaunted practicality, also made sure that this pain was not spread too widely.)

Ideally, in response to any act of injustice, punishment should be reserved for the guilty party, which explains the discomfort at killing a tailor for a blacksmith's crime. But we suspect that, in a pinch, anyone will do. Moreover, even though at a gut level most people understand and even sympathize with the need for revenge, it is also widely considered disreputable. Justice, yes; revenge, no. As we shall see, one might even equate the degree of civilization with the extent to which pain-passing is administered by civil authority rather than by the aggrieved party. A powerful reason for having police, laws, prisons, and even executioners is to prevent wronged and vengeful people from taking the law into their own hands.

The Bible enjoins: "Avenge not yourselves, but rather give place unto wrath: for it is written, Vengeance is mine; I will repay, saith the Lord" (Romans 12:19). Less widely appreciated, however, is that this is not only an admonishment but also a promise: We should content ourselves with something other than revenge, because God will obtain it, thereby saving us the trouble, the ignominy, the social disruption—but in the process, denying us the gratification.

According to H. L. Mencken, there is indeed an abiding pleasure that comes from inflicting pain on wrongdoers, a relief and release that lies at the heart of punishment in general, and of capital punishment in particular. Here is discomfort indeed: However one is permitted to respond to the infliction of pain upon others, taking pleasure (or even satisfaction) from it is not admissible in polite company. Especially dismaying is the exorbitant glee shown by some of those who witness punishment of others, notably the oafs and thugs who celebrate a state-sanctioned execution. (Public dismay at such despicable pleasure, although understandable, is also reminiscent of Thomas Macaulay's observation that, for Puritans the real harm of bear-baiting was not the pain caused to the bear, but the pleasure afforded the onlookers. Are executions especially odious if they bring pleasure to others?)

For his part, Mencken maintained that crime victims and members of society at large are concerned only indirectly with deterring other criminals:

> The thing they crave primarily is the satisfaction of seeing the criminal actually before them suffer as he made them suffer. What they want is

the peace of mind that goes with the feeling that accounts are squared. Until they get that satisfaction, they are in a state of emotional tension, and hence unhappy. The instant they get it they are comfortable. I do not argue that this yearning is noble; I simply argue that it is almost universal among human beings.[5]

When it comes to killing people officially/legally/judicially, the real motivation, for Mencken, is the satisfaction that victims derive from passing their pain to others; ideally, the perpetrators.[**] The death penalty, more than any other punishment, can therefore be assumed to reflect maximum anger and injury. As for Christian charity, forgiveness, and turning the other cheek, here is Mencken again: "In the face of injuries that are unimportant and can be borne without damage it [punishment] may yield to higher impulses; that is to say, to what is called Christian charity. But when the injury is serious, Christianity is adjourned, and even saints reach for their sidearms."

With such opinions, one might expect him to have opposed capital punishment, but Mencken (who reveled in his contrarianism), came out strongly in favor, basing his argument on *katharsis*, á la Aristotle—although he could as well have been talking directly about redirected aggression:

> Commonly, it is described as revenge, but revenge is really not the word for it. I borrow a better term from the late Aristotle: katharsis. Katharsis, so used, means a salubrious discharge of emotions, a healthy letting off of steam. . . . This is katharsis. What I contend is that one of the prime objects of all judicial punishments is to afford the same grateful relief (a) to the immediate victims of the criminal punished, and (b) to the general body of moral and timorous men.

* * *

It is distasteful but at least possible for many people to acknowledge that revenge, for all its primitive brutality, can also boast a certain cruel logic, based more on self-protection (especially for "moral and timorous men"?) than upon self-gratification, *á la* Mencken. As Mario Puzo put it in *The Godfather*, "Accidents do not happen to people who take accidents as a personal insult." More difficult, we suspect, is our suggestion that the pursuit of justice may reflect something even more unsettling than revenge; namely, an inclination to pass one's pain along, and not necessarily to the original troublemaker. That is, the point of

---

[**] Even Mencken, a notorious cynic, did not consider that the "squaring of accounts" might not even require collaring the actual culprit, and limiting punishment to those who "deserve it."

criminal justice may not be so much to punish the perpetrator, but to respond to injury by making someone, anyone, into the latest victim.

Psychologist Michael McCullough maintains that "the psychological common denominator among the severe, intentional harms that elicit the desire for revenge is that they violate the victim's sense of honor."[6] As McCullough points out, "honor" in this case does not refer to sexual virtue but rather to the primary definition listed in the Oxford English Dictionary: "High respect, esteem, or reverence, accorded to exalted worth or rank; deferential admiration or approbation." It seems likely that for most of humanity's evolutionary history, honor was a crucial part of one's interpersonal armor, a kind of "don't tread on me" badge that, for all its power, could readily be tarnished once a victim was perceived to be vulnerable. If so, then as we suggested earlier for animals, for a person to have been victimized means not only have they lost something specific (a meal, some property, a mate, an arm or a leg), but also to have been literally dis-honored, and therefore to have lost some or all of the public regard that all social species crave, and without which everyone is dangerously vulnerable.

Also vulnerable—at least in societies such as the United States, which has developed a notably punitive criminal system (and which, as already noted, is unusual in embracing capital punishment)—are politicians who seem less than punitive and potentially violent themselves. Some readers may recall when candidate Michael Dukakis, during a presidential debate in 1988, was asked how he would respond if his wife were raped and murdered. His answer: "I think you know that I've opposed the death penalty during all of my life. I don't see any evidence that it's a deterrent, and I think there are better and more effective ways to deal with violent crime. We've done so in my own state." He might have won the election had he responded, instead: "I'd tear the son of a bitch limb from limb."

Fear of just such vulnerability lies at the heart of most of the "blood feuds" that have bedeviled human history. Scratch the surface of an ongoing feud, and you are certain to find pain and the need to respond to it. And beneath that? The victim's fear of seeming dishonored, weak, and thus vulnerable. And this, in turn, can generate tension between an individual's yearning for honor and security on the one hand and society's formal mechanisms for assuring public safety via an "official" and "legal" justice system.

* * *

Man Monomania is an Albanian clan leader who tried for years to encourage his people to replace revenge with reconciliation. "People don't want to report killings to the police," he notes, "because then the accused would be protected by the state in prison instead of being available to kill."[7] This highlights a curious conflict between social means of justice and private, personal revenge-taking: the former serves, ideally, to reduce inclination toward the latter, but in the process, it can deprive aggrieved parties of the "satisfaction"—or honor—of taking the law into their own hands.

We thank Susan Jacoby[8] for drawing our attention to an important literary figure, based on a real-life character, whose tale has reverberated in one form or another for literally four centuries. Michael Kohlhaas was reputedly a solid, upstanding citizen who ran afoul of a local squire, who in turn detained two of Kohlhaas's horses while the dispute was to be adjudicated. The issue having been unsatisfactorily resolved, Kohlhaas returned to find that his animals had been abused, whereupon things rapidly spun out of control. Feeling maltreated and unable to achieve justice via the existing legal system, Mr. Kohlhaas proceeded to murder many innocents, in the course of which his own wife was killed; and he ended up leading a violent, destructive and ultimately unsuccessful rebellion, after which he was executed. Kohlhaas's rampage was powered by legitimate outrage, exacerbated by the authorities' initial refusal to give him justice. (Eventually, the legitimacy of his original claim was confirmed, but by that time, it was much too late.)

Michael Kohlhaas has had numerous modern incarnations, most notably in Charles Bronson's *Death Wish* movies, which were a kind of personal wish-fulfillment writ large for huge audiences in the 1970s and 1980s. Our hero's wife had been murdered and his daughter raped, after which the police were unable to apprehend the perpetrators. Bronson's character then proceeded to get a gun and kill hoodlums, willy-nilly, and with the enthusiastic approval of cheering moviegoers.

Even when redirected aggression is expressly abjured and the focus is explicitly upon punishing convicted malefactors, more of us are discomfited by an intense concentration upon payback, whether sanctioned by divine command or human insistence. "Who wants to be confronted by an Old Testament prophet, whether across the dinner table or on the evening news?" asks Susan Jacoby. "We are more comfortable with the notion of forgiving and forgetting, however unrealistic it may be, than with the private and public reality of revenge, with its unsettling echoes of the primitive and its inescapable reminder of the fragility of human order."

At the same time, it must be emphasized that passing one's pain to others—however disagreeable—is not a mental illness or sign of deviance. The biological background of retaliation, revenge, and redirected aggression, including their physiological, evolutionary, and animal manifestations, may seem to reinforce the notion that such activities are either a primitive vestige of a brutish past, or, at the other extreme, justify them as "biological" and therefore unavoidable and even good.

Here is Albert Camus, taking the former position, in his essay "Reflections on the Guillotine."

> Whoever has done me harm must suffer harm; whoever has put out my eye must lose an eye; and whoever has killed must die. This is an

emotion, and a particularly violent one, not a principle. Retaliation is related to nature and instinct, not to law. Law, by definition, cannot obey the same rules as nature. . . . Now, retaliation does no more than ratify and confer the status of a law on a pure impulse of nature.[9]

We have been hard-pressed to find comparable arguments on the other side—legitimating revenge because of its presumed "naturalness." We suspect, nonetheless, that this view lurks just below the surface among many supporters of violent retribution. One exception is the curmudgeonly Mr. Mencken, who, after identifying the penchant for *katharsis*, claimed that "it is plainly asking too much of human nature to expect it to conquer so natural an impulse" (more on the question of "conquering" human nature in the next chapter).

For now, our position is that revenge is not delegitimized by its biological roots, nor is it rendered either admirable or ineradicable as a result. The Three Rs are undoubtedly rooted in biology (and in much cultural practice as well), but the tendency to pass along one's pain is nonetheless also within the realm of human control. Roots are terrific as anchors and nutrient suppliers, but they do not dictate what grows above ground. We human beings do not need our large brains simply to do "what comes naturally." Rather, our cognitive, above-ground capacities provide *Homo sapiens* with the opportunity to be genuinely sapient, which, to paraphrase Reinhold Niebuhr's famous "Serenity Prayer," includes having the wisdom to know what is unalterable in our personal behavior (e.g., the automatic functioning of our kidneys), and what can and should be changed, if we so desire.

* * *

"Revenge is wicked, and unchristian and in every way unbecoming," wrote Mark Twain, "but it is powerful sweet, anyway."[10] Those such as Twain or Mencken, with the brazenness to acknowledge the attraction of revenge, typically do so under cover of black humor, hoping for, and generally getting, a knowing smile. Overwhelmingly, however, vengeance—"taking it out" on someone, even someone who has not injured you or yours—is not generally considered one of humankind's more admirable inclinations. Indeed, it is repugnant.

We hold no brief for revenge, nor its pain-passing relatives, retaliation and redirection; quite the contrary. But we are struck by its ubiquity, reflected in the abundance and vigor of efforts to subdue it. There would be no need to criticize the urge for vengeance were it not so widespread and also deeply ingrained. Indeed, nearly everyone takes issue with revenge.

Thus, Marcus Aurelius: "To refrain from imitation is the best revenge." And Francis Bacon, writing "Of Revenge," in his *Essays*: "A man that studieth revenge keeps his own wounds green, which otherwise would heal and do well"; a sentiment that is stated even more strongly in the Chinese proverb "when you go out to seek revenge, dig two graves." As for the oft-cited observation that "revenge is sweet," let us set the record straight, for this is a blatant misquote. The original, in Milton's *Paradise Lost,* actually reads:

Revenge, at first though sweet
Bitter ere long back on itself recoils.

Going now from the sublime to popular culture: "Hello. My name is Inigo Montoya. You killed my father. Prepare to die!" Myriad moviegoers thrilled to (and laughed at) these lines in the film *The Princess Bride.* But relatively few are likely to recall this shifting of Montoya's mantra, spoken after the estimable revenge-seeker finally achieved his retributive goal: "I have been in the revenge business so long, now that it's over, I don't know what to do with the rest of my life."

In Charlotte Brontë's *Jane Eyre,* the heroine acknowledges, "Something of vengeance I had tasted for the first time. An aromatic wine it seemed, on swallowing, warm and racy," but then she quickly adds, as though to make the experience more acceptable to her reading audience: "its first after-flavour, metallic and corroding, gave me a sensation as if I had been poisoned." And when a revenge-obsessed Prospero finally sees the light in Shakespeare's *The Tempest,* pointing out that "the rarer action is in virtue than in vengeance," the Bard leaves no doubt which half of the virtue/vengeance dichotomy is aligned with the angels.

Nor are such perceptions limited to imaginative fiction. Recent experimental research by social psychologists lines up similarly, suggesting that people often overestimate the satisfaction that they would be likely to derive from revenge.[11] Thus, instead of feeling better after obtaining vengeance, people not uncommonly continue to ruminate about the offence and about the perpetrator; whereas those who refrain are more likely to "move on." In addition, there are differences, for the most part unanticipated by the revenge-taker, between witnessing punishment and actually instigating or inflicting it oneself. The researchers conclude that "people punish others, in part, to repair their negative mood and to provide psychological closure to the precipitating event, but the act of punishment yields precisely the opposite outcome."

Not surprisingly, serious defenders of revenge are among humanity's most unsavory characters, such as Josef Stalin. Thus, according to one report from a participant,

At a boozy dinner, Kamenev asked everyone round the table to declare their greatest pleasure in life. Some cited women, others earnestly replied that it was the progress of dialectical materialism towards the workers' paradise. Then Stalin answered: 'My greatest pleasure is to choose one's victim, prepared one's plans minutely, slake an implacable vengeance, and then go to bed. There's nothing sweeter in the world.[12]

Justice is another matter. It may not be sweet, but it is widely acknowledged savory. Over and over, when victims are permitted to testify at a perpetrator's trial, or interviewed while attending legal proceedings, or arguing for the legitimacy of severe criminal punishment, they claim to be "shocked shocked" when asked whether they might possibly be out for revenge. And as for redirected aggression, that seems so illogical, implausible, and indefensible that the very idea is never even raised. It is beyond the scope of this book to engage a fully satisfying examination of justice; indeed, this has, so far, been beyond the capacity of brilliant philosophers and legal scholars—from Plato to John Rawls—who have devoted entire careers to the topic. But given the terrain we have thus far traversed, it would be irresponsible not to gesture in that direction.

"Blood cries out for blood" is the iconic cry for revenge. And for justice? As Gilbert and Sullivan's Mikado famously announced, "let the punishment fit the crime," with the "fit" determined by the sense of satisfaction and closure experienced by society's participant onlookers.[††] The famous *lex talionis*, derived etymologically from the same root as "retaliation" and traceable at least as far back as the Code of Hammurabi, specifies that the punishment should not exceed the crime. Hence, the claim "an eye for an eye, a tooth for a tooth," and so on—which occurs in only slightly different form in Leviticus, Exodus, and Deuteronomy—can accurately be seen not as a *demand* for violent recompense, but rather a *restraint* against going further; it thus endeavors to inhibit any tendency to indulge punishment that is more severe than the transgression.

At the same time, appropriate punishment is not only condoned, but actively encouraged, often as a means of cleansing the social fabric. And so, let us consider the case of John Billington, who came over to America on the *Mayflower*.

Mr. Billington and his family were troublesome, to put it mildly. In December 1620, while the Pilgrims were still living aboard the *Mayflower* at anchor, one of his sons started a fire by shooting a fowling piece in his father's cabin, setting off sparks and a near-catastrophe. A few months later, John Sr. was publicly arraigned "for contempt of the Captain's lawful command with opprobrious speeches" (i.e., disobedience and cursing), and was sentenced to have his heels tied to his neck but "upon humbling himself and craving pardon, and it being the first offence, he [was] forgiven." By 1624, Billington had been implicated in a failed revolt against the Plymouth Church, but once again avoided punishment. Then, in 1630, he had a dispute with one John Newcomen, whom Billington killed with a blast from his blunderbuss, after which he was arrested,

---

[††] In an ideal world, the punishment would *fix* the crime, and we applaud modern jurisprudence insofar as it has become increasingly open to restitution rather than punishment as a goal in itself. At the same time, we suspect that even though effective restitution would in fact diminish the pain of victims, the strong pull of the Three Rs keeps painful punishment the most common outcome.

tried, and found guilty, and became the first white immigrant to be put to death, legally, in the New World. According to then-Governor William Bradford, the Plymouth authorities "took the advice of Mr. Winthrop and others, the ablest gentlemen in Bay of the Massachusetts . . . who concurred with them that he ought to die, *and the land to be purged from blood.*" [our italics][13]

Think about those scales of justice. They offer a clear statement of balance and equalization, or at least the presumed restoration of equilibrium after they have been upset by a transgression. At the same time, of course, those scales can be unbalanced by too much pain for the perpetrator. Thus, criminal punishment is often reduced by various indications that the perpetrator has "suffered enough." Enough for what? Enough, we suspect, to satisfy the victims and society at large. Most commonly, however, the complaint is that villains "get off too easily."

The genocidal Cambodian leader Pol Pot died in 1998. By most estimates, his murderous Khmer Rouge regime had been responsible for the murder of approximately 2,000,000 of his countrymen. Along with the predictable retrospective about Cambodia's "killing fields," which Pol Pot had masterminded, his demise—peacefully, in his sleep, rather than in a gas chamber or in front of a firing squad—evoked immense frustration: a world-class villain had escaped justice. Youk Chang, head of a research center that had been accumulating evidence to present at the expected trial of Pol Pot: "[We] are sad because we have lost a criminal we cannot punish. I wish to see him in court. I wish to see him in handcuffs. I wish to see him suffer the way he made me suffer."[14] An accompanying article in *The New York Times* quoted Diane Orentlicher, professor of law at American University, as follows: "By not having a trial and not punishing Pol Pot and the Khmer Rouge over the past two decades we have, in effect, told the Cambodians that what happened wasn't a crime. If there was no punishment, there was no crime."[15] What Professor Orentlicher really meant, we suspect, is that if there is no punishment, there is no satisfaction for the victims.

Our argument, in short: Whatever else they may be, crime victims are in a sense no different from individuals who have been victimized by others, regardless of the details, whether the acts in question involve illegal actions, being bested in an argument or a fight, or simply having been insulted, slighted, or otherwise physically or emotionally hurt. The consequence is typically some form of subordination stress (proximately), and a need to maintain social status (ultimately), resulting in a need to pass along the resulting pain, whether by retaliation, revenge, or redirected aggression. As for "justice"—at least when applied to efforts at making amends following a serious social transgression—we suggest it is *also* the feeling of satisfaction that results when that need is satisfied.

Supreme Court Justice Potter Stewart, writing of pornography, famously noted that "I may not be able to define it, but I know it when I see it." Similarly, when it comes to justice, philosophers, ethicists, and legal scholars may not be able to define it, but nearly everyone knows it when they see it . . . or, better yet, when, having been wronged, they feel it. Revenge is rough, raw, crude, and—at least in part—literally hormonal; justice is supposed to be smooth and well-cooked, a carefully prepared and deeply considered product of sophisticated civilization. Revenge is to justice as lust is to erotic love.

Lust exists as a basic biological mechanism to facilitate projecting one's genes into the future. Revenge exists as an equally basic biocultural mechanism, also for projecting one's genes into the future. Social niceties often require that lust be obscured (albeit not eliminated); so, too, for revenge. Moreover, the transformation need not be dishonest. Although lust can exist without love, and love (of country, children, a good book, and so forth) without lust, the reality is that the two often coexist quite nicely. So can revenge and criminal justice.

Conventional wisdom identifies at least six reasons for punishing a criminal: (1) to deter other would-be malefactors, (2) to keep society safe by removing or at least temporarily restraining the offender, (3) to rehabilitate him or her (a payoff that presumably does not apply to capital punishment),[††] (4) to reaffirm the priority of social rules and values at least in part by italicizing the power of the state, (5) to achieve a moral balancing of the scales, and (6) to satisfy the psychological needs of victims. Of these, the first four—deterrence, public safety, offender rehabilitation, and social reaffirmation—are not powered by concern for "justice" as such, but rather by presumed societal benefit. When it comes to deeply residing, subjective sensations of justice, we need to consider numbers five and six; which is to say, the intimate if unpleasant reality of how we treat wrongdoers (those who have caused pain) in an effort to diminish that pain by passing it to someone else.

Take the case of Adolf Eichmann, the Nazi official who had been responsible for organizing and overseeing much of the bureaucratic machinery that carried out Hitler's murder of more than 11,000,000 Jews, gays, Roma ("Gypsies"), and others. Eichmann escaped from Germany and was living in Argentina when he was apprehended by the Israeli secret police and was brought to trial in Jerusalem, where he became the only person jurisprudentially executed by the state of Israel. The legal proceedings did not include any serious consideration of whether Eichmann could or should be rehabilitated, whether his punishment was justified as a deterrent to would-be future Eichmanns, or whether public safety or Israel's legitimacy would somehow be enhanced by his incarceration or execution. Rather, the issue was "justice," pure and simple; which is to say, whether

---

[††] In the movie *My Little Chickadee*, W. C. Fields's character, Cuthbert J. Twillie, is asked, just before being hanged, if he has anything to say concerning his execution: "It's going to be a great lesson to me."

Adolf Eichmann deserved to die for what he had done, and whether his punishment was mandated, at least in part, by the pain he had inflicted. Was this revenge? Probably—but maybe not despicably.

The picking of pockets was a capital offense in England for 245 years, between 1565 and 1810. We can be assured that during this extended period, those pickpockets hanged for their crimes were not executed out of retaliation, revenge, or redirected aggression, as Eichmann was, but rather for more practical motives, largely centered on simple—if grotesquely exaggerated—deterrence, as well as perhaps some yearning by the state to exhibit its power. In any event, justice does not always entail the passing of pain in general or revenge in particular. But to a degree that most people would rather not acknowledge, it often does.

Susan Jacoby, in her superbly argued book *Wild Justice: The Evolution of Revenge*,[16] made an especially persuasive case that human revenge is intimately connected to justice, and, moreover, that although the yearning for vengeance is unseemly and perhaps even immoral, it is also deeply fixed in human nature, maybe even irrevocably so. Redirected aggression, as such, does not appear in Jacoby's book, which takes its title from Francis Bacon's contention that "revenge is a kind of wild justice, which, the more man's nature runs to, the more ought law to weed it out." And this, in turn, leads to an interesting ambiguity, along with an intriguing idea.

First, the ambiguity: How "ought law to weed it out"? By forbidding revenge altogether, stifling any prospect of victims' passing their pain to perpetrators? Or by establishing norms and procedures for punishment, whenever possible, by actually carrying out said punishment, thereby making justice less personal and therefore less "wild"? This suggests the intriguing idea that civilization itself has progressed in proportion as it has done the latter, replacing interpersonal pain-passing, whenever possible, with violence administered by the state.

* * *

"The conviction of Timothy McVeigh in a Denver federal court," according to *The New York Times* in 1997, brought "cheers and sobs of relief at the lot where a building once stood in downtown Oklahoma City." At the same time, "the victims of the most deadly attack of domestic terrorism in U.S. history learned what they had suspected all along: That justice in a far-away courtroom is not satisfaction. That healing might come only at McVeigh's grave." The article went on:

> "I want the death penalty," said Aren Almon-Kok, whose daughter, Baylee, was killed by the bomb one day after her first birthday. Pictures of the baby, bleeding and limp in the arms of a firefighter, became a symbol of that crime, of its cruelty. "An eye for an eye. You don't take lives and get to keep your own."

Almon-Kok saw the announcement of the verdict on television at her mother's house, then went immediately to the site of her daughter's death, where she was joined by people who had lost children in the bombing and by others who had just felt drawn there. She said how happy she was with the verdict, but her face was stricken, haunted. "I cried and I cheered," she said. "I don't think there will ever be closure." . . . The survivors and victims talked hopefully of another victory in the penalty phase. How, once the jury is privy to so much pain, can it deny them McVeigh's life?

Before the verdict, accounts of the survivors and their families were consistent in stressing the universal insistence on a guilty verdict, and their fear that maybe McVeigh would get off (a hung jury was the greatest anxiety), which would do what? Somehow, it would devalue their own pain. Even though it became de rigueur to acknowledge that McVeigh's conviction would not bring back their loved one. . . .

"We were holding hands and praying and crying," said Katherine Alaniz, whose father, Claude Medaris, died in the bombing. "My mom reached into her purse and handed me his wedding ring and, of course, I . . . started crying. It was wonderful."[17]

Shortly after the guilty verdict came the judge's ruling that sentenced McVeigh to death. Here, once again, is *The New York Times*: "People . . . started to cry, to laugh. Some just said, 'Thank God.' People hugged on sidewalks, in hotel lobbies. . . . But even while some of Mr. McVeigh's victims quietly rejoiced at the prospect of his death, others were struck anew by how little real joy it caused."[18]

When McVeigh was eventually executed, the entire nation watched in fascination, many hoping for "closure" that never really came, because the Oklahoma City bomber remained stoical, refusing to acknowledge that his impending execution caused him the pain that so many of his victims demanded. Nor did he ever show any remorse, something that is also important when juries are deciding on how severely to punish a criminal.

One reason that contrition is often helpful in deflecting anger and calls for revenge or harsh punishment is that by being apologetic and remorseful, a perpetrator is acknowledging that he or she is already feeling pain, if only pangs of remorse, thus defusing clamor for the infliction of yet more. But to the frustration of many, McVeigh seemed to feel no pain. (It is also worth noting that McVeigh's act was itself an example of redirected aggression, in that he was responding to the earlier deaths of cultists associated with David Koresh in Waco, Texas, at the hands of the FBI—or so McVeigh claimed.)

Six months later, when a federal jury convicted Terry Nichols, McVeigh's collaborator, of conspiracy and manslaughter but spared him the death penalty, the anger was nearly as deep and widespread as had been the celebration at

McVeigh's conviction and sentencing. But for most of the victims, it was taboo to admit their deeper disappointment.

According to an account in *The New York Times*:

> The most painful thing, the families of victims of the Oklahoma City bombing said, was not that Terry L. Nichols had escaped, for now, death by lethal injection. They said they wanted justice, not vengeance. One woman, who lost her infant daughter in the bombing, was quoted as saying, with relief: "At least we're still going to get a punishment."[19]

Legal systems are not directed toward eliminating the desire for revenge, but toward satisfying it—but doing so in a way that is socially acceptable. Whatever else it involves (and of course, it involves quite a lot), civilization also requires the domestication of retaliation, revenge, and redirecting aggression. It is not merely that things would be chaotic if everyone took the law into his or her own hands (although that is certainly true), but law itself owes much of its existence to the social acknowledgment that transgressions, especially violent ones, must be adjudicated by society and not simply by each aggrieved party. Vengeance is mine, quoth the Community.

Supposedly, it is not merely the victims who are entitled to revenge, but society as a whole that can and must demand "justice." Punishment for the crime is thus distinguished from vengeance for the victim. For some philosophers, such as Immanuel Kant, punishment—and with it, the infliction of pain on a perpetrator—is readily legitimated, not because the crime inflicted pain on the victim, which must be balanced or otherwise redressed, but because a crime is, by definition, wrong.

Should it ever be the role of a judge and jury to "feel the pain" of a crime victim, or is it simply to administer disinterested justice? And can justice ever be disinterested? Even if crimes "need" to be punished, independent of the needs of society or of the immediate victims, to understand the Three Rs is to understand that victims (perhaps more than society at large) have a particular need to have their injury acknowledged. In the United States, an important change in criminal law involved the admission in the sentencing phase of "victim impact statements" from relatives of murder victims, ever since a Supreme Court decision known as Payne *v.* Tennessee,[§§] in 1991. Although extremely popular, at least among "victim's rights" groups, this policy has moved American criminal justice closer to the older, presumably less civilized status of private feuds rather than the seemingly neutral and more modern proceedings of public justice. It is also

---

[§§] We cannot take credit for the Payne/pain parallelism, but also cannot help noting the coincidence.

distinctively American; nothing comparable exists, for example, in current European legal systems.

Islamic criminal law, however, provides an interesting exception, one that is little known in the Western world and toward which U.S. criminal law has (unbeknownst to most Americans) begun to converge. Under Islamic criminal law, the most serious category of illegality, known as *hudud*—which includes theft, adultery, and apostasy—cannot be pardoned by the victim, the victim's family, or a judge. By contrast, *qisas* crimes are a different story. These include assault, battery, and murder, all of which involve a direct act of aggression against someone else. In such cases, the Islamic state's role is quite limited, with the victim and/or victim's family often allowed—indeed, encouraged—to decide the perpetrator's punishment. To be sure, like its Western counterparts, *shari'a* law provides guidelines for appropriate criminal punishment, but if they wish, the victims can nonetheless choose, for example, a lighter jail sentence, or even imprisonment instead of execution.

The path from victimhood to criminal jurisprudence has been significantly different in the West. One definition of the state, especially among European and American theorists, is that it exists for no other reason than to prevent wrongdoing, and, should it fail in this respect, to apprehend the malefactor and then administer punishment. This view of government as "night watchman" essentially defines the state as that entity with legitimate power of life and death over its citizens, death presumably being the ultimate in sanctioned infliction of pain. This definition dates at least as far back as Thomas Hobbes, in the mid-seventeenth century.

Sociologist Norbert Elias, in *The Civilizing Process*, provided a groundbreaking analysis of the decline in lethal violence in Western Europe from the Middle Ages until the present.[20] His basic argument is that, ironically, this decline occurred as strong political states emerged, each having "a monopoly of force." Elias argued that citizens are much less likely to engage in personal violence— much of it in response to violence visited upon them or their relations—when the state promises to do so: "When a monopoly of force is formed, pacified social spaces are created which are normally free from acts of violence." Homicide rates plummeted in Europe, for example, from the fourteenth to the twentieth century, in parallel to the skyrocketing power of the state.

As University of Miami psychologist Michael McCullough points out, the converse also holds: When the government's ability to kill—or at least, to punish—is hobbled, citizens are more likely to do it themselves:

> Before the March 2003 invasion of Iraq, there was approximately one violent Iraqi death per ten thousand residents per year.¶ In the forty

---

¶ Our note: this refers to street crime, not the "organized terrorism" of Saddam Hussein's despotic regime itself.

months between March 2003 and June 2006, this figure had soared to seventy-two per ten thousand per year. Extrapolating from these results, epidemiologists estimate that six hundred thousand Iraqis died violent deaths between the beginning of the invasion and June 2006. However, less than a third of those six hundred thousand violent deaths were directly attributable to the actions of Coalition forces. Of the remaining two-thirds, untold thousands (probably hundreds of thousands) were due to revenge-fueled sectarian violence at the hands of militias representing the Kurdish-Shia and Arab-Sunni factions.

Saddam's repressive state tyranny, for all its horrors, effectively kept a lid on Shiite-Sunni revenge-fueled violence. When this monopoly of force was removed following the U.S.-led invasion, the resulting power vacuum opened the door to a lethal reciprocating cycle of violence, some of which was fueled by the earlier violence of Saddam's regime, especially toward the Shiites.

A similar pattern has been working itself out in the killing fields of Juarez as well as elsewhere in Mexico, where grossly underpaid and thus notoriously corrupt local police forces, combined with a historically weak army, have permitted feuding drug cartels to act out their most homicidal antipathies and tit-for-tat murders.

At the same time, there is a deep and widespread ambivalence when it comes to the punishment of criminals, especially when that punishment is extreme: namely, capital. Consider this historical footnote. In the late nineteenth century, at the same time that authorities in the United States were looking for a way to perform executions that was less gruesome, more reliable, and more "humane" than hanging or the firing squad, Thomas Edison was vigorously competing with George Westinghouse for primacy in the brave new world of electricity. Edison (who, incidentally, was opposed to capital punishment), urged that "electrocution" (a word he coined) be used to dispatch condemned prisoners. He further proposed that Westinghouse's alternating current be employed for this purpose, since it was more lethal and thus quicker than Edison's own direct current. Ever the entrepreneur, with an eye toward public relations, Edison was presumably not simply being modest when he recommended that this method of execution be termed "Westinghousing."

* * *

Sociologists have deployed vats of ink over the question of criminality: what causes it, what to do about it, and how it fits into more general conceptions of "social deviance." Combining this extensive debate with a focus on retaliation, revenge, and redirected aggression yields the following possibility: Perhaps criminality and its punishment is a means whereby society keeps itself intact, not merely by punishing deviants out of a yearning for deterrence, a desire to balance the cosmic scales of right and wrong, or to reaffirm social norms and the power of the state. Rather, they serve to unite its own members in shared redirected aggression toward perceived outsiders, not unlike Konrad Lorenz's observations of the mated pairs of cichlid fish who attacked neighboring animals instead of each other.

According to Emile Durkheim, founder of modern sociology, the form of crime "is not the same everywhere; but everywhere and always, there have been men who have behaved in such a way as to draw upon themselves penal repression."[21] Durkheim's perspective (and that of sociologists generally) is quite different from that espoused in the present book, in that it focuses on the macro level—that of society as a whole—instead of on individual cases and personal motivation. Deviance, Durkheim famously argued, was a "social fact," a cultural phenomenon independent of biology and even psychology, and something that needs to be understood on its own terms since it resists reductionism.

Nonetheless, for most sociologists, "social facts" are not purely arbitrary or capricious; they serve a social function, and in that sense one might consider them at least analogous to biological traits that must be at least minimally adaptive if they are to persist. If so, then perhaps one adaptive function of punishing offenders is that it brings people together in social solidarity. This would help explain the widespread persistence of spectacles of public punishment (e.g. the stocks, burnings at the stake, breaking-on-the-wheel, hangings, being drawn and quartered) throughout history. According to this view, the process, driven by enthusiasm for shared redirected aggression, has been not only gruesome and brutalizing, but carried out against innocent individuals whose guilt or innocense is actually irrelevant, and whose primary offense has simply been their departure from group norms. If so, this would substantially narrow the difference between the punishment of genuine or perceived malefactors and the ancient phenomenon of scapegoating, which we have already considered. The primary difference between these would simply be that scapegoating involves redirected aggression to compensate for pain experienced by society (climatic disasters, bad economic times, and so forth), whereas criminal punishment is, ironically, more "positively" motivated: by the need to enhance social solidarity.

In his influential book *Wayward Puritans: A Study in the Sociology of Deviance*, Kai Erikson developed a more traditional sociological theory, arguing that communities have an innate desire to retain their "cultural integrity" by developing structures that control deviance, regardless of whether the transgressive acts are harmful in themselves. Their benefit, to society, lies in the opportunity to punish. He writes:

> This raises a delicate theoretical issue. If we grant that human groups often derive benefit from deviant behavior, can we then assume that they are organized in such a way as to promote this resource? Can we assume, in other words, that forces operate in the social structure to

recruit offenders and to commit them to long periods of service in the deviant ranks?[22]

And of course, Erikson's "delicate theoretical issue" fits into a conception whereby social outrage and punishment, powered by redirected aggression, might also serve to enhance social cohesion. Erikson goes farther, albeit in a more controversial direction, arguing that penal institutions do more to *perpetuate* criminals than to rehabilitate them, and that this apparent "failure" is actually an unacknowledged if perverse *success* of a system that is actually designed to maintain deviance.

Whatever the role of society in "setting up" deviant and criminal behavior, what about the perpetrators themselves? Insofar as people hurt others "because" they have themselves been hurt, does that diminish their responsibility or subsequent guilt? Should we pity the poor perpetrator? Are all victimizers themselves previous victims? And what if they are? Does that excuse their behavior? In short, what about the self-justifying claim of victimization as a way of avoiding accountability? When does passing the pain become passing the buck? It has been claimed that American culture has increasingly become one of self-perceived victims, and it is assuredly not our intent to further this development, to justify villainous behavior by perpetrators whose actions are attributable—even partially—to their prior victimization. Yet there may indeed be a risk that the Three Rs in general, and redirected aggression in particular, will replace "The devil made me do it" or the notorious "Twinkie defense,"*** as an excuse for victims to lash out at others or to dodge responsibility after doing so.

Explanation is one thing; exculpation is another. Unless someone is acting under obvious compulsion, like with a gun to her head, we must consider her to have free will; which is to say, to be fundamentally responsible for her actions.[†††] (Isaac Bashevis Singer was once asked whether he believed in free will, to which he replied, "I have no choice!") This is not the venue to resolve the ancient free will versus determinism debate, and even if it were, we are not up to the task. But it is worth noting that despite the universal subjective feeling on everyone's part that he or she possesses free will, the reality is that every behavior, and indeed, every thought and perception, must have been caused by something: in particular, molecules in motion across nerve membranes, which in turn are

---

*** The defense attorneys for Dan White, who shot San Francisco Supervisor Harvey Milk and Mayor George Moscone, argued that his behavior was partly attributable to having consumed large quantities of high-sugar junk food. The strategy was successful: White was convicted of voluntary manslaughter rather than murder.

††† Of course, there are exceptions and extenuating circumstances, such as intoxication, mental illness, etc., but it is a prerequisite for normal human functioning to assume that most people, most of the time, are not androids.

affected by previous movements, collisions, osmotic gradients, electric fields, genes, experiences, and so forth. It has been said (although we have been unable to confirm it) that when juries are shown studies pointing to the role of various regions in the central nervous system when it comes to generating specific behaviors, they are less likely to subsequently convict a criminal defendant. "His brain made him do it!"

The French have a saying, *tout comprendre, c'est tout pardonner* ("to understand completely is to pardon completely"). We prefer this: *To explain is to understand.* Period. We would add, however, that to understand is to be better prepared to intervene, perhaps even to modify and prevent . . . but not to let perpetrators off the hook.

* * *

This has been a difficult chapter, in which we have sought to acknowledge the importance of pain-passing as part of the biological, psychological, and social structure that undergirds justice, but without legitimizing retaliation, revenge, and redirected aggression, as such. The problem is in balancing an understanding of propensities that are less than admirable with the reality that they exist, are stubborn, but are nonetheless subject to modification. No one has ever claimed that it is easy to be a sentient being, especially because to be sentient (and thus, to recognize the wrongness of the Three Rs) conflicts with being—if nothing else—a *being*, and thus, subject to some of the same inclinations as other living beings, many of them neither particularly sentient nor admirable.

One way to proceed from here, while also pointing to a hopeful resolution, is via the work of Nobel Prize–winning Irish poet Seamus Heaney. Part of his translation of an ancient play by Sophocles examined the dilemma of Philoctetes, a Greek warrior during the Trojan War. Poor Philoctetes had been bitten by a snake, which not only caused him immense recurring pain, but also produced a foul odor that made him *persona non grata* among his military colleagues, who responded by abandoning him on an island.

After many years of isolation and misery, Philoctetes was visited once again by his former associates, seeking his assistance (it turns out that Philoctetes had Hercules' magic bow, which was to prove useful in eventually conquering Troy). Philoctetes' challenge, then, was to put aside his pain, his anger, and his yearning for revenge, in order to meet his social obligations . . . to choose a route other than payback, and, not coincidentally, to be cured himself in the process.

Here, without further commentary, is an excerpt from Heaney's *The Cure at Troy*:

> Human beings suffer.
> They torture one another.

They get hurt and get hard.
No poem or play or song
Can fully right a wrong
Inflicted and endured.
History says, Don't hope
On this side of the grave,
But then, once in a lifetime
The longed-for tidal wave
Of justice can rise up
And hope and history rhyme.
So hope for a great sea-change
On the far side of revenge,
Believe that a farther shore
Is reachable from here.[23]

References

1. Morris, Herbert (1968). "Persons and Punishment," *The Monist*, 52: 475–501.
2. Robert C. Solomon (1995). *A Passion for Justice*. Lanham, Md: Rowman & Littlefield.
3. Elizabeth Hankins Wolgast (1987). *The Grammar of Justice*. Ithaca, NY: Cornell University Press.
4. Amartya Sen (2009). *The Idea of Justice*. Cambridge, MA: Harvard University Press.
5. H. L. Mencken (1926; 1977). *Prejudices, Series Five*. New York: Octagon Books.
6. Michael McCullough (2008). Beyond Revenge: The Evolution of the Forgiveness Instinct. San Francisco: Jossey-Bass.
7. April 14, 1998, by Jane Perlez. Pg. A3.
8. Susan Jacoby (1982). *Wild Justice*. New York: Harper & Row.
9. A. Camus (1961). Reflections on the guillotine. In *Resistance, Rebellion and Death*. (Transl. J. O'Brien.) New York: Alfred A. Knopf.
10. Mark Twain (1949). "Letter to Olivia," quoted in D. Wechter (ed.), *The Love Letters of Mark Twain*. New York: Harper & Brothers.
11. Kevin M. Carlsmith, Timothy D. Wilson, and Daniel T. Gilbert (2008). The paradoxical consequences of revenge. *Journal of Personality and Social Psychology* 95(6): 1316–1324.
12. Simon S. Montefiore (2007). *Young Stalin*. New York: Knopf
13. William Bradford (1991). *Of Plymouth Plantation* (1620–1647), ed. Samuel Eliot Morison. New York: Knopf.
14. Seth Mydans, "The Demons of a Despot." *New York Times*, April 17, 1998.
15. Elizabeth Becker, "Pol Pot's End Won't Stop U.S. Pursuit of His Circle." April 17, 1998.
16. S. Jacoby (1983). *Wild Justice: The Evolution of Revenge*. New York: Harper & Row:.
17. June 3, 1997.
18. Rick Bragg, "Many Find Satisfaction, But Few Find Any Joy," *New York Times*, June 14, 1997.
19. Bill Dedman, "Families' Anger at Outcome Is Scalding," *New York Times*, Jan. 8, 1998, pg. A16.
20. N. Elias (1939; 1969). *The Civilizing Process, volume 2*. New York: Pantheon.
21. E. Durkheim. (1895; 1982). *The Rules of Sociological Method*. New York: Free Press:.

22. K.T. Erikson (1966). *Wayward Puritans: A Study in the Sociology of Deviance*. New York: Macmillan Publishing Company.

23. Excerpts from *The Cure at Troy: A Version of Sophocles' Philoctetes* by Seamus Heaney. Copyright © (1990) by Seamus Heaney. Reprinted by permission of Farrar, Straus & Giroux, LLC.

Overcoming

Shall We?

"There are some crayfish souls," wrote Victor Hugo, "forever scuttling backwards into the darkness."[1] He was thinking of Napoleon III. The sad truth is that when it comes to passing one's pain along, many people are crayfish souls indeed. But not all. And even those who are, don't act that way all the time. Moreover, although it is easy—indeed, natural—to scuttle backwards into the darkness of endless pain-passing and redirected aggression, such payback is not mandatory. This chapter will examine some of the most important ideas that promise, or at least propose, a way out.

At the same time, we caution against unrealistic expectations. The Chinese reform leader Deng Ziaoping once summarized his policy as "crossing a river by feeling for the stones with your feet." His practical motto stands in marked contrast to Mao Zedong's unwavering and disastrous certainty.* Pain-passing is a river of formidable dimensions; best to cross it carefully, feeling for the stones as we go.

* * *

The world's great ethical systems have long struggled to define responses to victimization that preserve personal and collective security, without falling into the excessive violence of unbridled payback. This challenge is particularly appropriate at a time when the word "evil" is bandied about to condone violence, terrorism, and war, no less than wars *against* terrorism.

The nineteenth-century American transcendentalist Margaret Fuller once famously announced, "I accept the universe," to which the Scottish historian Thomas Carlyle is reputed to have observed, "Gad, she'd better!" The universe does many things to us, including the transmission of pain. If we are to accept the universe—and we'd better!—then we had better also accept that we shall

---

* And may also have been intended to contrast with Mao's famous swim in the Yalu River.

experience pain, and that in the process everyone would be best served if we refrained from passing it unnecessarily to anyone else.

At this point, however, it should be clear that for most people it isn't simply a matter of "just saying No." After all, nearly everyone has a crayfish—or the equivalent—inside. Therefore, for all its negative consequences, redirected aggression and its relatives cannot merely be ethically disdained and self-righteously disavowed. Although neither revenge nor redirection are human universals, inaction after victimization demands more than most people can muster, and it also presents problems. As we have seen (more to the point, as most people intuitively recognize), doing nothing after having been victimized may invite further encroachments. There is an old Bedouin saying, "If a man takes your camel and you ignore it, bid goodbye to your daughter." But at the same time, to overreact—that is, to kill someone and his family for stealing your camel—or to target an innocent bystander is not only counterproductive but downright villainous. Even plain garden-variety revenge is widely acknowledged to be deeply hurtful, and not only to the party upon whom vengeance is wrought.

Earlier, we discussed how the Iliad is especially concerned with the "wrath of Achilles." Here is Homer's Achilles once more, reflecting on his fury at Agamemnon, and yearning for it to be otherwise: "Why, I wish that strife would vanish away from among gods and mortals, and gall, which makes a man grow angry for all his great mind, that gall of anger that swarms like smoke inside of a man's heart and becomes a thing sweeter to him by far than the dripping of honey."[2]

We must ask, therefore, how normal people might possibly overcome the temptation of this "gall" and "smoke," which seems sweeter than honey yet is ultimately profoundly bitter—which is to say, how can a well-meaning person, who lacks the strength of Achilles and the determination of a saint, stop short of being a violent, pain-inflicting son of a bitch and yet also avoid being a sucker.

In this chapter, we point to an array of possible crossing-stones, á la Deng Ziaoping. The result is a rather wild compendium of thoughts, words, and potential deeds that may be useful to those who seek to cross the river and stop the cycle of pain-passing. We will list certain schools of thought (religious, philosophical, academic), calling them each a *Way*, in the Taoist sense of "path," the Buddhist sense of "dharma," or the plain English notion of a route or street. According to the devout Christian antiwar activist A. J. Muste, "There is no way to peace. Peace is the way." We are confident that the Three Rs work differently: Pain-passing is *not* the way. Moreover, there are ways out of its trap. Toward that end, we shall identify and label an eclectic mix of psychological tools, like the various devices in a Swiss army knife, inviting the reader to draw upon them as needed, with the caveat that no individual method will fit all people or all circumstances. Our goal is not to complete the task of enumerating the ways that people may disavow and disconnect from redirected aggression, but rather to begin a conversation that we hope will endure beyond the covers of this book.

Every great religion includes processes and procedures for forgiveness and reconciliation. The authors of this book are Jewish atheists, not religious scholars. We shall nonetheless do our best to identify answers within religious traditions that might be useful to readers who, by now, are interested in stopping the cycle of retaliation, revenge and redirected aggression, and who may be committed to one religious tradition or another.

The Jewish *Way* (*Halakah*)

Halakah literally means "The Way" in ancient Hebrew, and it refers to the entire body of Jewish law, including the 613 *mitzvot* or "commandments" in the Torah—the five books of Moses—as well as classical rabbinic literature, especially the Mishnah and the Talmud (the "oral law"), plus the Jewish code of law. Those who thought the Ten Commandments were "it" should note that Jewish law, like Shar'ia law in Islam, is a comprehensive system that does not discriminate between civil and religious duty, and that includes literally hundreds of commandments. Some 248 are prescriptive, telling people what to do, while 365 are prohibitive, detailing what *not* to do. The Old Testament is such a huge compendium of stories and styles that one can find nearly any admonishment or instruction about how to live and how to respond to wrongs, from vigorous retaliation and revenge, to nonviolence. Not surprisingly, therefore, the search for a comprehensive, practical scheme that deals with relationships to God as well as to other people has not resulted in a single, agreed-upon court or actionable doctrine to which all Jews seek recourse. Furthermore, since Judaism has split into factions that vary in age as well as orthodoxy, there is no single comprehensive source of advice for all of them. The most famous summary, however, remains Rabbi Hillel's admonition, "What is hateful to you, do not do to your neighbor."

For the spirit of Jewish morality, we recommend the Passover tradition, a ritual dinner that Jews around the world have practiced for thousands of years, which recounts their liberation from Egypt. Part of the story of Exodus describes ten plagues (frogs, lice, boils, death of the first-born sons, etc.) that God ostensibly inflicted upon the Egyptians, thereby forcing them to release the Jews. In the Passover recounting of these disasters, an interesting thing happens: Rather than describe these terrible events with an air of triumphalism, it is customary to dip a finger into one's glass of wine and remove a few drops as each plague is named, thereby symbolically diminishing the pleasure (the amount of wine) of the celebrants. To be sure, there is joy in the eventual liberation but none to be derived from the suffering of the Egyptians—only regret that freedom was obtained at the price of others' pain.

Even the Old Testament itself, usually more inclined to bloodthirstiness than compassion, reflects how disconcerting it can be when the imposition of pain evokes generosity rather than violence. Here is Proverbs (25: 21–22): "If thine enemy be hungry, give him bread to eat; and if he be thirsty, give him water to drink. For thou shalt thus heap coals of fire upon his head, and the Lord shall reward thee." The "coals of fire" thereby heaped are, of course, metaphorical. Rather than passing pain, Proverbs urges us to confront evildoers with the confusion and disorientation experienced when a foe, anticipating the passing of pain, unexpectedly encounters nonviolence, or—more troublesome yet—love.

A similar message can be derived from the story of Joseph in Genesis. In brief, we are told that Joseph had been horribly treated by his jealous brothers, and eventually sold by them into slavery in Egypt. But years later, he rose to a position of great power and was eventually visited by his brothers, who in the meanwhile had been reduced to starvation and beggary, whereupon—to their great surprise—he forgave them, choosing love over vengeance.

There is also a compassionate prayer before sleep that is said by orthodox Jews, which explicitly rejects both revenge and redirected aggression. In this "bedtime Shema," the devout not only pray for personal forgiveness, they also explicitly ask God not to punish anyone on account of any hurt or injury they may have suffered that day. Part of the underlying theology derives from an ancient belief that while asleep, one's soul leaves the body, whereupon the sleeper suffers a little death. Since it is important to die with a clean slate, so to speak, it is important to go to sleep without grudges, hard feelings, or anger, because it is only by God's whim and mercy that we wake up in the morning.

Tool #1: The Bedtime Shema

Master of the universe, I hereby forgive anyone who angered or antagonized me or who sinned against me—whether against my body, whether against my property, whether against my honor, or whether against anything that is mine; whether he did so accidentally, whether willfully, whether carelessly, or whether purposely; whether through speech, whether through deed, whether in deliberation, or whether with fleeting thought; whether in this transmigration or whether in another transmigration, I forgive every Jew. May not be punished any person because of me. May it be the will before You, HASHEM, my G_d and the G_d of my forefathers, that I not sin any more, and that I not return to them and that never shall I again anger You, and that I not do what is evil in your eyes. Whatever sins I have done before You, may You erase in Your mercies that are abundant, but not through suffering or illnesses that are bad. May they find favor—the expressions of my mouth and the thoughts of my heart—before You, HASHEM,[†] my Rock and my Redeemer.[3]

To our knowledge, this is the only prayer—in any religious tradition—that explicitly asks God *not* to punish someone who has hurt the one who is praying, that asks God to forgive the perpetrators as the praying person does. What we especially admire about this prayer is that it does not differentiate between suffering caused by intention or accident, to body or spirit or property. It is a blanket request, asking God to refrain from initiating any more suffering. (At the same time, we have been told that many Jewish traditions abandoned this prayer after the Holocaust, because the magnitude of that murderous transgression was so great. And we are less than entranced by the statement "I forgive every Jew" . . . but presumably not every Gentile.)

Some Christian *Ways*

Christianity relies heavily on the imagery of pain and may indeed be the only major religion whose divine figure is said to have suffered mightily and died in agony at the hands of human beings. Not coincidentally, Christianity may also exceed other religions in the centrality of forgiveness, responding to pain with the explicit request that the perpetrators not be made to suffer in turn: "Father, forgive them, for they know not what they do." It may be noteworthy, however, that in this famed utterance, Jesus asks God to forgive his killers, but does not specifically do so himself. And would the offending Romans have been entitled to forgiveness if they knew precisely what they were doing, but did it anyway?

There can be no doubt, however, that Christian tradition is suffused with exhortations for forgiveness: "Then Peter came and said to Him, 'Lord, how often shall my brother sin against me and I forgive him? Up to seven times?' Jesus said to him, 'I do not say to you, up to seven times, but up to seventy times seven'" (Matthew 18:21–22). One's personal salvation may well depend upon doing so: "And when you stand praying, if you hold anything against anyone, forgive him, so that your Father in heaven may forgive you your sins" (Mark 11:25). Perhaps the most widely repeated such injunction comes from Matthew 6:9–13, better known as the Lord's Prayer:

Our Father which art in heaven, Hallowed be thy name. Thy kingdom come, Thy will be done in earth, as it is in heaven. Give us this day our

---

[†] "Hashem" is the expression that Orthodox Jews use, rather than uttering the unspeakable name of God.

daily bread. And forgive us our debts, *as we forgive our debtors*. And lead us not into temptation, but deliver us from evil: For Thine is the kingdom, and the power, and the glory, forever. Amen.

(We added italics to emphasize a phrase oft-overlooked because of its familiarity.)

In a masterpiece of painfully accurate revelation, G. K. Chesterton once wrote that Christianity has not been tried and found wanting; rather, it has been found difficult and left untried. Never has this been more evident than in cases of personal pain and the all-too-human reaction to it. Thus, in the Sermon on the Mount (Matthew 5:38–42, NIV), we are told the following:

> You have heard that it was said, "An eye for an eye, and a tooth for a tooth." But I tell you, do not resist an evil person. If someone strikes you on the right cheek, turn to him the other also. And if someone wants to sue you and take your tunic, let him have your cloak as well. If someone forces you to go one mile, go with him two miles. Give to the one who asks you, and do not turn away from the one who wants to borrow from you.

This message was evidently considered important, since it is essentially repeated in the Sermon on the Plain (Luke 6:27–31. NIV), which we designate,

Tool #2: The Sermon on the Plain

> But I tell you who hear me: Love your enemies, do good to those who hate you, bless those who curse you, pray for those who mistreat you. If someone strikes you on one cheek, turn to him the other also. If someone takes your cloak, do not stop him from taking your tunic. Give to everyone who asks you, and if anyone takes what belongs to you, do not demand it back. Do to others as you would have them do to you.

And in a similar note, here is Luke 6:35–38 and 6:42

> Love your enemies, do good to them, and lend to them without expecting to get anything back. Then your reward will be great, and you will be sons of the Most High, because He is kind to the ungrateful and wicked. Be merciful, just as your Father is merciful. "Do not judge, and you will not be judged. Do not condemn, and you will not be condemned. Forgive, and you will be forgiven. Give, and it will be given to you. A good measure, pressed down, shaken together and running over, will be poured into your lap. For with the measure you use, it will be measured to you." . . . How can you say to your brother, "Brother, let me take the speck out of your eye," when you yourself fail to see the plank in

your own eye? You hypocrite, first take the plank out of your eye, and then you will see clearly to remove the speck from your brother's eye.

Perhaps Jesus did not entirely appreciate the magnitude of the demand he was making upon *Homo sapiens*. In asking his followers to refrain from retaliation—to absorb pain without passing it on to someone else—he was asking people to inhibit their personal inclinations, while simultaneously going against a deep-seated tendency of living things generally. As we have seen, for millennia, both before Christ and after, we and our animal brethren have been far more likely to respond to pain and injury with a retaliating barrage of the same sort: more pain, more injury. On the other hand, it presumably would not have required special sermonizing to get people to do "what comes naturally." No one has seriously claimed that just because something is difficult, or goes against human (or animal) nature, it is not possible, or desirable.

It can also be transformative

For reasons we have explored, love is not easy, especially love that goes beyond the sloppy, sentimental variety, or its erotic or lustful alternative, but rather, is evoked—at least according to the Christian ideal—in the aftermath of pain and injury.

There can be no doubt, moreover, that Christian tradition in particular venerates and validates precisely this phenomenon, with Christ's agony widely taken as crucially related to God's redemption of humanity. Indeed, Christian commentators have historically viewed the following passage from the Old Testament (Isaiah 53:3–5), sometimes treated as a self-contained poem called "The Suffering Servant," as prefiguring the suffering of Christ and His/its redeeming impact:

He was despised and rejected by men, a man of sorrows, and familiar with suffering. Like one from whom men hide their faces he was despised, and we esteemed him not.

Surely he took up our infirmities and carried our sorrows, yet we considered him stricken by God, smitten by him, and afflicted.

But he was pierced for our transgressions, he was crushed for our iniquities; the punishment that brought us peace was upon him, and by his wounds we are healed.

Hidden within dense layers of interpretive theology is this equation, one that is, however, rarely made explicit: The more pain (the more suffering on the part of Jesus), the more redemption for the rest of us.

But *why*? Perhaps because the crucifixion of Christ, revered as the epitome of innocence—the "Lamb of God"—provides an especially potent example of scapegoating as route to social cleansing. It is also possible that insofar as Christ suffered ("for our sins"), His pain enhances the social, personal, and even biochemical status of the rest of us, helping to overcome subordination stress among His followers.

For some, the above interpretation will doubtless be controversial (for others, blasphemous), although there can be no doubt that blood sacrifice and blood atonement for sins loom large in the Old Testament. Moreover, in the person of Jesus' suffering and death, they are if anything even more central to the New Testament, where it figures prominently in the promise of redemption. A small sampling: In the Book of Revelations (1:5), Jesus is described as "him that loved us, and washed us from our sins in his own blood." Paul's letters to the Hebrews (9:22) state that "without the shedding of blood there is no remission of sin"; and at the Last Supper, Jesus is reported to have added, "This is my blood of the covenant, which is poured out for many for the forgiveness of sins" (Matthew 26:28). In Ephesians 1:7, Paul wrote, "In him we have redemption through his blood, the forgiveness of sins, in accordance with the riches of God's grace."

For an even more explicit example of benevolent, biblically based "bloody-mindedness," here is the classic nineteenth-century Gospel song "Nothing But the Blood."

What can wash away my sin?
Nothing but the blood of Jesus;
What can make me whole again?
Nothing but the blood of Jesus.
Oh! precious is the flow
That makes me white as snow;
No other fount I know,
Nothing but the blood of Jesus.
For my pardon, this I see,
Nothing but the blood of Jesus;
For my cleansing this my plea,
Nothing but the blood of Jesus.

Scholars, notably René Girard in his monumental work *Violence and the Sacred*, have examined the anthropology of religious sacrifices and "substitute violence." One conclusion is that in their effort to make sense of a world filled with incomprehensible suffering, people have long assumed that when disaster comes upon them, it is because some higher power has been offended, and that a deity, either the one and only, in the Jewish, Christian or Islamic tradition, or one of many—among Hindu or pantheistic belief systems—is passing its pain along to the rest of us. Hence, the bloody history of sacrifices, propitiatory offerings to mollify a divinity who must have been angered if not downright injured in order to be moved to treat his or her subjects so badly.

Girard's basic point—powerfully consistent with the Three Rs—is that human societies tend to seek "surrogate objects," which they then subject to sacramental violence as a way of establishing social order. Girard's trail-blazing study did not specifically mention redirected aggression, and was developed without reference to the underlying physiological and evolutionary bases that are only now becoming clear. What was new in Girard's day remains equally fresh today, however, and all the more compelling since it can be connected to a growing body of theory and evidence concerning the potency of pain-passing. But it is one thing to identify a central figure such as Christ as the recipient of pain—whether His own or humanity's—and quite another to absorb our own pain and "respond" by not responding. Of course, turning the other cheek is a possible response, and one that is profoundly pro-active, courageous, and demanding, while also flying in the face of much biology and psychology. It is in fact *more* difficult than indulging the Three Rs because, as we have seen, turning the other check is literally more "unnatural" than is responding to pain by inflicting yet more.

Observant Catholics regularly practice confession, wherein the penitent confesses his or her transgressions to a priest who has the power to assign a penance that will result in God granting forgiveness. Psychologically, this is very astute, since in the process people are made aware of social norms and values, while also being given the opportunity to reflect on their failures and to achieve forgiveness by paying a price in words and deeds. The imposition of penance reflects a deep recognition that having transgressed and caused pain to another—possibly to God as well—the penitent must himself "make up" for his misdeed, often by suffering in turn. One problem with confession and penitence, however, is that violent or malevolent perpetrators may then feel that they can readily earn God's forgiveness, without making restitution or apology to those whom they have harmed.

Moreover, there is the risk that an expectation of future forgiveness will facilitate misbehavior. Philosopher Daniel Dennett quotes the comedian Emo Phillips as follows: "When I was a child, I used to pray to God for a bicycle. But then I realized that God doesn't work that way—so I stole a bike and prayed for forgiveness!"[4]

Obtaining God's forgiveness is one thing, whereas soliciting it from a third party, notably a victim, is quite another. A perpetrator's confession, whether or not it benefits the confessor, does not help his or her victim achieve recompense or relief. To be sure, even a malefactor deserves support and at least the prospect of redemption. But what about the poor guy whose bike was stolen?

No one doubts the difficulty of responding to the immediate infliction of pain—say, a literal slap in the face—by turning the other cheek. But it is no understatement that merely forgiving those who caused us pain can be nearly as challenging as exposing oneself to yet more. Whereas the retaliatory impulse is powerful, so is the temptation to respond later, typically after brooding on the pain, loss, and insult. Forgiveness is to revenge (and to a lesser extent, redirected aggression) as restraint is to retaliation. The fact that it is so difficult probably helps explain why it is considered so laudable—although exhortations to forgive sometimes come across as irksome, even despicable, because forgiving is not only emotionally strenuous but, at least in such cases, potentially demeaning. Listen to this rumination from Fay Weldon's novel, *Female Friends*:

> Understand and forgive, my mother said, and the effort has quite exhausted me. I could do with some anger to energize me, and bring me back to life again. But where can I find that anger? Who is to help me? My friends? I have been understanding and forgiving my friends, my female friends, for as long as I can remember. . . . Understand Hitler and the bank of England and the behavior of Cinderella's sisters. Preach acceptance to wives and tolerance to husbands. . . . Grit your teeth, endure. Understand, forgive, accept, in the light of your own death, your own inevitable corruption. . . . Oh mother, what you taught me! And what a miserable, crawling, sniveling way to go. . . .

We can all understand the yearning to be let off the hook for our own misbehavior. But doing the forgiving is another thing, quite distinct from soliciting it from a third party, notably God—and then announcing the reassuring words, "I am forgiven." One problem with forgiveness, as we have seen, is that it deprives the offended party of the opportunity to confirm her status in the aftermath of a social, psychological, and biological "take-down," a situation from which God is presumably exempt.

But as Weldon's lament makes clear, the rest of us are often less generous, even as we typically recognize the moral high ground occupied by those able to forgive. Even here, however, the extremes are pejorative: Revenge aside, a stubborn refusal to forgive even a small affront comes across as perversely intransigent, stuck in the past, and outrageously self-centered. At the same time, too-eager forgiveness can seem spineless; one need not actually advocate the Three Rs to feel that injurious behavior should be noted and protested, not only in the service of self-defense and/or justice, but in what might be a realistic hope of making a repeat performance less likely.

Hannah Arendt wrote about the "predicament of irreversibility,"[5] the fact that what has been done literally cannot be undone, just as one cannot step in the same river twice. To convey full and complete forgiveness comes perilously close to suffering full and complete amnesia, a cheap way out of the predicament of irreversibility. But if what has been done cannot be undone, what then *can* be done when it comes to dealing with pain and injury? Are there no ways out of that other predicament, the one that results from giving in to the Three Rs?

In his poem "Gerontion," T. S. Eliot asks, "After such knowledge, what forgiveness?" More to the point: After pain, what to do?

Maybe it is too much to ask for complete Christian forgiveness, at least in the aftermath of great wrongs. More accurately, it is all right to ask for forgiveness, but maybe too much to *expect* it. In any event, given human nature and thus our species-wide susceptibility to being hurt, perhaps the most anyone can hope for—and it is actually quite a lot—is that even if people cannot bring themselves to forgive, they can at least refrain from the Three Rs. This is essentially the take-home message of two famous sermons "Upon Resentment" and "Upon Forgiveness of Injuries," delivered by the eighteenth-century English bishop Joseph Butler. His point is that, when it comes to forgiveness, a realistic goal is the forswearing of revenge.[6] Butler distinguished between "sudden" and "deliberate" anger, pointing out that the latter in particular, since it is susceptible to thought, reason, and ethical remonstrance, should also be open to Christian restraint.

It falls short of turning the other cheek, but Butler's advice is at least an improvement on "doing what comes naturally." In a sense, it is a realist's ethical compromise, of the sort recently discussed by political philosopher Avishai Margalit,[7] who makes a verbally bold distinction between two problems: the case of a "fly in the ointment," which can at least be solved and lived with, and a "cockroach in the soup," which cannot.

The *Way* of A.A.

One of the best models for forgiveness lies in the Twelve Steps approach of Alcoholics Anonymous. Alcoholics, almost by definition, are guilty of social sins. Liquor typically anesthetizes the conscience of many alcoholics, making them liable to do terrible things to others, things that often seem terrible even to themselves when they sober up enough to evaluate their behavior. The Twelve Steps are a systematic approach to character building, based on Protestant Christianity, but not limited to it. The Steps have proven themselves effective for many alcoholics and also for people addicted to other drugs and dysfunctional behaviors (overeaters, workaholics, sex addicts, and so forth).

Here they are,

Tool #3: The Twelve Steps

- Step 1—We admitted we were powerless over [our addiction]—that our lives had become unmanageable.
- Step 2—Came to believe that a Power greater than ourselves could restore us to sanity.

- Step 3—Made a decision to turn our will and our lives over to the care of God *as we understood Him*.
- Step 4—Made a searching and fearless moral inventory of ourselves.
- Step 5—Admitted to God, to ourselves and to another human being the exact nature of our wrongs.
- Step 6—Were entirely ready to have God remove all these defects of character.
- Step 7—Humbly asked Him to remove our shortcomings.
- Step 8—Made a list of all persons we had harmed, and became willing to make amends to them all.
- Step 9—Made direct amends to such people wherever possible, except when to do so would injure them or others.
- Step 10—Continued to take personal inventory and when we were wrong promptly admitted it.
- Step 11—Sought through prayer and meditation to improve our conscious contact with God *as we understood Him*, praying only for knowledge of His will for us and the power to carry that out.
- Step 12—Having had a spiritual awakening as the result of these steps, we tried to carry this message to other [addicts], and to practice these principles in all our affairs.

Look particularly at Steps Four to Ten. Beginning with a fearless personal moral inventory of exactly how others have been harmed, the alcoholic is then supposed to tell someone else exactly what these problems have been, focusing on personal responsibility, not blame or self-justification. Then after asking for divine help, the transgressor is to list those people he or she has hurt and make personal amends to each, unless doing so would cause further harm. This process is supposed to become a lifelong practice of reflection, responsibility, making amends, and living mindfully.

It is not uncommon for people practicing the Twelve Steps to take years to go through them all, and to repeat them, especially in times of stress. Of the various Steps, making amends turns out to be especially difficult. For example, if someone commits adultery while under the influence, and truly regrets it, should that person tell the betrayed spouse and ask for forgiveness (even if the other would be traumatized by the information)? What about child abuse? Should a repentant child abuser contact the victim, even after many years have gone by, to express sorrow and ask to make amends? Would having any contact with an abuser simply exacerbate the victim's mental wounds? People in A.A. struggle with these questions all the time, and there are no easy answers, but we submit that the process itself is a very good one, because it builds one's conscience and creates an environment for amends and reconciliation. Furthermore, although the penitent asks God for help in building his character and removing personal flaws, God is neither expected nor asked to intervene as a broker in the transaction. God presumably helps the penitent, but the penitent nonetheless has to place the phone calls, write the letters, pay the debts, and otherwise make amends without direct divine assistance.

We submit that in the case of the Twelve Steps, the relationship of the "sinner" to his or her Higher Power is an antidote to the narcissism of drug and alcohol abuse, with the sinner acknowledging that he or she is not the center of the universe. It must be noted, nonetheless, that an apology, or even an apology plus amends, does not automatically result in forgiveness. Not uncommonly, the process—especially Steps Four through Ten—must be repeated over and over before something even approaching "success" is achieved.

In most cases, the more a perpetrator sincerely asks for forgiveness, admits the damages, and attempts to make amends, the easier it is for the victim to let go his or her anger and move forward. Nonetheless, perpetrators nearly always find themselves complaining (if only to themselves): "There, I've done it. I said I was sorry. I've done what I can. What more does he/she want?" without realizing how difficult it is to compensate for inflicted pain. Perhaps the sticking point is the necessary rebalancing of the dominance hierarchy and its attendant hormones. The initial pain-inflictor put something over on the victim, and in that sense became dominant. For the victim to recover, the malefactor has to abase him- or herself sufficiently that the roles are reversed, with stress hormones going up in the malefactor and down in the victim. The humility of the penitent rebounds as improved self-esteem in the former victim. This may be why a simple apology—even if heartfelt—is rarely enough for any really substantial transgression.

The *Way* of Islam

We are not sufficiently learned in Islam to fairly present its subtle teachings when it comes to the appropriate response to victimization generally and to forgiveness in particular. According to Dr. Amir Ali, managing director of the Institute of Islamic Information and Education, forgiveness is demanded of Muslims not only because it is the will of Allah, but for one's own sake. Revenge— or "recompensing" or "requiting" evil—is considered permissible under Islamic teaching, but only within strict limits, and it appears that forgiveness is to be preferred. Thus, here are two translations of the same verse of the Qur'an, the first more literal, and the second, more interpretive:

> The recompense for an injury is an injury equal thereto (in degree): but
> if a person forgives and makes reconciliation, his reward is due from
> Allah: for (Allah) loves not those who do wrong. 42:40 (A. Yusuf Ali)

> But [remember that an attempt at] requiting evil may, too, become an evil: hence whoever pardons [his foe] and makes peace, his reward rests with God—for, verily, He does not love evildoers. 42:40 (Muhammad Asad)[8]

As we have seen repeatedly, it is terribly easy for a victim to become an offender, an outcome against which the Qur'an explicitly warns.

It must be stated, with regret, that although all three great Abrahamic religions have gone on record as opposing the tendency to pass along one's pain, the sad reality is that injunctions to forgive enemies and leave revenge to God are routinely ignored. Most likely, this is because the Three Rs are simply too sweet and too natural to disavow for long, no matter how wise and insistent the countervailing advice.

Gandhi's *Way*

Hindus speak of the endless pattern of death and rebirth, and of ways to break this cycle and achieve nirvana. In the Hindu worldview, each action has an effect, and this action-effect cycle is called "the law of karma." Nothing is without consequence. What comes around goes around, at a deeper level than Westerners normally assume. In some literalist schools, it is said that if you do a bad deed, you are liable to be reincarnated as a "lower animal." Murderers, for example, can look ahead to numerous lifetimes as flies, mosquitoes, or perhaps snakes. Alternatively, the payback may be direct: Kill a cow, and come back just in time to become someone else's pot-roast. According to ancient Hindu precepts, cruelty begets suffering for the perpetrator, if not in this life, then in the next. The Hindu concept of karma is thus remarkably like Arendt's predicament of irreversibility: Every action has consequences that cannot be undone.

One of the most powerful responses to the problem of the Three Rs came from a man well-schooled in Hindu theology, although he was also a lawyer, a teacher, and a political activist. If anyone has shown the Way in modern times, perhaps it is this small, brilliant, colossally stubborn, spiritually gifted, nearly naked mahatma out of India, Mohandas K. Gandhi, whose pioneering of nonviolence as a religiously-based model for real-world action was explicitly developed with an eye toward *not* demanding an eye for an eye. (Gandhi once observed that if everyone followed the Old Testament adage, the world would end up blind and toothless.)

Gandhi emphasized that a nonviolent response not only offers the prospect of breaking the chain of anger and hatred—analogous to the Hindu chain of birth, death, and rebirth—but that it carries its own here-and-now power since it puts the initial attacker in an unexpected position: unbalanced and disoriented when the victim responds, not with aggression but with love and nonviolence.

In short, although he did not say it in so many words, Gandhi recognized the ubiquity and danger of pain-passing, and he struggled to replace it with something much more difficult, but also more hope-filled: Pain acceptance, combined with the eventual transformation of the perpetrators. "I seek entirely to blunt the edge of the tyrant's sword," wrote Gandhi, "not by putting up against it a sharper-edged weapon, but by disappointing his expectation that I would be offering physical resistance."[9] Accustomed to counter-violence—and even, perhaps, hoping for it—the violent person becomes a "victim" of a kind of moral jiu-jitsu when he encounters a nonviolent opponent who is courageous and respectful, even loving, willing to suffer but also firm and unyielding. The attacker's energy is thus unexpectedly redirected, but this time in a way whose outcome is benevolent instead of malevolent.[†]

For our purposes, perhaps the most important Gandhian concept is *satyagraha*, literally "soul-force" or "soul-truth," although it has often been rendered into regrettable English as "passive resistance," which omits its positive, creative, and most demanding component, and is equivalent to translating *light* as "nondarkness," or *good* as "absence of evil." *Satyagraha* is passive only insofar as it espouses self-restraint rather than the active injuring of others. In all other respects, it is active and assertive, requiring great energy, initiative, and courage—more than most people can muster.

Gandhi felt strongly that *satyagraha* must be distinguished from passive acquiescence or the desire to avoid pain at any price, and thus, to refrain from violence not out of conviction but rather cowardice. According to one observer,

> This cowardice shows itself in what may be called the mercenary impulse, the impulse to hire others to fight one's own battles. This impulse has such concrete manifestations as hiring additional police to suppress domestic unrest or in spending money for a so-called all volunteer army, rather than personally accepting the obligations of citizenship. While many people see such practices as sensible and less conflictual approaches to social problems, they represent what Gandhi called the nonviolence of the weak. Such nonviolence he took to be

---

[†] For all its relevance to the question of how one might overcome the Three Rs, Gandhian *satyagraha* is unique in several respects, not least because it was primarily developed in the context of political strategizing (specifically, with the goal—ultimately successful—of freeing India from British rule). As a result, it differs from the usual situation in which an injured party has been unwillingly hurt; instead, the "victim" goes out of his or her way to court injury, after which retaliation, revenge, and redirected aggression are specifically disavowed. What is left is a unique dignity.

counterfeit, a cloak for passivity and cowardice, a form of apathy and indifference.[10]

Gandhian nonviolence at its best is the negation of the Three Rs by the strong, the courageous, the outraged—not mere passive resistance by the weak, the cowardly, or the comfortable. Easier said than done.

A key to understanding Gandhi's way of overcoming is embodied in the word for nonviolent love, *ahimsa*, which is the bedrock of *satyagraha*. As Gandhi expressed it, "*Ahimsa* and Truth are so intertwined that it is practically impossible to disentangle and separate them. . . . Nevertheless, *ahimsa* is the means; truth is the end."[11] *Ahimsa* is often defined as "nonviolence." As with the term *passive resistance*, however, this usage itself does violence to the underlying concept, which instead is far more active: In the case of *ahimsa*, it means active love.

It is closer to Albert Schweitzer's principle of "reverence for life," a concept that is not only negative—determination not to destroy living things—but also positive, a commitment in favor of life, especially the life of other human beings. *Ahimsa* requires deep respect for the pain-causer's humanity, an insistence upon meeting the other with sympathy and kindness, but also with unwavering firmness. It is not meek, mild, or retiring. It implies nothing less than the willingness of each individual *satyagrahi* to take unto her- or himself the responsibility of absorbing pain without passing it onto anyone or anything else.

Hence, as Gandhi emphasized,

> *Ahimsa* in its dynamic condition means conscious suffering. It does not mean meek submission to the will of the evil-doer, but it means pitting of one's whole soul against the will of the tyrant. Working under this law of our being, it is possible for a single individual to defy the whole might of an unjust empire to save his honor, his religion, his soul, and lay the foundation for that empire's fall or its regeneration.[12]

And so, we offer the words of Mohandas K. Gandhi:

Tool #4: Ghandian Nonviolence

Suffering is the law of human beings; war is the law of the jungle. But suffering is infinitely more powerful than the law of the jungle for converting the opponent and opening his ears, which are otherwise shut, to the voice of reason. Nobody has probably drawn up more petitions or espoused more forlorn causes than I, and I have come to this fundamental conclusion that if you want something really important to be done you must not merely satisfy the reason, you must move the heart also. The appeal of reason is more to the head, but the penetration of the heart comes from suffering. It opens up the inner understanding in man. Suffering, not the sword, is the badge of the human race.[13]

For Gandhi, this suffering (termed *tapasya*) is crucial in several ways. First, unless one is prepared to suffer, the depth of one's commitment can be questioned, especially when the path to be followed involves accepting pain and not responding with corresponding violence. Moreover, since any serious conflict must lead to suffering, the nonviolent resister's devotion to justice will almost certainly precipitate suffering. *Tapasya* therefore indicates willingness to undergo this suffering, and not to shift its burden onto anyone else—including the opponent—as a consequence of one's commitment to the truth of nonviolence.

Gandhi's emphasis on suffering is especially difficult for many people to understand or accept. Probably more than any other aspect of his thought and practice, it tends to make nonviolence particularly inaccessible to many Westerners. And yet, *tapasya* should not be altogether foreign, especially to the Christian tradition, given the central importance attributed to Christ's redeeming agony on the cross. In addition, it is not stretching Gandhi's concept too greatly to substitute "courage" for "willingness to suffer." This has the added benefit of helping dispel the frequent misunderstanding that practitioners of nonviolence are simply seeking an easy way out of conflict, an excuse rather than a reason for not indulging in either retaliation, revenge, or redirected aggression.

The reality, of course, is that when it comes to retaliation, revenge, and redirected aggression, non-indulgence is by far the more rewarding route—but also the most challenging and, in a real sense, the *least* self-indulgent.

The Buddhist *Way*

Buddhism stands in relation to Hinduism as Christianity does to Judaism; it is a more recent offshoot of an older religious tradition. And like Christianity, Buddhism is deeply suffused with teachings derived from pain and committed to overcoming the human tendency to respond to pain with the infliction of yet more. Whereas Christ is believed by Christians to have "died for our sins," and thus to have suffered pain on our behalf, the Buddha is believed by Buddhists to have been deeply moved by the pain he witnessed in others: old age, sickness, poverty, and death. Especially in the Mahayanna Buddhist tradition, those who have achieved perfect understanding of how the world works and who have the option of escaping from the cycle of birth and rebirth into *Nirvana* often opt instead to reenter the world to heal it; these Enlightened Ones are called *bodhisattvas*.

It is no overstatement to note that Buddhism is founded on the recognition that pain or suffering (*dukkha*) is ubiquitous and unavoidable: "birth is suffering, aging is suffering, illness is suffering, death is suffering; sorrow, lamentation, pain, grief and despair are suffering; union with what is displeasing is suffering; separation from what is pleasing is suffering; not to get what one wants is suffering; in brief, the five aggregates subject to clinging are suffering." This is the first of Buddhism's "Four Noble Truths," which together constitute the Buddha's first discourse after he attained enlightenment.

The Buddha's second Truth concerns the origin of suffering in craving or clinging (*samudaya*): "This is the Noble Truth of the origin of suffering: it is this craving which leads to renewed existence, accompanied by delight and lust, seeking delight here and there, that is, craving for sensual pleasures, craving for existence, craving for extermination."

The third Truth is that suffering can be minimized, and even in some cases, ended (*nirodha*): "This is the Noble Truth of the cessation of suffering: it is the remainderless fading away and cessation of that same craving, the giving up and relinquishing of it, freedom from it, nonreliance on it."

And finally, the fourth Noble Truth is the renowned Eightfold Way (*magga*) that leads to suffering's cessation: "right view, right intention, right speech, right action, right livelihood, right effort, right mindfulness, right concentration."[14]

A modern elaboration of this, written by Vietnamese Buddhist master Thich Nhat Hanh, is

Tool #5: Buddhist Vows

- Aware of the suffering caused by the destruction of life, I vow to cultivate compassion and to learn the ways of protecting the lives of people, animals and plants. I am determined not to kill, not to let others kill, and not to condone any act of killing in the world, in my thinking, and in my way of life.
- Aware of the suffering caused by exploitation, social injustice, stealing and oppression, I vow to cultivate loving-kindness and learn ways to work for the well-being of people, animals and plants. I vow to practice generosity by sharing my time, energy, and material resources with those who are in real need. I am determined not to steal and not to possess anything that should belong to others. I will respect the property of others, but I will do everything in my power to prevent others from profiting from human suffering or the suffering of other species.
- Aware of the suffering caused by sexual misconduct, I vow to cultivate my responsibility and learn ways to protect the safety and integrity of individuals, couples, families and society. I am determined not to engage in sexual relations without love and long-term commitment. To preserve the happiness

of myself and others, I am determined to respect my commitments and the commitments of others. I will do everything in my power to protect children from sexual abuse and to protect families from being broken by sexual misconduct.

• Aware of suffering caused by unmindful speech and the inability to listen to the suffering of others, I vow to cultivate loving speech and deep listening in order to bring joy and happiness to others and relieve others of their suffering. Knowing that words can create happiness or bring suffering, I vow to learn to speak truthfully, with words that can inspire self confidence, joy and hope. I am determined not to spread news that I do not know to be certain, and not to criticize or condemn things I am not sure of. I will refrain from uttering words that can cause division or discord, or that can cause the family or the community to break. I will make every effort to reconcile and resolve all conflicts, even small.

• Aware of the suffering caused by unmindful consumption, I vow to cultivate good health, both physical and mental, for myself, my family, and my society by practicing mindful eating, drinking, and consuming. I vow to ingest only items that preserve peace, well-being and joy in my body, in my consciousness, and in the collective body and consciousness of my family and society. I am determined not to use alcohol or any other intoxicants, or to ingest foods or other items that contain toxins, such as certain T.V. programs, magazines, books, films and conversations. I am aware that to damage my body and my consciousness with these poisons is to betray my ancestors, my parents, my society, and future generations. I will work to transform violence, fear, anger, and confusion by practicing a diet for myself and for society. I understand that a proper diet is crucial for self-transformation, and for the transformation of society.[15]

Among the *"Six Paramitas"* (fundamental teachings of Mahayana Buddhism) is the *kshanti paramita*: "the capacity to receive, bear and transform the pain inflicted on you by your enemies and also by those who love you." This is worth meditating upon, both for its clear identification of the problem—the importance of receiving, bearing and transforming pain (not "transmitting" it)—and for this concluding wisdom: that no one is immune.

The *kshanti paramita* also highlights the first of the Four Noble Truths: the unavoidability of pain, since it notes that even those who love you are going to cause you pain—albeit in most cases unintentionally—for example, by being occasionally critical, or thoughtless, by dying, or simply being late for dinner. Just as no one gets out of here alive, no one avoids pain, which makes it all the more important to be able to "receive, bear and transform the pain inflicted on you," regardless of its source, and with full recognition that the existence of pain does not necessarily confirm the presence of a malefactor.

Buddhist thought offers additional insights; some of them—as with Gandhian *tapasya* and Christian forgiveness—as challenging as they are inspiring. We are thinking particularly about compassion.

Thich Nhat Hanh, for example, asks people to perform the following meditation: Visualize a dark ocean, and a small boat bobbing in the waves. Picture upon the boat a group of ragged immigrants, in flight from a terrorist regime. They have suffered and are seasick and weary. A larger boat appears from nowhere, manned by sea pirates. The pirate captain climbs aboard, and while his crew pillage the desperate refugees, he rapes one of them, a twelve-year-old girl. In mortification, she throws herself into the ocean and drowns. Now, develop compassion . . . not only for the girl, but for the sea pirate captain!

This exercise inspired Hanh to write a poem, "Call Me By My True Names," from which this is an excerpt:

> I am the frog swimming happily in the clear pond,
> and I am also the grass-snake who, approaching in silence,
> feeds itself on the frog. . . .
>
> I am the twelve-year-old girl, refugee on a small boat,
> who throws herself into the ocean after being raped by a sea pirate,
> and I am the pirate, my heart not yet capable of seeing and loving. . . .
>
> Please call me by my true names, so I can wake up,
> and so the door of my heart can be left open, the door of compassion.[16]

For Buddhists, the key to compassion is the stunning recognition that all things are connected: The frog and the grass-snake who kills and eats it—they both deserve the same name. Ditto for the twelve-year-old girl, her sea pirate rapist, and Thich Nhat Hanh himself, as well as everyone else. How can one not be compassionate when the "object" of our compassion is oneself? Even here, the concept of compassion may be inadequate, since it, too, implies a relationship to an "other." Thus, most people do not avoid touching a hot stove because they are compassionate toward their hand but rather, because they intuitively recognize that their hand is literally a part of themselves; no more need be said.

In another priceless meditation, Thich Nhat Hanh locates compassion, not in a sympathetic feeling of another's pain, but in the physical nature of reality itself. He urges the reader to look deeply into the sheet of paper on which his words appear:[§]

> If you are a poet, you will see clearly that there is a cloud floating in this
> sheet of paper. Without a cloud, there will be no rain; without rain, the

---

[§] Presumably, his insight applies equally to anyone reading via a computer screen, or e-book reader, etc.

trees cannot grow; and without trees, we cannot make paper. The cloud is essential for the paper to exist. If the cloud is not here, the sheet of paper cannot be here either. So we can say that the cloud and the paper inter-are. "Interbeing" is a word that is not in the dictionary yet, but if we combine the prefix "inter-" with the verb "to be," we have a new verb, inter-be.

If we look into this sheet of paper even more deeply, we can see the sunshine in it. Without sunshine, the forest cannot grow. In fact, nothing can grow without sunshine. And so, we know that the sunshine is also in this sheet of paper. The paper and the sunshine inter-are. And if we continue to look, we can see the logger who cut the tree and brought it to the mill to be transformed into paper. And we see wheat. We know the logger cannot exist without his daily bread, and therefore the wheat that became his bread is also in this sheet of paper. The logger's father and mother are in it too. When we look in this way, we see that without all of these things, this sheet of paper cannot exist.

Looking even more deeply, we can see ourselves in this sheet of paper too. This is not difficult to see, because when we look at a sheet of paper, it is part of our perception. Your mind is in here and mine is also. So we can say that everything is in here with this sheet of paper. We cannot point out one thing that is not here—time, space, the earth, the rain, the minerals in the soil, the sunshine, the cloud, the river, the heat. Everything coexists with this sheet of paper. That is why I think the word inter-be should be in the dictionary. "To be" is to inter-be. We cannot just be by ourselves alone. We have to inter-be with every other thing. This sheet of paper is, because everything else is.[17]

Insofar as things "inter-are," there is no separation between subject and object, organism and environment, victim and perpetrator; hence, there is no basis—rational or emotional—for passing one's pain to someone else, since such an act is as inappropriate as biting off one's own arm. "If only there were evil people somewhere insidiously committing evil deeds, and it were necessary only to separate them from the rest of us and destroy them," wrote Aleksandr Solzhenitsyn. "But the line dividing good and evil cuts through the heart of every human being. And who is willing to destroy a piece of his own heart?"[18]

For all its appeal, however, deep Buddhist compassion based on "interbeing" is simply beyond the reach of many. So how about its milder companion, empathy?

Empathy has been defined as "the intellectual identification with or vicarious experiencing of the feelings, thoughts, or attitudes of another." It often involves projecting one's personality onto someone else, so as to understand the other more clearly. Empathy stands in relation to compassion roughly as Bishop Butler's "forswearing of revenge" does to Christian forgiveness. Interestingly, empathy derives from the Greek *paschein*, "to suffer," and therefore has the same root as the theological term "passion." It implies sharing the feelings of another, if need be, to the extent of suffering along with that other.

Perhaps, for those of us still inclined to see a difference between perpetrator and victim, one way to begin transcending the Three Rs is to understand—not just as an intellectual exercise but as a gut-level shared recognition—the motivations and the pain of another. In his novel *Dune*, Frank Herbert imagined the existence of "mentats" who possess mental skills that enable them to exceed normal cognitive capacity. Is it merely wishful thinking to imagine the training of "empaths," empowered not only to comprehend how they came to be hurt in the first place, but also to understand what it would mean for an innocent party in particular to be victimized in turn? Although such empathy, based on Buddhistic compassion, will not guarantee an end to pain-passing, it seems likely to make redirected aggression (and perhaps even aggression in general) less frequent and less intense.

* * *

Although religious doctrines have notably—and in some cases, nobly—attempted to deal with pain and forgiveness despite the powerful bio-psychological pull of the Three Rs, there is nothing in the problem or its potential solution that mandates an approach that is specifically "faith-based." Moreover, there is no reason to think that there is a single solution or unitary perspective, whether religious or secular, to a problem that is so hydra-headed. Mark Twain once noted that it was easy to stop smoking: He had done it hundreds of times! By the same token, it is easy to overcome the Three Rs: There are many ways of doing so (or at least, many ways to try). Having devoted respectful if too-brief attention to the Jewish Way, Christ's Way, the Twelve Steps, Islam's Way, Gandhi's Way, and the Buddha's Way, we now present some non-theological "ways" that also offer the possibility of avoiding retaliation, revenge and redirected aggression.

The *Way* of Psychology and Physiology

There are innumerable schools of relaxation training and meditation: Eastern, Western, psychotherapeutic, religious, empirical, expensive, and free. Pick one that suits you, and practice it. For example, many people who cannot sit for formal Zen meditation enjoy running, swimming or other vigorous exercises that demand regular breathing and awareness of the breath. It doesn't matter what you call it. If you do something that allows you to exhale deeply, and stop holding your breath, it will probably allow you to think more clearly and behave less impulsively.

Here, then, is a do-it-yourself tool that is entirely secular.

Tool #6: Breathing Meditation

Inhale, slowly. Exhale, very slowly. Notice the point at which your exhalation stops, and your entire body rests, before another inhalation follows. See if you can prolong (but not to the point of discomfort) that moment of suspension before you inhale, when you are completely at rest. The exhaled breath is one element of physiology that is always available, and it is a powerful tool for relaxation and mental clarity. You can see for yourself what it accomplishes, if you put your pointer finger on your wrist above the thumb and feel your pulse. Observe your pulse for several minutes, and notice that it is systematically irregular: When you inhale, your pulse speeds up. When you exhale, it slows down. This "sinus arrhythmia" is perfectly normal. Each inhalation is accompanied by a slight surge in the sympathetic nervous system, releasing the stress hormones norepinepherine (noradrenaline) and epinephrine (adrenaline). The heart speeds up, digestion slows, and there is a moment where the body is prepared to fight or flee. Immediately afterwards, the parasympathetic system kicks in, releasing acetylcholine, which slows the heart via the vagus nerve. The parasympathetic system stimulates digestion, metabolism, and rest. Fear and anger drive the sympathetic system, while rest and tranquillity drive the parasympathetic system.

Thus, we suggest that the first way to inhibit retaliation and redirected aggression is something already familiar as an injunction: *take a breath*. Literally. No need to count to ten—rather, focus on the exhalation, allowing your body to down-regulate any stress. Repeat as often as you wish; there are no negative side-effects. Breathe, exhale, be still for a moment, then gather yourself up. Repeat.

Breathing forms the core skill of many forms of meditation, including many forms of Yoga as well as the Buddhist tradition of *Vipassana*, and it owes its effectiveness, not to mysticism, but to physiology.

The Game Theorist's *Way*

Just as individuals frequently overdo pain-passing, it is also possible to go too far in attempting to *avoid* it. Thus, some people are insufficiently self-protective, essentially "too nice." They are themselves victims of co-dependency and "enabling," ending up as a doormat instead of a *mensch*. Riding to the rescue, or at least helping to clarify this problem, is game theory, a notoriously hardheaded branch of research that is heavily indebted to mathematics.

Imagine the following: Stanley and Oliver have each had a bad day, although through no fault of the other. But now they are standing close to each other, and each has a choice: Stanley could hit Oliver, or refrain from doing so, while Oliver has the same two options. Assume, for the sake of simplicity, that it would feel good to be the hitter and bad to be the one hit. So, there are four possibilities: (1) Stanley could hit Oliver while Oliver refrains, (2) Oliver could hit Stanley while Stanley refrains, (3) each could hit the other, or (4) both could refrain. Imagine, further, this admittedly cynical but nonetheless physiologically likely situation: that the best payoff for each would be to hit the other and not be hit back. By the same token, however, the worst payoff might well be to get hit, without hitting. If each hits the other, then each receives whatever benefit comes from hitting but also suffers the cost of getting hit. Finally, if both refrain, then neither gets the pleasure of passing along his pain, but at the same time, neither suffers the cost of being hurt.

This admittedly oversimplified situation can be made to approximate the most famous situation analyzed by game theory, known as the Prisoner's Dilemma, if the payoffs are arranged as described above, with the highest payoff coming from hitting and not being hit, next highest from neither hitting nor getting hit, followed by the relatively bad payoff of hitting *and* getting hit, and then, worse yet, being hit and *not* hitting. Assuming that neither one knows what the other is going to do, Stanley's logical "move" is to hit Oliver, because by doing so, he protects himself against the worst outcome (getting hit while doing nothing), and at the same time, provides himself the possibility of getting the highest outcome, namely hitting without being hit back. And of course, the same applies to Oliver. So they end up trading punches.[¶] What makes this "game" especially maddening is that as a result, they each suffer what game theorists call the punishment of mutual defection, which is after all a rather poor outcome, whereas both could have been better off—enjoying the reward of mutual restraint or cooperation—if each had only kept his anger and pain to himself.

As just presented, the Stanley and Oliver situation is not a formal Prisoner's Dilemma in the game theoretician's sense, but it is close enough for our purposes. Stanley and Oliver are both tempted to pass their pain to the other, and each is worried lest he be taken advantage of if he holds back. So the two become pain-passers, with each suffering mightily as a consequence.

At first blush, it would seem that the paradoxical logic of a Prisoner's Dilemma would urge anyone at risk of being "too nice" to be downright nasty instead, to inflict pain on others in an effort to protect one's self. In the iconic Prisoner's Dilemma, it pays individuals to respond to pain (in game theory terms, to the other player's "defection") by defecting, which is equivalent to passing one's pain along, either to the initial perpetrator or to an innocent bystander. The initial

---

[¶] After which Oliver would be at least one-half justified in saying "Well, here's another nice mess you've gotten me into!"

defector—or malefactor, troublemaker, criminal, pain-causer, etc.—may be acting out of previous injury, hope of taking advantage of a pacifist victim, and/ or fear of being victimized by the other individual. And that other individual, in turn, is under similar pressures, including the downside of appearing to be a wimp.

To repeat, the dilemma in such cases is that the outcome, mutual pain-passing, would have been considerably better if both had cooperated instead of defecting; that is, if each had somehow restrained his pain-passing inclinations. The problem is that even when this potential shared payoff is made clear, the temptation still looms to take advantage of the other's forbearance, just as there arises fear of being suckered as a consequence of self-restraint while the other is uninhibited.

We will not undertake a detailed explication of game theory in this book,[19] but its basic perspective not only speaks to the pain-passing problem, but also points to ways out, identifying alternatives to being either a sucker or a victim-izer. One of the most promising derives from a simple strategy known as "tit-for-tat," which was elaborated in an influential book titled *The Evolution of Cooperation*[20] by political scientist Robert Axelrod. Tit-for-tat is a non-predatory rule-of-thumb, in that its default setting is for cooperation, or—in our terms— restraint and refusal to inflict pain on the other player. Tit-for-tat is also self-protective, since it instructs a player to do whatever the other fellow did the last time around; as a result, if you are following tit-for-tat, and your partner/ opponent has just defected—caused pain to you—your next move will be to cause pain to him. But it accepts the other side's "apology," which is to say, it responds to cooperative, non-injurious overtures by being cooperative and non-injurious in turn, even if the other player had previously defected, as long as he or she has returned to cooperation. In short, tit-for-tat is forgiving: "Take heed to yourselves," we read in Luke 17:2–4. "If your brother sins, rebuke him, and if he repents, forgive him."

The intent of tit-for-tat is essentially to train the other player (who is, after all, a fellow prisoner in the world's vast pain-passing dilemma) to be nice, but to do so without sacrificing one's own security, self-respect or—again, in our terms—social standing and reputation. It may be noteworthy that tit-for-tat is not literally a "winning strategy," in that it never defeats its opponent; rather, by a simple combination of rewards and punishments, it encourages the other player to be nice, while also robustly protecting itself from exploitation. (It is worth noting that even Gandhi and the Buddha condoned violence on occasion, to restrain or if necessary kill a rabid dog or someone "running amok.")

Insofar as it offers a way out of what otherwise seems to be a logically intrac-table dilemma, tit-for-tat is immensely promising. It may if anything be too punitive, however, since if confronted with another individual who is somewhat stubborn, or who, following tit-for-tat, has simply made a mistake and as a result has behaved more aggressively than intended, both sides can get stuck in that all-too-familiar cycle of endless mutual pain-inducing defection. Tit-for-tat begins by instructing its followers to cooperate. Thus, had they been following tit-for-tat, both Stanley and Oliver would have kept themselves in check, and no one would have gotten punched. The second tit-for-tat rule is that in any subsequent interaction, do to the other what he did to you the last time around. As a result, although cooperation (non-painful behavior) evokes cooperation from a tit-for-tatter, defection (precipitating pain) by Stanley in round "t" generates corresponding defection by Oliver in round "t + 1." Tit-for-tat is thus a way out of the nightmare of mutual pain-passing, but only sometimes, since in its eagerness to protect itself it is vulnerable to mutual "defection" in which pain caused by Stanley generates pain-passing by Oliver, which in turn produces yet more defection by Stanley, and so on.

Other game theory strategies have been developed and are being evaluated, through both computer simulations and laboratory studies. One of the most promising of these is also quite simple: Play tit-for-tat, but refrain from defection unless the other player has done so more than once, which is to say, engage in tit-for-two-tats.[21] This helps avoid the quagmire of continuing tit-for-tat defection in cases when, for example, either player may have been "nasty" simply as a result of error or carelessness, after which both sides, if following tit-for-tat, would be hopelessly stuck, although neither side intended any nastiness.

Another worthwhile candidate has been called "generous tit-for-tat" because it randomly grants unconditional forgiveness for past transgressions, behaving cooperatively—at least sometimes—even when the other player has behaved "badly."[22] In short, such a strategy, which can at least in theory have evolved purely via mechanical and mathematical processes, will, on occasion, lead one to turn the other cheek.[23] Yet another strategy induces Stanley to tolerate defection by Oliver—i.e., the other individual is allowed a "free," unpunished bout of nastiness—if Oliver's behavior occurred after Stanley started defecting in the first place without having been justified. This strategy has been dubbed "contrite tit-for-tat."[24]

Despite considerable research effort, however, game theory has yet to offer a guaranteed optimum strategy that provides for personal and "social security" while avoiding the pitfalls of the Three Rs. Nonetheless, it offers at least a glimpse at possible solutions. So while the search continues for a middle ground between being a saint and a sea pirate, here are Tools 7a and 7b:

Tool #7a: Original Tit-for-Tat

Start off being nice, then respond as you are treated. If someone with whom you are in a relationship is nice, be nice in return. If nasty, be nasty. But if the other changes and becomes nice, be nice in return; don't hold a grudge.

Tool #7b: Generous Tit-for-Tat

Once again, if your partner is nice, be nice. If nasty, be nasty, but in addition, randomly offer complete forgiveness and repair, with the prospect of ongoing cooperation. Don't be a sucker who is always forgiving, regardless of the other's behavior, but at the same time, provide occasional opportunities to get out of a pointless and endless cycle of mutual hurt.

The Economist's *Way*

There are other ways. By inhibiting retaliation, revenge, and redirection one can contribute to the development of long-term "economies of gain." No surprise here, since after all, much of effective social life involves mutual benefit rather than the destructiveness of pain-passing: "A rising tide lifts all boats." When the prospect exists for fruitful ongoing interactions—as tit-for-tat guru Robert Axelrod puts it, when "the shadow of the future" is long—cooperative strategies develop; these may have competitive components, but they are also characterized by rules and order, as well as mutual benefit. In fact, the development of complex civilization depends not merely on exploitation, but on the acceptance of norms and values of restraint and inhibition, albeit mixed with ambition and exploration. In short, people pass the *gain* along. Readers depressed by the ubiquity of pain-passing as well as of pain itself would do well to remind themselves of this.

Similarly, it is important to examine and to celebrate how, in most cases, individuals respond with civility, decorum, and even good humor to life in a crowd. In short, why don't we hurt or kill each other more often? There is much to learn from how most people, most of the time, handle freeways, subways, and the Christmas rush, most of which do not result in mayhem. Gandhi was acutely aware that such nonviolent cooperation was far more pervasive in ordinary human life than its violent, pain-passing alternative. The problem is that, in the journalist's epigram, "if it bleeds, it leads," which is to say that people are more attentive to defection (in the game theorist's terminology) or to pain-passing (in ours), than to successful cooperation. Here are Gandhi's words:

> The fact that there are so many men still alive in the world shows that it is based not on the force of arms but on the force of truth or love. Therefore, the greatest and most unimpeachable evidence of the success of this force is to be found in the fact that, in spite of the wars of the world, it still lives on. Thousands, indeed tens of thousands, depend for their existence on a very active working of this force. Little quarrels of millions of families in their daily lives disappear before the exercise of this force. Hundreds of nations live in peace. History does not and

cannot take note of this fact. History is really a record of every inter-
ruption of the working of the force of love or of the soul. Two brothers
quarrel; one of them repents and re-awakens the love that was lying
dormant in him; the two again begin to live in peace; nobody takes note
of this. But if the two brothers, through the intervention of solicitors or
some other reason, take up arms or go to the law—which is another
form of the exhibition of brute force—their doing would be immediately noticed in the press, they would be the talk of their neighbors and
would probably go down in history. And what is true of families and
communities is true of nations. . . . History, then, is a record of an inter-
ruption of the course of nature.[25]

We rarely encounter news reports that announce "Ecuador and Peru did not
go to war today," or "friends Ellen and Sarah continued to get along," or "cooperation between the development, sales, and production departments at XYZ
Manufacturing resulted in a net profit for the company." As a result, it is easy to
discount and devalue the mutual payoffs that derive daily from cooperation and
restraint of violence. It is typically the failures, what Gandhi called the "interrup-
tions of the course of nature," that receive attention. Perhaps greater awareness
of this reporting bias will help shape that course of nature in a more fruitful
direction. If pain can be shared, why not joy? What about passing *it* along? To be
sure, misery loves company (which, incidentally, is yet another "take" on the
seductive power of pain-passing), but laughter, too, is infectious.

Tool #8: Passing the Gain Along

Don't look only at the possible downsides of interactions (the chances of being
hurt or taken advantage of). Notice, as well, the potential upsides, and be aware
of the payoffs that come from peaceful, mutually beneficial cooperation.

The Psychiatrist's *Way*

Physicians practice two kinds of medicine: preventive (public health) and restorative (therapy for illness). When it comes to the Three Rs, psychiatrists and psychologists may have a lot to say about both prevention and treatment.

In the first place, it is clear that psychological resilience and mental health are
the products of genes, early learning, peer pressures, and social circumstances.
People of even temperament, who work well with others and have at least average intelligence and resources, are more able to "play by the rules" and avoid
impulsive aggression toward themselves or others, while also eschewing ruminative thoughts of revenge. A goal for parents and for societies should therefore

be to equip everyone with good "shock absorbers," which can help people deal with trouble without excessive personalization, rage, or depression. According to Steven D. Levitt and Stephen J. Dubner in *Freakonomics*, one of the major causes of reduced violent crime in the 1990s was the legalization of abortion some 30 years previously. Children who are wanted by their parents, who in turn have the ability and interest to provide for their offspring, have better outcomes than children who result from unwanted pregnancies. The take-home message is obvious: Help all children to be wanted and loved, and provide good experiences and resources for them. Permissive contraception and abortion rights, mandatory child support from both parents, good pediatric care, daycare and schools, as well as additional childcare benefits, and adequate social support for parents – these and other comparable common-sense programs should help create children with maximum mental stability, who would be less likely to precipitate trouble on their own and also less likely to respond to trouble by causing yet more.

However, there are those who seem to be born with disorders of empathy, conscience, and impulse control. Children with antisocial behaviors such as persistent bullying, torturing animals, stealing, and a low threshold for fighting are often on track to become sociopaths. We suggest that although on the whole, liberty and justice for all is a good thing, people who are insensitive to—or worse yet, who positively enjoy—the suffering of others should not be at liberty. Accordingly, a just society would deprive them of free-range aggression, especially since there is currently no reliable treatment for their disorder.

One of the hard messages of the Three Rs is that pain-passing is so pernicious that although kindness, compassion, and prevention are to be strongly encouraged, incorrigible pain-passers ought not be tolerated, whether at the level of individuals or larger groups. Hence, we believe that an especially potent case can be made for protecting society from sociopaths: Lock them up and—if necessary—throw away the key, thereby insuring that society will be spared their depredations. We realize that this recommendation may be harsh, illiberal, un-Christian, un-Gandhian, and un-Buddhist, but sadly, we fear that it is necessary. Similarly, it appears not only justifiable but essential to strengthen international law and also to discipline rogue states, and restrain sociopathic leaders as well as disruptive, pain-passing groups within and between states.

The early identification of sociopathy and its childhood antecedents should be an important social priority. Various studies of sociopathy estimate its incidence at about one percent of the general adult population. This is considerably lower than the proportion of adults who are incarcerated, and consistent with the finding that not all convicts are sociopaths. (Nor are all sociopaths criminals.) Ideally, the public should become familiar with the *Diagnostic and Statistical Manual* (*DSM*) of the American Psychiatric Association, especially Version 5, due for release in 2013. Particular attention ought to be paid to personality disorders, known as "Axis 2," because people with these problems are almost by definition poor cooperators, and some are violent and dangerous. We do not believe in the sunny Rousseauian vision that human nature is essentially "good," any more than we are persuaded by the dark, Hobbesian alternative that people are essentially "bad." Rather, individuals behave in ways that are more or less good depending upon their temperaments and circumstances.

It is comparatively easy to lock up the really bad guys. The tougher question is what to do with people like Andrea Yates, the 45-year-old mother of five who killed all of her children on June 20, 2001, by drowning them in a bathtub. Yates had a long history of depression with psychotic features, along with a peculiar religious fixation, and she was eventually found not guilty by reason of insanity and committed to long-term psychiatric care. There is no reliable evidence as to the cause of Mrs. Yates's pathology, but it is clear from her own words that her sense of being a bad or evil mom was redirected toward her children. She apparently drowned them to "save" them from herself.

According to the World Health Organization, in the year 2002, depression was second only to HIV/AIDS as the world's most disabling condition. Depression is primarily a disorder of persistent and debilitating low mood, with various physical manifestations including poor sleep, changes in appetite, and low energy. But along with depression comes its not-very-kissing cousin—rage— sometimes against the self, but against others as well. Added to this unholy alliance is unhappy rumination, which we have already identified as a risk factor for injustice collecting, grudge holding, and delayed acts of revenge and redirected aggression at the level of social groups as well as individuals.

We are appalled by the misuse of psychiatric language and treatments to "medicalize" problems that do not deserve such responses; for example, medicating two-year-olds with tranquilizers for their hyperactivity and purported bipolar disorders. Nonetheless, there is a strong case to be made that aggressive treatment of severe depression can prevent the kind of catastrophe created by Andrea Yates. Furthermore, substance abuse, including alcoholism, increases the risk for aggressive behavior, and in many countries, substance abuse— including binge and chronic drinking, and poly-drug abuse—involves more than ten percent of the population.

Let us imagine that Hamlet was treated for his depression. Would an accordingly less-melancholy Dane have then "gotten it together" and eloped with Ophelia to start a new life somewhere away from his too-compliant mother and his murderous uncle? What if Farrington were sent to a chemical dependency treatment center, so that he cleaned up and was then treated for his symptoms secondary to subordination stress? We suspect that he would not have beaten his little boy. Picture Captain Ahab on Prozac, which decreases obsessional thinking. Would he have acceded to First Mate Starbuck's wise counsel and come home with a good amount of high-value whale oil rather than losing the *Pequod* and its crew? Or imagine Othello with enough cognitive therapy to see through

Iago's lies and understand that Desdemona was not really unfaithful after all. Could a good shrink have prevented her murder? Following the efforts of a talented team of orthopedic surgeons, physical therapy, and an antidepressant regime, would Richard III—humpback removed—be more benevolent and relaxed? How much can supportive care treat depression and various malignant obsessions in the non-fictive world, especially as they may relate to subordination stress, thereby reducing the frequency of revenge and redirected aggression?

We don't know. But it seems worth a shot, at least when it comes to real people. If even a fraction of the depressed, vengeful, and unhappy human beings on this planet could be helped to become more forgiving, cooperative, and flexible, that would certainly be a step in the right direction. But issues of funding (and insurance) aside, here is a caveat: Throughout the maze of *DSM IV* and its forthcoming sibling, *DSM V*, a key distinction is made between "states" and "traits." A *state* is a disorder that is typically transient, such as a panic attack due to fear of flying. Such mental states are designated "Axis 1," which is basically a compendium of major psychiatric disorders from autism to xenophobia. To varying degrees, nearly all are treatable. However, next are the Axis 2 disorders, which involve personality *traits*. These are persistent, harmful to social and occupational function, and often lifelong. Give someone enough alprazolam for her fear of flying, and she will probably make it through the flight without panicking. But it is virtually impossible to make a person with obsessive-compulsive personality disorder into a flexible playmate. And there is no current treatment for those most prone to induce pain in others: the sociopaths among us.

Personality traits are matters of temperament and disposition. Just as there are dogs that are phlegmatic while others are energetic, there are people who are stodgy and others who seek novelty and stimulation. There are horses who are brave, and others who are fearful; similarly with people. One can teach a timid horse to do new things, and help a comparably timid child to make new friends or be more enterprising, but it takes work. Neonatologists can often predict human temperament by the time babies are six months old, with fairly good reliability. Some babies are fretful and hard to console; others are afraid of strangers; and some are pacific and generally "easy." These are early markers of temperament that may persist for a lifetime.

Our view of the Shrink's Way is bound to be controversial, especially when it comes to prescribing the following:

Tool #9: Psychiatric Responses

Vigorously treat psychiatric conditions such as depression, schizophrenia, and other such disorders of mood and cognition. At the same time, expend resources on improving the lives of people with personality disorders, within their limits.

But acknowledge these limits. In addition, educate the public about those with poisonous Axis 2 personality disorders, how to recognize them, as well as how to avoid and when possible, restrain them.

Tool #10: Self Protection

Be alert for the early warning signals that Gavin De Becker, in his book *The Gift of Fear*, calls "pre-incident indicators" of potential violence. If something feels very wrong in a situation, it probably represents real danger and requires attention. Get out of abusive or corrupt relationships. You cannot get bread at Radio Shack: You cannot get love, affection, cooperation, and honest reciprocity from someone with a severe personality disorder. Don't even try!

This is not to claim that intervention is useless; quite the contrary. But it takes careful discrimination to identify when it is likely to be helpful. As a general rule, early intervention works better than later. Take the case of bullying: In the aftermath of the Columbine shootings and other schoolyard outrages, public attention focused to some extent on the harmful effects of bullying and other behavior leading to childhood alienation: from social ostracism to threats and genuine physical injury. Not surprisingly, the bottom line in such cases is likely to be the infliction of pain, with potentially negative consequences for the victims of bullies, as well as for the bullies themselves (who are often responding to their own prior victimization). Hence, an important policy proposal involves early identification and sanctions against bullies, carefully calibrated to inhibit such behavior but without instilling a motivation for yet more. This should involve early assessment and treatment of psychiatric disorders: brain damage, ADHD, bipolar disorder, alcoholism and substance abuse, as well as "poisonous personalities." Once again, those suffering from Axis 2 disorders who cannot be successfully treated need to be restrained so that they do not hurt others and initiate a "Three Rs" cascade. An important correlate would be early identification and support for the weak, timid, different, and vulnerable.

In short, block bullies.

The *Way* of Apology

If, as we have argued, pain is not only a result of bad behavior but also a cause, then it is important to minimize—or even, when possible, to abolish—punitive damages and attitudes, and to make restitution, not punishment, the law of the land.** At the same time, it would be both desirable and feasible to formalize

---

** Also, as we have noted, restraint—when it comes to incorrigible pain-passers.

non-sectarian apology and forgiveness procedures, the former for criminals and the latter for victims. This approach can and should be extended to non-criminal transgressions as well, leading to organized teaching of forgiveness protocols in schools, starting in kindergarten.

This would mean blazing a new pedagogical trail, but not altogether in the wilderness. There has recently been substantial interest in forgiveness and its beneficial effects, ranging from physiological to societal. On the political front, South Africa's "Forgiveness and Reconciliation Commission"—conceived and carried out especially by Nobel Peace Prize winner Desmond Tutu—has been particularly effective.[26] Tutu's book, *No Future Without Forgiveness*, is a notable manifesto, couched in specifically Christian language, but accessible and persuasive to non-believers as well. Indeed, anyone familiar with the Three Rs should be able to understand not only the impulse for retaliation, revenge, and redirection, but also why forgiveness and atonement are so difficult, and also so important, at levels ranging from the physiology of individuals to the welfare of neighborhoods, societies, and, without exaggeration, the world.

Just as everyone is the recipient of pain—sometimes intended, sometimes not—everyone is also a pain transmitter. Asking for forgiveness and getting it is therefore one of the most effective tools for stopping pain-passing in its nefarious tracks. One of the authors of this book has developed a guide for those seeking forgiveness. It has helped many of her patients and might well help you, or someone you care about. Here, then, is Dr. Judith Lipton's Forgiveness Protocol (or, how to make an apology). It shares many features with the Twelve Step program described earlier, but with no spiritual overtones.

Tool #11: Forgiveness Protocol

1. Say you are sorry.
2. Make a detailed list of how your behavior might have hurt or harmed someone. Err on the side of overestimating rather than underestimating. Ask the other person if the list is complete, and correct your list to reflect a complete account of the costs of your behavior.
3. Say you are sorry again. Be prepared to say this many times.
4. Tell the other person exactly how you understand the costs of your behavior, and allow the other person to ventilate, elaborate, or reiterate as needed so that the other person really feels "heard."
5. Clarify with the other person if the behavior was a simple accident, a mistake, a mistaken calculation of costs and benefits, or a deliberate deed. This part is especially difficult and takes time and attention. "Thoughtlessness" is one of the most common sources of problems, and may reflect recurrent self-centeredness. Intentional acts of revenge or malice also require great insight to acknowledge.

6. Fix what can be fixed. Repair what is broken, replace what is lost, augment that which has been diminished.

7. Humbly ask forgiveness. Describe your inner state of guilt, remorse, sadness, grief, anger or whatever. (Note that saying you are sorry—items #1 and #3—are not the same as asking forgiveness, and that it is premature and presumptuous to ask forgiveness before having completed #1–#6.)

8. Describe what you have learned from the incident. Show insight and awareness, of yourself and your mistake, and of the other person and his or her pain.

9. List what you will do or change so as to avoid a repetition of the incident.

10. Clarify what penalties to expect if you make a mistake, or transgress again. Discuss what each of you will do to avoid a repetition.

11. Return to step #1 and repeat as needed . . . which will almost certainly be more often than the apologizer would expect, or like.

The *Way* of the World

It may be necessary to intervene so as to minimize the propagation of pain, but it is not sufficient. Also required is to affirmatively *reduce* the amount of pain in the world, albeit with the recognition that it will never be eliminated. In his wonderful essay "The Myth of Sisyphus," Albert Camus revisited the iconic image of Sisyphus, condemned to push a heavy rock up a steep hill, only to have it roll down again, forcing him to start over . . . and over, and over, eternally struggling and never succeeding. Camus argued that Sisyphus is heroic in performing this impossible task. He also added this stunning conclusion: "One must imagine Sisyphus happy."

Sisyphus had no choice. According to Greek mythology, he was condemned by the gods to perform his fruitless but (in Camus's view, at least) ennobling labor. Anyone who elects to pursue the Sisyphean task of eliminating the world's pain might consider rolling the following rocks: Affirm and encourage the legitimacy of nonviolence and forgiveness, through media, spiritual practices, education, and personal example; support social and economic structures that reduce inequity and promote maximally widespread well-being; encourage the pursuit of environmentally sustainable and respectful policies; support systems that privilege restorative justice over punitive procedures. In short, take seriously the ancient Hebrew injunction, *Tikkun Olam:* "repair the world."

In the process, we urge greater awareness that *Homo sapiens* has not cornered the market on pain and suffering; animals also suffer. Although it is clear (painfully so) that human beings are especially prone to injure each other when they engage in the Three Rs, a strictly human-centered perspective does not yield unquestioned examples in which the infliction of pain upon animals redounds to the obvious and immediate disadvantage of human beings themselves. But, by the same token, there is no obvious and immediate sense in which the pain of a person in, say, Zimbabwe is detrimental to an American reading this book. Hence, we maintain that just as the goal of pain minimization must not be limited to reducing one's personal distress or that of one's friends and family, it should not be restricted by a myopic species-centrism.

In short, the less pain the better: for you, for us, for all people, and – as Buddhists like to say – for all "sentient beings."

* * *

On the evening of April 4, 1968, Robert F. Kennedy was about to speak to a largely African-American audience in Indianapolis, Indiana, when he was notified that Martin Luther King, Jr., had just been murdered. Kennedy proceeded to deliver an extemporaneous eulogy to Dr. King, in which he quoted from Aeschylus: "In our sleep, pain that cannot forget falls drop by drop upon the heart and in our own despair, against our will, comes wisdom through the awful grace of God." We are not as sanguine as Aeschylus, in that we are less confident that wisdom reliably comes after pain . . . although we wish it were so.[tt]

In any event, there are at least some inspiring real-life cases in which it does. Here is one, recounted in a book subtitled *Inside the World of Palestinian Women Suicide Bombers*. An Israeli man had been mortally wounded in a suicide bombing attack, whereupon his wife decided to forego payback and to donate his organs so that others might live:

> As arranged with the hospital, his heart, liver, kidneys, and corneas had been donated to the hospital's organ bank. In an extraordinary set of circumstances, her doctor called her after she had signed all the legal forms to ask her a very specific question. "A Palestinian man in the hospital was next on the list for my husband's heart . . . and the doctor wanted to know, given the circumstances of my husband's death, if I had any objections." She had no objections and even agreed to meet the recipients after he had successfully undergone transplant surgery. The scene in his hospital room was one of those moments when blood feuds, biblical prophecies, and political grievances disintegrate under the weight of pure human emotion. The Palestinian man, his wife, and the Israeli widow embraced, the three of them, their arms intertwined as the two women leaned over the patient's hospital bed. There was nothing any of them, or any of us who witnessed the moment, could do except cry.[27]

[tt] We are also skeptical of the claim that when wisdom comes, it necessarily comes from God. (But that is another matter.)

References

1. Quoted in Graham Robb (1999). *Victor Hugo: A Biography*. New York: W. W. Norton.
2. *Iliad* (1961). Translated by R. Lattimore. Chicago: University of Chicago Press.
3. Menachem Davis (ed.) (2002). *Siddur for Weekdays* (The Schottenstein Edition). New York: Mesorah Publications, Ltd.
4. Daniel C. Dennett (2006). *Breaking the Spell: religion as a natural phenomenon*[New York: Viking.
5. H. Arendt (1958). *The Human Condition*. Chicago: University of Chicago Press.
6. J. Butler (1896). *The Works of Joseph Butler, vol. 2* (W. E. Gladstone, ed.). London: Clarendon Press.
7. A. Margalit (2010). *On Compromises and Rotten Compromises*. Princeton, NJ: Princeton University Press.
8. Accessed at http://www.hawaiiforgivenessproject.org/library/Forgiveness-in-Islam.pdf.
9. *Young India*, October 8, 1925.
10. J. P. Hanigan (1984). *Martin Luther King, Jr., and the Foundations of Nonviolence*. New York: University Press of America.
11. Quoted in E. Easwaran (1978), *Gandhi the Man*. Petaluma, CA: Nilgri Press.
12. Easwaran (1978).
13. Quoted in N. K. Bose (ed.) (1957). *Selections from Gandhi*. Ahmedabad, India: Navajivan.
14. B. Bodhi (trans.) (2000). *The Connected Discourses of the Buddha: A Translation of the* Samyutta Nikaya. Somerville, MA: Wisdom Publications.
15. Thich Nhat Hanh (1993). *For a Future to Be Possible—Commentaries on the Five Wonderful Precepts*. Berkeley, CA: Parallax Press.
16. Reprinted from *Call Me by My True Names* (1999) by Thich Nhat Hanh, with permission of Parallax Press, Berkeley, California, www.parallax.org.
17. Thich Nhat Hanh (1992). *Peace Is Every Step: The Path of Mindfulness in Everyday Life*. New York: Bantam.
18. A. Solzhenitsyn (1974). *The Gulag Archipelago*. New York: Harper & Row.
19. For a non-technical introduction to game theory, see D. Barash (2003), *The Survival Game: How Game Theory Explains the Biology of Cooperation and Competition*. New York: Henry Holt.
20. R. Axelrod (1984). *The Evolution of Cooperation*. New York: Basic Books.
21. M. Nowak and K. Sigmund (1994). The alternating prisoner's dilemma. *Journal of Theoretical Biology* 168: 219–226.
22. M. Nowak and K. Sigmund (1992). Tit for tat in heterogeneous populations. *Nature* 355: 250–252.
23. H. Godfray (1992). The evolution of forgiveness. *Nature* 355: 206–207.
24. J. Wu and R. Axelrod (1995). How to cope with noise in the iterated prisoner's dilemma. *Journal of Conflict Resolution* 39: 183–189.
25. M. K. Gandhi.(1993). Gandhi, an Autobiography: The Story of My Experiments with Truth. Boston: Beacon Press.
26. D. Tutu (2000). *No Future Without Forgiveness*. New York: Doubleday.
27. B. Victor (2003). *Army of Roses: Inside the World of Palestinian Women Suicide Bombers*. Emmaus, PA: Rodale Press.

‖ 8 ‖

Conclusion

The Principle of Minimizing Pain (an 11ᵗʰ Commandment)

Longer version—Pain and suffering are inevitable, since there will always be bullies, cheats, and jerks, as well as plain old bad luck, accidents, and unfortunate natural events. But whenever and however I am hurt, the pain stops with me. Enough is enough. I will not pass it along. I may seek restitution and amends insofar as they may be necessary for healing, and I will attempt to forgive, but I will refrain from retaliation, revenge, and redirected aggression. I will try to be a "just" person, which means that I will attempt to absorb some of the world's pain, without passing it on or adding to it. At the same time, I will not be a sucker, because to allow myself to become a victim also increases pain, and I will actively stand up to cheats, haters, and bullies, and will advocate for those who lack power and the means to protect themselves. I will practice this on a daily basis, and teach it to my children, students, clients, and anyone else who will listen.

Shorter version—When evaluating alternative actions, I will ask myself whether each is likely to increase or decrease the total amount of pain in the world, and I will always choose the latter.

INDEX